Genius of Geneva

A Popular Account of the

LIFE AND TIMES OF JOHN CALVIN

JOHN CALVIN

[*Frontispiece*

Genius of Geneva

A Popular Account of the

LIFE AND TIMES OF JOHN CALVIN

by

L. Penning

With Twelve Full-page Plates

WM. B. EERDMANS PUBLISHING COMPANY
Grand Rapids   1954   Michigan

Translated from the Dutch by
Rev. B. S. Berrington, B.A.

PHOTOLITHOPRINTED BY CUSHING - MALLOY, INC.
ANN ARBOR, MICHIGAN, UNITED STATES OF AMERICA
1954

CONTENTS

CONTENTS

LIST OF ILLUSTRATIONS

LIFE AND TIMES OF CALVIN

CHAPTER I

THE DARK NIGHT

FORTUNATELY we have left behind us the damp houses and tortuous streets of Paris. And yonder —outside the gates—between the trees, rises stately and impressive, the abbey Saint-Germain des Prés, where the kindly abbot, William Briçonnet, sways his sceptre.

Like a fortress the abbey is surrounded by deep moats to prevent surprise from any sudden and unexpected attack ; and a sweet resting - place it affords to the man, who worn out by the moil and toil of the great city, wishes here to end his days in tranquillity and peace.

There in the great hall with its costly library, sits a solitary man. The friendship of Briçonnet brought him to the place. And on the parchment, that is lying before him on the massive writing-table, he writes : " Anno 1509."

For it is the year 1509.

His hand trembles with age as he writes.

Yes, that solitary man is old; along that face run deep furrows; his hair is blanched by the seventy-four winters which have passed over it.

He stands up, stiff from sitting, goes to the window and stares through the cross-leaded panes into the Herbary, where grow the simples, used by the monks skilled in medicine, for sick and suffering humanity.

Now you see that the man is short of stature; he does not even reach to the shoulder of his king, who is called Louis XII.

Nevertheless, he is a king—O deny him not that title!

As a king he rules in the domain of minds, as Louis rules in the domain of the French kingdom.

That face of his attracts us; at the first sight of it we feel sympathy for the man; those eyes express intelligence, reconciliation, love.

Speak, noble old man! Of what are you thinking?

He does not answer; more and more thoughtful grows his face; all the remembrances of a long life, perhaps, are passing before his mind's eye.

He was eighteen years of age when European Christendom turned pale with terror at the tidings that Constantinople had fallen under the furious attacks of the Turk's crooked sword; he was not forty-four, when the Sultan snatched Moldavia away from the Polish kingdom.

The pitiful end of Charles the Bold, who, stripped naked, was found at Nancy, sticking frozen in the ice, was not unknown to him. Laurence Koster and John Gutenberg, the inventors of printing, were his contemporaries, and his life's sun was already declining in the western horizon, when Columbus discovered America.

A new world—son of Rome! cover your face!

For the army of Franciscan and Dominican monks, that went to America to convert the heathens, murdered those heathens by thousands and made the survivors ten times worse than they ever were before.

Hark! there is another cry going up to heaven: the cry of a hero and martyr, who is fast bound to the strangling-post. It is Savonarola, who preferred the gallows to a Cardinal's hat, offered by the hand of a pope, and whose only crime was, that he preached a poor sinner and a rich Christ.

THE POPES!

Is it unknown to you, O son of Rome! that Europe once saw the unheard-of spectacle of two, three popes, who at the same time laid claim to the chair of St. Peter, and hurled at each other the thunders of the Vatican? That Innocent VIII made himself notorious by introducing into Germany trials for witchcraft, and as being the father of sixteen illegitimate children?

And Alexander VI, who died six years before—

did he do anything else than neglect, to his own advantage, the interests of the Church, which are dear to your heart ? Was his son not a Cain, a fratricide ? And did not the people consider him guilty of incest with his own daughter ?

Degenerate, corrupt, sick to her very life's core has the Church become ; the immorality of the monks and the shameless ambition of the priests cry to God ; the traffic in indulgences and image-worship has assumed revolting proportions.

True it is that the incursion of the Turks and the fall of Constantinople caused Greek literature to seek refuge in Italy and Western Europe ; in those regions it became a rich source of civilisation and brought with it treasures of knowledge.

A revival of knowledge is discernible ; new universities are founded ; the names of Reuchlin and Erasmus will be spoken of with honour even after centuries to come.

In another department, too, Art shows what she can do, when her efforts are approved by God.

It is fifty-nine years since, in the city of Rome, the foundations were laid of St. Peter's Church, and they will have to go on building for more than a century before that imposing production of human art and of Michael Angelo's genius will be completed. This old man has seen the unfinished church, and, dumb with astonishment and admiration, he claps his hands together in ecstasy at the sight of the splendour before him.

Yet appearances are deceptive; this St. Peter's Church, built in honour of the Almighty and true confession of faith, is a lie; and the hundred and forty-four million guilders, which the building of the church will cost, will, for the greatest part, have to be covered by the sale of indulgences.

The atmosphere is sultry, oppressive; the air is infected; centuries before, the necessity had been felt of a reformation.

The noblest minds have pleaded for that reformation; every nation of the Christian West has had its martyrs, whose conscience-cry has re-echoed through the dark night like a wail for help.

But the reformation has not come; councils, convened for that object, broke up without result; and the synod of Constance could do no more than erect a stake, on which to burn God's holy witness, John Huss.

The piety of the old man, spoken of in the beginning of this chapter, is renowned. The Roman Catholic Church, that burns heretics, lets scoffers live; yet in the seat of scoffers this old man, this le Fèvre (or Fabri) has never sat. He is a faithful son of his church; never has any one sung the Mass with more reverence than he; kneeling before the images he reads his prayers.

But in his soul, which none can see save God, it seethes and foams—it is the storm, by God awakened; the storm that is beginning to blow over Western Europe, and, breaking the dry branches, foretells the spring.

Le Fèvre is not unacquainted with the history of the Middle Ages. Better than any one else does he know how Dante, who with angels and devils alike held intercourse, met on his terrible journey to hell more than one pope in the abodes of the damned—and that more than one mouth uttered the awful words : " The Pope is Antichrist ! "—O, this is not unknown to him !

The old man sits down again.

Once more we are struck by the shortness of his stature, the meanness of his appearance, his insignificance. And yet Erasmus, the great scholar of Rotterdam, who even in the saddle pursues his studies, once said of this man : " That Le Fèvre—that pious, good, and learned man, who has rendered such great services to science and to all learned men, deserves to remain always young ! "

This same Le Fèvre shall, with the strength of a Samson, attack the Sorbonne and fell it to the ground. There he sits and muses. Then suddenly the eyes under those grey brows light up, and over that furrowed face runs a thrill of silent, pent-up enthusiasm.

Of what is he thinking ? Is his patriotic heart aglow at the thought that his king Louis XII has just destroyed the power of the proud Republic of Venice ?

Is it the brilliant light of national glory, which makes his old heart beat faster ?

He is thinking, indeed, of a brilliant light, and taking up the pen to write the preface to his five-fold version of the Psalms, he speaks thereof.

But yet it is another, a higher, a more blessed light, the splendour of which makes his old eyes rejoice ; it is the discovery of a new world, compared to which the discovery of Columbus, of seventeen years before, sinks into insignificance.

And he writes :

" For a long time I have devoted myself to classical studies, and scarcely touched upon theology, for it is of exalted nature and must not be taken in hand without serious reflection.

" But in the distance such a brilliant light has already shone upon my eyes, that in comparison with what theology offered, the humanities seemed to me darkness, and the study of theology to diffuse such a sweet fragrance, that on earth there is nothing that can be compared to it."

It is remarkable, that in the year 1509 the regeneration of the noble Le Fèvre took place, and, in the same year, the last and greatest of the Reformers of the sixteenth century was born.

CHAPTER II

THE SON OF FISHERS AND SAILORS

LE FÈVRE had spoken of a brilliant light—no, Gerard Calvin, the father of the Reformer, perceived little of that heavenly light. The man had something else to do. With him it was working hard all day; he wanted to get on in the world; to be independent, a substantial citizen of the town of Noyon—that was his ambition.

Gerard Calvin was born in the little fishing village of Pont l'Evêque, not far from Noyon. Following the old road, in half an hour you reach the town, the towers of which rise up pleasantly above the high trees. And in the background the eye is agreeably struck by an undulating line of little hills.

Calvin was in heart and soul a son of his country, a real Picardian: of that race, from which sprang the celebrated hermit, Peter of Amiens, who, by his flaming words, had once set all Christian Europe on fire.

The Picardians have a warm temperament. They are warlike; the spirit of contradiction rests on them; they are the Frisians of the French nation: resolute, hardy, obstinate, and with strong demo-

8

cratic tendencies. In them the Reformation and the Revolution found their staunchest defenders ; this province was the cradle of the French Protestantism, which attacked the Roman Catholic Church in her very vitals, and of the Ligue, that with blood and steel strove to root out Protestantism. Gerard Calvin had seaman's blood in his veins. Although his father was a cooper—the family of the Calvins were a seafaring people, with a love for adventure. And that seaman's blood was of service to his son, the Reformer, for none of his forefathers ever went through such a storm as he did before his little barque reached the haven in safety.

Gerard Calvin knew what he was about when he turned his back upon the little fishing village. In his father's workshop he had learned something more than how to knock the staves round the barrels. He was a writer ; clever moreover, quick and discerning. And his heart yearned for the town.

He was suited for Noyon. And Noyon was the cradle of his fortunes. He became successively apostolical notary, procurator fiscal, clerk of the Ecclesiastical Court of Justice, secretary of the Diocese, and *promoteur* of the Chapter.

" He has so many irons in the fire," wrote one of his opponents, at a later period, " that all his life long he never knew which way to turn."

He took everything he could get—that is true, but it required a good deal to perplex him.

As actuary he had a great name ; he was held in high repute by the nobility, and was respected as a citizen of Noyon.

There he married, and his neighbours said that this cooper's son of Pont l'Evêque had made good use of his eyes when he knocked at the door of Mr. Johannes le Franc.

Le Franc had been an hotel-keeper at Cambrai, had sold or let the business and become an inhabitant of Noyon. People said, that this Cambrai hotel-keeper had feathered his nest well, and they were right. The man's ship had come home, he became one of the leading men of the town, member of the corporation, and paid four pounds a year income-tax, whilst his future son-in-law's was never more than fourteen pence.

Johanna, his daughter, was a desirable match. She was lovable, winsome, and of a beauty calculated to make the hearts of the young unmarried men of Noyon beat faster.

Gerard Calvin was the lucky man who led her to the altar, and from there to his own dwelling, close to the Corn-market, in the neighbourhood of her parents' house.

In character and way of thinking, they were different. The mother of the Reformer was a quiet woman, deeply attached to the Church, whilst one has a strong impression that Gerard Calvin's eyes were firmly set on earthly things.

His ideals were not exalted. He loved his wife

and his children, but his desire to get on in the world overruled everything else. And although the heavenly lights were burning, we have not a single proof that his eye saw those lights.

It was not an unhappy marriage, but there is reason to conjecture that the severe social struggle maintained to the end by the father with such indomitable and admirable perseverance was but too frequently like a thick mist, that intercepted the joyous light of the Sun. One of the biographers of Calvin has said, that his father's system of education consisted in concealing his love from his children, whom he really loved. This is perhaps an exaggeration. But yet it is to be feared that the children had to suffer through the endless cares of their father, and experienced but little of that affection which to a young heart is like dew and summer rain.

We are sorry and grieved to say that it was so. We are grieved more especially about that little Johannes.

For he was a very impressionable child, with a sensitive soul. In his little body beat a heart. And on account of his father's many occupations it was impossible for that heart to receive what it was entitled to.

So we see the stamp of suffering already imprinted on Calvin's childhood. Suffering indeed followed him like a shadow all through his life and with scorn and revilings. And have not that scorn and those revilings—side by side with passionate love and veneration—been his lot to the present day ?

Of the three sons Charles was the eldest, Johannes the second, and Antony the third.

Amazed and startled at the elasticity afterwards displayed by Johannes Calvin, his enemies have examined his genealogical tree, taken notice of the swarm of gnats which flew up at his birth, and even consulted the stars, in order to explain his wonderful and extraordinary influence. And to these astrologers we are indebted for the hour of his birth being settled with horoscopical exactitude as having taken place on the 10th of July, 1509, at twenty-seven minutes past one in the afternoon.

Johannes was brought up by his mother, who probably died early, in all the solemnities and ceremonies of the Roman Catholic Church. He took part in the processions ; he pressed his lips with reverential awe on the relics of the saints ; it did not trouble him much, that from time immemorial the town of Noyon had been divided, with regard to the relics of St. Eloy, into two hostile camps, who were always at war with each other.

Who really possessed the true genuine remains of St. Eloy ? The chapter of the Cathedral or the abbey of St. Eloy, for both laid claim to them ? The people wanted to know this ; they would know it, for it was a matter that affected their eternal interests, and, furious with rage, they asked who were the falsifiers and deceivers : the clergy or the monks ?

For two generations a lawsuit went on about it ; the Parliament had acted as judge between the two ; a decision had been given and new decisions followed. But the uncertainty was not removed.

The violent disputes did the Church no good. The respect for the clergy decreased alarmingly. A spirit of doubt and mockery was awakened. The sharp-sighted Gerard Calvin must have had difficulty in suppressing a scornful laugh, and, more than thirty years later, the son who had sprung from his loins lashed image-worship with whips and scorpions.

In that remarkable writing, Johannes Calvin enumerates the principal relics in order then to make the following observations :

The wooden cross : if you were to collect all that has been found of it, you would have a good shipload.

The three nails of the cross : there are fourteen of them.

The point of the spear : you must assume that the crucible of the alchemist has quadrupled them.

The crown of thorns : you must take for granted that they have been planted again in order to produce new ones—or else how could they have increased so ?

" Everything is so contradictory and confused," says Calvin, " that you cannot worship the bones of a martyr without running the risk of reverencing the bones of some thief or robber, or of an ass, a dog, or a horse. And one cannot worship a ring, a comb, or girdle of the Blessed Virgin Mary, without being in danger of bowing the knee to the ornaments of some shameless woman."

Gerard Calvin saw clearly the advisability of giving his children a sound education. His idea was that the money spent on the education of one's children is well invested, and it was a load off his mind when he was in a position to send his boys to a good boarding and day-school just outside the gates of the town.

Especially for the second son, who was one day to attract the attention of Europe, he began to entertain great expectations.

He was a child of quiet and retiring disposition, weak, delicate and pale ; nervous, timorous and irritable. Yet the penetrating eye of the father saw through all those externals ; and he was surprised at the judgment, the intelligence, and the quick, cheerful spirit which animated this child.

He was a peculiar child ; into those pale cheeks of his came colour and glow when he sat poring over his books ; and the powerful aristocratic family of Montmor was so struck by the wonderful talent of this extraordinary boy, that he was educated with their children.

Here Johannes came into a new and strange world ; his heart yearning for love, was refreshed

by the charming kindness of this excellent household, and all his life long he thought of them with
deep-felt gratitude.

In this circle he quickly learnt the first principles
of science ; there, too, he acquired those refined
forms and distinguished manners, which afterwards
enabled him to associate with the highest aristocracy, even with princes and kings.

By Gerard Calvin, who was busy night and day
in order to help his children on in the world, it was
soon settled that Johannes should be educated for
the Church.

The seriousness of the boy and his talent, fitted
him for this ; the worldly side of the matter would
not be lost sight of by the father. By his connections he succeeded indeed in getting his son appointed
chaplain when only twelve years of age ; he received
the tonsure, and enjoyed a yearly income of three
bushels of corn and the produce of twenty grain
fields.

Does it sound strange, that a boy of this age
could be chaplain ? In the eyes of the world, such
as it was then, there was nothing strange in it ;
people did not know better ; the state of things
was so bad that they would have been astonished
at the man who had dared to make remarks about it.

In the century before, there had been popes of
eighteen years of age ; Benedictus IX was a boy
of twelve when the triple papal crown was placed
upon his head ; John of Lotharingia, who in 1502

was appointed Bishop of Metz, was a child of ten ; and Leo X had no scruples about appointing cardinal —another child of eight.

There was almost as great a traffic then in Church appointments as there is now in Russian and American Consols at our Exchanges. The house of God was made a house of merchandise ; the Pope and money ruled there, but for Christ there was no place. And whilst, abusing what is sacred, a man became purchaser of an ecclesiastical office, that sacredness had to be profaned a second time in order to obtain money for a substitute.

Later on, Calvin was loaded with reproaches for not having fulfilled the duties connected with his office.

But the reproaches were silly. He could not do so. He had not the right to say Mass and administer the sacraments. For that he had to be a priest, and he could not be a priest till he was twenty-five years of age.

Time did not stand still. Johannes was now fourteen years old, and the father's eye began to rest with pride and pleasure on his child. He saw himself reflected in that boy : the same resoluteness of will ; the same perseverance ; the same unflagging energy. There was something in that boy ; he gave promise of becoming a great man— he would be his father's glory, his father's crown.

Gerard Calvin, no doubt, consulted wise men of his surroundings, as to where he should then send the boy. And the advice to send Johannes to the University of Paris coincided with his own views.

This University, founded in the beginning of the thirteenth century, owed its greatness to the struggle which it maintained against the despotism of the Church, and in the short period of half a century had become the glory of France and of Western Europe. The Sorbonne and the Pope were in that century considered indispensable ; they formed the two pillars of the Church ; the Sorbonne looked after the unity of doctrine, the Pope after the unity of authority.

The Sorbonne was the beaming sun in the scientific world ; it was the Mecca of studious young men ; it would have sounded like a strange contradiction if any one had become a learned man without having attended the lectures of the professors in Paris.

Yet this University, whose morning had foretold such a gladsome and bright summer day, fell into the same despotism that it had suppressed with so much glory. It became reactionary, as stubborn as a self-willed pony, the violent opposer of all real progress.

The age of sophism reigned in the seats of the audience-halls : the question whether it was an apple or a pear that Adam had eaten was eagerly discussed ; the authority that was to be given to the testament of Lazarus after his resurrection, called forth the most passionate disputes. And in the sixteenth century the University had gone down so far, that Erasmus could not resist the temptation of shooting at it his sharpest arrows dipped in mockery and contempt.

" At this worm-eaten gate then," says Dou-mergue,[1] " Calvin knocked in 1523, when the plague and heresy were threatening Noyon and Picardy."

[1] *Calvin's Youth*, by E. Doumergue.

CHAPTER III

THE GREAT DAY OF THE REFORMATION

MUCH had happened in Europe during the last six years ; the dark thunder-clouds had begun to gather rapidly, and over Wittenberg the first storm had burst, when, on October 31st, 1517, a former Augustine monk, in the strength of his God, nailed to the principal door of the Wittenberg Schloss-kirche, his ninety-five theses against the traffic in indulgences.

On the market-place of Jüterbock, Tetzel threw Luther's theses into the fire ; Luther answered by burning the papal bull outside the gate of Elster. And at the diet of Worms, before an assembly of princes and prelates more brilliant than Europe had scarcely ever seen before, he sealed his conviction with the immortal words : " Here I stand ; I cannot do otherwise ; God help me, amen ! "

The day of the Reformation had come ; over Europe passed a breath of God ; the hearts of men were moved as the sea in a storm. It was a stream, that could not be turned aside ; it was another Nile stream, which flowing far over its banks, fertilised the arid and sunburnt lands.

This stream was irresistible ; it knew no bounds ; the writings of Luther and his brave helpmates were disseminated like strong germinating seed, over the field of the world, and in the spring of 1519 Luther wrote triumphantly that his letters were read in Paris and gave satisfaction to many.

But if he for one moment imagined that among those well-wishing readers the professors of the Theological Faculty were included, he was greatly mistaken.

The Sorbonne was terribly incensed. Luther was in its eyes worse than Mohammed ; against such a cursed heretic nothing could avail but sword and fire. And mad with rage, the Sorbonne issued an edict, that whoever possessed a book of Luther's and did not bring it within a week, should be imprisoned and fined a hundred livres.

Is Luther, then, the father of French Protestantism ?—Not so !

In 1512, when the Augustine monk on his bare knees, bewailing with tears of blood his sins and misery, had climbed Pilate's staircase at Rome, without a kindly star to illumine his darkness, and Zwingli, like another crusader, had crossed the Alps to risk his life and all that he had before the Pope, Le Fèvre with increasing enthusiasm had followed the shining and everlasting light, that had appeared to him three years before.

He was the pioneer of Protestantism ; and the Exposition of the Psalms, which was printed in

LUTHER BURNS THE BULL

[Face page 20

LUTHER AT THE DIET OF WORMS

[Face page 21

1512, was the first Protestant book that appeared in France and in Europe.

He did not, indeed, possess Luther's heroic courage. It never entered his head to burn a papal bull, whilst the resolute consistency of John Calvin was nothing for this grey-headed old man, inclined to silent speculations. He was a Protestant in the monk's cowl, and whilst Luther fought with heroic courage against priests and devils, the soul of Le Fèvre longed for rest and reconciliation.

Yet the fire that burned there on the altar of his heart had been lit by God ; he had gazed upon the unveiled face of Christ ; and his spirit had accepted the sacred secret of reconciliation through Christ's blood.

Le Fèvre did more ; by his instruction he won his first pupil : a man who, for burning zeal, untiring energy, and matchless intrepidity, was excelled by none of the Reformers.

That man was William Farel.

" My son ! " said the grey-headed old man of nearly eighty, in the year 1512, whilst his aged eyes were illumined with prophetic glow, " God is going to renew the world, and you will live to see it ! "

With all the strength of his young, passionate heart, Farel had clung to the Roman Catholic Church, but she had not been able to satisfy the yearnings of his soul. Then he had turned to Aristotle, but the Greek philosophy brought him no light. And the Bible had left him just as perplexed, since it was impossible for Farel to place the authority of God's Word higher than the authority of the Church.

Then on his life's path he met Le Fèvre, and, as if by inspiration, he understood that this man possessed the herbs wherewith to cure his sick soul.

The two so totally different characters attracted each other with strong magnetic power ; in the gentle and lovable old man, whose one foot rested on the earth, whilst the other stood on the golden strand of eternity, there was a charm which William Farel could not resist.

Did Le Fèvre lead the child of Rome, thirsting for righteousness, immediately to the fountains of life ?

Alas ! Le Fèvre himself was still tossed to and fro like a reed in the storm. He took the young man by the hand and together they knelt before the mother of Jesus, the Virgin Mary.

There in earnest worship they lay absorbed, and then with flowers they would adorn the object of their veneration.

Yet Le Fèvre could not remain standing where he was ; truth drove him on with irresistible force, and he took his pupil with him on the way.

" My son ! " he once said, " it is all grace ! "

They were four simple words, and they struck Farel with the strength of a flash of lightning. The scales fell from his eyes ; his soul drank in the words as the parched traveller in the desert drinks the cool water. He was saved, redeemed, blessed ; in the twinkling of an eye it had been done. And from that time forth Farel would declare to the four corners of the earth, that all our merits are like a garment, that is only fit to be cast aside. He took the pilgrim's staff in his hand and preached the word of life ; he came to the great city of Paris and there founded a community—in the same year that Calvin had entered the city and taken up his abode with his uncle Jacob Calvin, the locksmith, in order to attend the lectures in the College Cordier.

CHAPTER IV

TWO METHODS OF PEDAGOGY

" WHAT do you know ? " asked Cordier.

And overcoming his bashfulness, Calvin replied : " Nothing that I do not think to learn better from you ! "

Never could Calvin have been more fortunate ; Cordier was the ideal of a teacher : learned, acute, full of patience, the originator of a new pedagogy.

He had his own way of looking at things, and said that more could be done by gentleness and love, than by the whip and harsh words. A strange and singular assertion at a period when the scholars, if they did not learn, were thrashed like dogs.

He tried to implant in their youthful hearts the love of God ; they should be imbued with the spirit of Christ ; he longed to write the sacred name of the Saviour in their hearts with ineffaceable letters, and went on the hypothesis, *that the fear of the Lord is the beginning of wisdom.*

From this excellent master, Calvin learned the elegant Latin that awakened the admiration of his enemies, and that vigorous, temperate, and lucid French with which he exercised such powerful influence over the French nation.

From Cordier College, Calvin went to Montague College. It was a leap over a precipice. Cordier represented progress, spring, gentleness ; Montague, winter, the old method, the strictest conservatism and the whip. The whip was the commonest means in resort to make young men learn ; more than once the rectors of the University impressed seriously upon the minds of the teachers the necessity of thrashing their pupils well ; Margaret of Valois, sister of Francis I, received in her youth many bloody stripes from this terrible whip.

Erasmus paid particular attention to the life scholars had in the notorious Montague College, and thus describes it : " Thirty years ago I was at a college in Paris, where you swallowed so much theology that the walls were impregnated with it ; but I took nothing else of it away with me than a cold disposition and a number of vermin. The beds were so hard, the food so wretched, the sitting up and studying at night so difficult, that in the first year of their stay in that college many young men of great promise became bandy-legged, blind or leprous, if they did not die. Some bedrooms, near which were the privies, were so dirty and infected that nobody who had slept in them came out alive or without the germ of some terrible sickness. The punishments consisted in flagellations, which were dealt with a severity that can only be expected from a hangman.

" The Principal wanted to make monks of us all,

and so to teach us fasting, he gave us no meat at all ! O, how many bad eggs did I eat there ! "

When Calvin went to this college, the gloomy, fanatical Noël Béda was at the head of the institution. And this Béda was the successor of the celebrated Dutchman Standonck, of whom it is said that when young he had reached Paris in the greatest poverty, and at night climbed into the tower to study by the moonlight, as he had no money for candles.

It was a hard school this, that Calvin had to go through, but he went through it with heroic courage. His mind was polished ; he became the first in his class, and here learned the art of debating, after Cordier had taught him the art of writing.

There were, indeed, bright sides to that stay at Montague College. Calvin formed the central point of a circle of sociable young men, among whom were the three young Montmors, the comrades of his childish years, and the son of the celebrated King's physician, William Cops.

It is true Calvin did not mince matters ; he was not afraid to express his opinions whenever his companions did things which were not in accordance with his serious views of life. But it was not censoriousness, and the Calvin of the legends flees to the land of mists and lies when we watch him in company with his friends. In him were united the energy of his father and the charm of his mother ; his innate bashfulness gave him that nice modesty, which forms the ornament and the crown of a young man, whilst his great attractive power accounts partly for the wonderful influence, which at a later period he exercised.

He could laugh and jest ; by his amiability he conquered hearts, and by his uprightness he retained them. His disinterestedness and unselfishness struck every thoughtful person ; and the charm which emanated from this noble character was so strong, that it afterwards induced the grey-headed Cordier to go and live at Geneva.

The young Montmors followed Cordier and so did the sons of Cops out of sincerest affection for the man, who has been done the most horrible injustice by the most scandalous falsification of facts.

CHAPTER V

A BATTLE AND ITS CONSEQUENCES

A PERPETUAL treaty of peace, made at Noyon in
1516 between France and Germany, had become
waste paper. And Calvin's peaceful studies were
disturbed by the cries of war and the clash of arms.

Two young men with ambitious and passionate
blood in their veins, had ascended the two most
powerful thrones of the Christian West. One was
Francis I, King of France ; the other, the Emperor
Charles V. The King was scarcely twenty-seven
years of age when the war broke out ; the Emperor
was six years younger.

The French King, decked with the laurels of
Marengo, where, seated on a cannon-carriage, he
had drunk a cup of water mingled with dust and
blood to quench his thirst, felt hurt and offended
when he lost the German imperial crown. He never
forgave Charles V, and the bloody strife of arms
should decide who was the more powerful.

In 1521 the strife began, and in the middle of the
war a pope came and died. He was the well-known
Adrian VI, son of a common weaver and washer-
woman from Utrecht ; a modest, sober-minded, and

sensible prelate, who was perfectly well aware of
the corruption that had attacked the sheepfold of
Christ, but lacked the energy to take the reformation in hand. Twenty months only did he wear
the papal crown. His days were already numbered
when his reign began. And whilst he gave nothing
to true Christians but fine promises, he was mocked
and laughed at by the Italians for the candid confession of his faith.

The energy which Adrian VI lacked Luther
possessed in double measure. The monk's cowl
he laid aside for ever and was as happy as a prince
when Catherine von Bora gave him her hand and
heart.

That joy, however, was not without alloy, for
the clear water of the Reformation was in danger
of being troubled by the stormflood of Revolution.

In 1524, the same year in which the victorious
army of Charles V drove the French from Italy, the
German peasants rose up to wreak their grievances,
real or imaginary, upon the nobles. These anarchists
of the sixteenth century fought like wild beasts ; the
flames of the rebellion spread with the rapidity of
a prairie fire—from the Alps to the Harz mountains
and from the French frontiers to Bohemia, to be
quenched in a sea of blood.

Horrible cruelties were committed in that peasant
war. A German margrave had the eyes of eighty-
five rebellious peasants put out because they had
declared that they would never regard him again

as their master. And from the devastated villages
of the peasants rose up to heaven the blood-red
flame with the lamentations of poor women and
children. With the enemy at their heels, the
remnant of the French army, led on by the Knight
Bayard, fled to the French frontiers. A shot
shattered Bayard's spine, and he died uttering the
words : " I die in an honourable fight for my fatherland ! "

And France and Europe bewailed him as their
bravest warrior.

Yet when the Imperials had crossed the French
frontiers, their glory waned. Attacked in their
rear, the Germans and the Spaniards were sent
home flying, after they had heroically and martially
stormed in vain the walls of Marseilles. Decimated
by continual skirmishes, hunger, and sickness,
General Pescara led his wasted and beaten army
back to Italy, without having fought a serious
battle.

In Paris the greatest joy prevailed, bonfires were
lit, and the good tidings from the South must have
done the heart of young Calvin good. For he was
a child of Picardy, of France, and never denied the
national tie which bound him to his fatherland.

A bright smile passed over the face of Francis I,
and the eyes of the whole French nation followed
him, when, at the head of his army, he crossed
the Alps at three points, and in ten days descended
into the smiling plains of Lombardy. Without

a battle or blow he reconquered the greatest part of his dukedom ; on the walls of the capital, Milan, he planted the French standard, and the Imperial army would have been scattered like chaff had it been followed.

But Francis I wanted something else ; the walls of Pavia were a hindrance to the King, and he led his army against the fortress. The fortress uttered a cry of distress, which was heard in Germany. The celebrated George von Freundsberg, the father of the young commander of Pavia and who had grown grey in arms, sprang up to save his son, and the town. He was the general who, patting Luther heartily on the shoulder at the diet of Worms, had spoken these remarkable words : " Little monk, little monk ! It is a dangerous game that you are playing to-day, but if you mean well and are sure you are right—then go on in God's name, and He will not forsake you."

By the beating of the drum, grey-headed Freundsberg called together his faithful lansquenets, and when he appeared before the walls of Pavia with twelve thousand soldiers, he was sure of victory.

The French King was resting on his laurels ; he set his soldiers the example of merry-making and carousing, and lodged in one of those Lombardian abbeys, where the monks, by their revels and drunkenness, had filled the soul of Luther with the bitterest indignation when he was on his way to the city of Rome.

It was on a gloomy February morning in the year 1525 that the Imperialists began the attack. The battle was excessively severe ; the King fought with desperate bravery, but his bravery was of little avail against the well-disciplined troops so ably commanded by Pescara and Freundsberg. The French were not defeated, but crushed ; their bravest soldiers covered the plain like corn-sheaves on the stubble-field in the time of harvest. Francis I handed his sword over to the Dutch general, Lannoy.

In one of the splendid rooms of the Palace at Madrid stood young Charles V, dressed in black velvet, waiting for tidings from the battlefield.

The Emperor was of medium height ; his forehead was broad and imperious, and his dark blue eyes, full of majesty and benevolence, gave a certain lustre to that plain face, of which the ugly, misshapen lower jaw was an inheritance from his fathers.

The Emperor was thinking of what Pescara had written : " We will conquer or die." And his face trembled from anxiety and painful impatience, when a courier, who had ridden his horse half dead, appeared at the gate of the palace.

" Where from ? " asked the porter.

" From Lombardy ! "

The courier was immediately admitted. And his tidings seemed somewhat like those of Cushi to King David : " *The enemies of my Lord, the King, and all that rise against thee to do thee hurt, be as that young man is."*

Motionless as a statue stood there the great grandson of Charles the Bold. The blood seemed to congeal in his veins. He spoke not a word ; no one spoke ; in silence his courtiers stared at him. Then the Emperor fetched a deep breath and muttered : " The King of France my prisoner ! "

He then disappeared in his bedchamber and threw himself on his knees before the image of the Virgin Mary, whilst words of the deepest gratitude flowed from his lips. To his astonished eye unfolded a brilliant future. His imperial hand was to be stretched out protectingly over the Catholic Church, which was being threatened by a late monk, was to plant the cross on the mosques of Constantinople and reconquer the holy sepulchre.

If Charles V were thinking of the Sultan, the captive King of France was thinking of the same man. Taking the gold ring from his finger he whispered to one of his confidants : " Let the Sultan see this ring ! "

But the Sultan was far away, and Margaret of Valois, the only sister of the King, knew of better help. She sent the King St. Paul's Epistles, and wrote : " These will be your deliverers ! "

There are two persons, who in the French Reformation tower far above the others, a queen and a plain son of Picardy. Margaret of Valois was one ; John Calvin the other.

We mention the royal lady first. Margaret Duchess of Alençon was the most charming and witty, the most intellectual and amiable, and if we except her daughter—the greatest woman of her age. She was the sister and mother of kings, afterwards herself Queen of Navarre and the grandmother of the man who is called France's greatest King.

The seed, sown by old Le Fèvre, had, in the case of the Duchess, fallen into good ground, and pure and undefiled in the midst of a corrupt court she had, in her quiet enthusiasm, set about the salvation of her brother. She had flattered herself that her work would not be in vain ; a change had already taken place in the King's heart ; even the blind eyes of her mother, the bitter and notorious Louisa of Savoy, seemed to open to the gloriousness of the Gospel.

But the war came and passed like a hurricane over the young blossoms, whilst the Duchess referred the King, who looked for help from Turkey, to the Pauline Epistles.

But Margaret of Valois did more. When she heard of the disastrous result of the battle of Pavia she could not rest, but started at once for Spain to see her captive brother. Her mind was a prey to the most violent emotion ; her brother, of whom she was passionately fond, was for her the symbol of beloved France, of the Reformation, of liberty. This King was then in the hands of a powerful

Emperor, who was surrounded by such advisers as
the Duke of Alva.

It was a long and tedious journey, and sometimes
she thought she would succumb from very weariness.
Yet like a heroine she rose up again, and seated in
a litter, passed through the fields of Catalonia.

On a Wednesday the Duchess reached the Spanish
capital. The Spanish grandees uttered a low cry
of admiration when they saw that eloquent and
lovely face. The Emperor took her reverentially
by the hand, and led her between two rows of
courtiers to the apartments of her brother.

The King had become seriously ill: he was
grieving about the hard conditions of peace which
the Emperor had imposed upon him. Yet at the
sight of her, the pressure of her hand, the look of
her eyes, his hope revived.

Margaret did not come alone. She brought with
her France, his native land, the charm and solace
of home, and the sweet remembrances of his
childish years. Her love, her devotion, and her
faith triumphed. She frowned a little when she
saw the treatment of the ablest court physicians and
prescribed another mode of cure, and watched like
the most faithful nurse at the bedside of the hero of
Pavia.

Did the Duchess make use of those silent hours,
as ministering sister, in the double sense of the
word, to attack Rome ?

Even in the days of her greatest zeal for the

Gospel she never did so. Whilst she believed in the suffering and death of the Saviour as an expiation for sin, her piety remained shrouded in the mists of Rome. She was a spiritual daughter of Le Fèvre ; her hand was more fitted to heal wounds than to deal them. She had set herself the impossible task of reforming the Church without destroying its unity.

It was an error of judgment, not of that noble heart, in which there was the deepest love for the Saviour of sinners. She spoke to her sick brother of that love. She urged him to celebrate with her the Lord's supper, and together they knelt down and received the bread and wine in remembrance that Christ died for them.

The battle of Pavia, which had made the Spanish people tremble from joy, had plunged France into the deepest mourning. The flower of the French nobility had remained on the fatal plains of Lombardy, and the storm of the panic raged through the streets of Paris. When young Calvin came from the University, he could see groups of excited people standing at the corners of the streets, in the squares, and before the churches. They could not conceive of a French King being a prisoner—it was a thing unheard of ; the Parliament called all able-bodied citizens to arms, and whilst the Imperial eagles were expected before the walls, command was given, that all the gates of the city except five should be walled up.

A reaction soon followed this terrible calamity.

The leaders of the people asked themselves what terrible crime the French nation had committed, that her army was annihilated. The fiery partisans of the Roman Catholic Church knew of no other reasons than the weak, irresolute attitude towards the *Lutherans*. And they considered it their duty to avert by bloody sacrifices the wrath of heaven, which had been kindled by the Protestant heresies.

The persecutions had begun some time before; in the same month in which young Calvin started for Paris, a Norman hermit had been burnt there on the Pig-market.

Yet the Royal Court had had no mind for these persecutions; the influence of Margaret of Valois stood the Protestants in good stead; and not till France was in danger of succumbing to her misfortunes did the hour strike for fire and blood.

Many Protestants took to flight; Le Fèvre, the meek and grey-headed old man, who was placed on a par with Luther, and called the precursor of Antichrist, fled to Strasburg with his sorrow and his burden of ninety years.

Johannes de Klerk was condemned to be whipped in public on three different days. Amongst the spectators was his own mother; her face shone with heavenly joy, because her child, whom she had brought with suffering into the world, was accounted worthy to endure reproach and pain for the name of the Lord Jesus.

"Keep up your courage, my child!" she said consolingly. And when the red-hot and hissing irons pressed the brand of infamy upon his forehead, this Kenau Hasselaar of the Huguenots, cried out: "Jesus and His standard-bearers shall live!"

In April (1525) De Klerk went to Metz, where, three months before, the body of a confessor of Christ was consumed by the flames. There he found a great number of kindred spirits, who received him with open arms. William Farel pressed his hand; the brand upon his forehead stamped him in the eyes of the Evangelists as a chosen one among the chosen. Yet, his days were numbered; his impetuous iconoclastic zeal brought him speedily in conflict with the Government, and in July he was led to the place of execution to be burnt. He was made to sit on sharp nails; and afterwards bound with iron chains.

Compassionate voices among the crowd cried out: "Pray to the Virgin Mary!"

But De Klerk shook his head, for he would not pray to the Virgin.

"I do not despise the Blessed Virgin," he said, "but I cling to the Lord Jesus Christ, who died for me."

When the executioner with his red-hot tongs wanted to pull off his nose, De Klerk, who was looking in a different direction, involuntarily turned his head away from the heat of the iron.

By this movement his lips were burnt off to the

teeth, but then he understood what they wanted to do and bore the cruel mutilation without uttering a cry of pain. The executioner then drew three circles round his head with the burning iron, as a punishment for having damaged the crown on the image of a Virgin Mary. His right hand was then torn off, and the faggot-fire was lit.

In the midst of the smoke and flames his face shone like that of an angel of God; Christ, who knows His own, had spread His hands over him to bless, and amidst the crackling of the wood, there rang forth from the lips of the dying man these words: "Their idols are silver and gold, the works of men's hands. They that make them are like unto them, and so is every one that trusteth in them. O Israel, trust thou in the Lord; He is their help and their shield!"

Pauvan, a young clergyman from Picardy and countryman of Calvin, was burnt alive on the *place de Grève* in Paris.

Much had happened before this.

When the officers of justice had seized him, he was frightened to death. And to save his life had followed the example of St. Peter and denied Jesus.

The clerical authorities were satisfied, and the scaffold was altered to imprisonment.

Yet in the gloomy vaults of that subterranean prison the look of Jesus penetrated, and the apostate wept bitter tears of repentance. He was deeply moved; no monk crossed the threshold of his prison to whom Pauvan did not proclaim the Gospel.

The clerical authorities were informed that the prisoner had lapsed into his former errors ten times worse than ever before. And to burn out this pestilential bacillus by fire, Pauvan was led to the *place de Grève.*

It was perfectly black with people when he appeared at the stake; there was a look of blessed peace upon his face, and when the flames rose up, he spoke to the people in the strength of the Holy Ghost.

William Joubert, a young man of twenty-eight and of good family, began to search the Scriptures, and once said at the office where he was engaged: "Neither Geneviève nor Mary—the Son of God alone can save!"

It was a bold declaration; the young man was put under lock and key, and the anxious father hastened from Rochelle to save his child. He did everything that could be done—went from one judge to the other and promised heaps of gold if the life of his son were spared.

But it was of no avail; William Joubert had to mount the dust-cart which was to convey him to the place of execution, and the people who came streaming up saw how the executioner bored through his tongue, bound him to the stake, and then set fire to the faggots.

CHAPTER VI

THE GLIMMERING LIGHT

WHAT a strange peculiar being is man! Gerard Cauvin (Calvin) had spared no pains to ensure his son a clerical career, and now that his ideal was about to be realised, suddenly came his order : " Don't do it ! Stop ! Go and study for the law, John ! "

But yet it is true, that unless the Lord give His blessing, our labour is in vain. Gerard Cauvin had toiled and moiled to get on in the world, and yet nothing that he did prospered. The neighbours of Corn Square, Noyon, said that he had buried his good luck in the grave with Johanna le Franc, and although he married again—the grim spectre of financial difficulties overshadowed his life.

From one misfortune another was born. As *procureur* he could not properly acquit himself of his duties ; as testamentary executor of a chaplain's bequest, he delayed to render an account ; again and again he came into conflict with the Church authorities, and angry and embittered, he bade his son lay aside theology and study for the law.

But would Johannes obey his father's command ?

He was then a young man of eighteen, with a determined, independent character and an opinion of his own, and was apparently qualifying himself with great zeal for his future career. His father's idea, that the law paid better than the Church, left him entirely cold ; he had a sovereign contempt for gold ; and the world of historic materialism, sketched by the socialistic democrat Marx in such brilliant colours, was for him nothing but a visionary region.

Johannes' answer pleased his father. It never entered his mind to disobey his command. His father wanted him to go to Orléans and study law. And he said, " Very well, I will go."

Indeed Johannes did not find it very hard to have to come to this decision ; the nimbus that surrounded his church had, in his eyes, lost much of its lustre ; and in the silent hours of night he began to study the Scriptures, called by the Sorbonne *a pest and a curse,* and by Olivetanus, *a source of Divine blessing.*

Olivetanus was a Picardian ; a son of Noyon and relative of Calvin. And whilst this defender of the truth was destined to become the heroic missionary of the Waldensian Alps, he guided Calvin into the path that was to lead to the highest seat in the most remarkable Republic ever known in profane history.

Untiring assiduity, the most dogged perseverance and a talent, brilliant and genial, combined to for-

ward Calvin with giant strides. And to his great
cheerfulness, his retentive memory, his perspicuity,
he added a wonderful aptitude for clothing the
lectures of his teachers in an agreeable style, full
of sensible and witty conceits. He was animated
with a deep and earnest desire for knowledge ; and
even then he showed that almost anxious love for
order, which he retained all his life. This same
precision he expected from his friends ; he did not
like parting with a book that belonged to him, and
would ask for it back, although he did not want it,
simply not to be vexed at a gap in his bookshelf and
the lack of scrupulousness in his friends.

He began then to study divinity, and Thomas
Aquinas was his man. This thinker charmed him ;
and had he remained in the Roman Catholic Church,
then he would have become a follower of Aquinas.
And he raised scholasticism to the queen of sciences.

It was the time that the breath of the Gospel
passed over France like the smell of spring ; the
names Le Fèvre and Erasmus, Luther and Melanchthon filled the air ; and the new idea that nothing
but grace can save man found its way even through
the strong walls of the cloisters.

Olivetanus professed this doctrine and Calvin
contested it. He regarded it with aversion, for
its novelty hurt him, and his pride could not bear
the thought that he had erred like a blind man.
He trembled for the fate of his cousin Olivetanus,
who had dared to touch the fathers, the priests, the

holy Church with his heretical hands, and he invoked the saints to bring back the lost sheep to the true sheepfold.

But was Olivetanus a lost sheep ?

Calvin began to doubt ; disquietude filled his soul, and the bright ray of light that flashed through him revealed to him his sins. He was the pilgrim who was portrayed a hundred years later in the immortal book of John Bunyan ; there was a mountain of sin, which threatened to crush his weak shoulders, whilst all his good works and all the saints, with the queen of heaven at their head, were powerless to help him.

Then a shudder went through his soul ; the thought of God frightened him, and he cried out, " O God ! Thou holdest me hemmed in as though Thou wouldst dart Thy lightning on my head ! "

By the advice of Olivetanus he began to examine the Bible, and wherever he opened the Word of God—he saw the crucified Saviour. Then he began to dry his tears ; he took heart, and the Lord *passed by him with a still small voice.*

" O Father ! " cried he in adoration ; " the sacrifice of Thy Son has turned away Thy wrath ; His blood has washed away my sins ; His cross has borne my curse ! "

But with strong ties he was bound to the Church of his fathers ; there was a mist before his eyes, although above the mountains shone the light. He stood in the midst of the movement, in the turmoil,

in the surge ; more than once he looked with perplexity about this turbulent world, and whilst
Olivetanus had become his friend, Béda, the fanatical pioneer of the Jesuits, was his teacher.

THE JESUITS !

When in 1528 Calvin left the capital to take up
his abode at Orléans, a dark Spaniard entered the
gates of Paris. He was a man of middle age. He
was on foot, and drove an ass, which carried his
books, whilst his purse was filled with gold pieces,
given him by rich and charitable people.

It is possible that Calvin and the Spaniard met
each other in one of the tortuous streets of Paris
such as it was then ; that the Spaniard asked the
way, and that Calvin with his inborn willingness
showed it him.

That man, that Spaniard was—Ignatius Loyola !
Strange ! wonderful ! extraordinary !

Calvin and Loyola were to be the armed leaders
of two principles, who were to strangle each other
in a deadly and desperate struggle. Their names
express two world-ruling thoughts. Calvin was the
embodiment of the Reformation, Loyola of the
Roman Catholic Church. And whilst Calvin was
to become the father of the Huguenots, and Loyola
the father of the Jesuits, the children of Rome
collected together to defend to the uttermost the
authority of the Pope.

CHAPTER VII

THE CAPTIVE POPE AND THE TRIUMPHANT GOSPEL

YET the Pope and Rome no longer existed. At least, the affrighted burghers told one another so.

What had happened ?

The Imperial army had marched to the South to punish Pope Clement VII for an act of perfidy. The dreaded German lansquenets formed the kernel of that army ; booty, glory, and honour were promised them, and Bourbon, who commanded them, had said : " Look, soldiers, yonder is rich Italy ! It is for you—take it ! "

And they took it.

In the month of May, 1527, the Imperial army reached the city of seven hills ; it was in the evening ; the sun had just gone down.

Next morning the attack began ; the scaling-ladders were made fast to the walls, and the Duke of Bourbon was the first to climb to the top. He received a shot right in his breast. His fall made his soldiers mad with rage ; nothing could resist the impetuosity of their attack, and they poured into the streets of the eternal city like a torrent that cannot be turned aside.

Then from the city there went up a long cry of grief; like Vandals the soldiers made havoc of everything; the most splendid works of art were destroyed and the archives plundered.

In the Pope's vestry, the cavalry horses were stalled, and as there was a scarcity of straw, the lansquenets collected all the valuable documents they could find there, and tearing them to pieces, strewed them under the horses like straw.

The despoilers kept holiday; they got down into the graves of the Popes and stole the ring from the finger of the dead body of Pope Julius II. A booty of more than ten million guilders was taken, and the soldiers gambled for gold, as silver and copper had lost their value.

It is said that the German lansquenets were the leaders, and this opinion is founded on the fact that the majority of those soldiers were Lutherans. And yet it is true that the Roman Catholic Spanish soldiers far surpassed the Germans in roughness and cruelty, and in the desecration of churches and graves could not be matched.

The Germans indulged in their love of ridicule to their hearts' delight. They were seen on asses riding through the streets of Rome in red clothes and with cardinals' hats on their heads. One of the troop was dressed up like the Pope and adorned with the triple crown; he was conducted to the front of the Angel's Tower, where he was done homage to; and the soldiers shouted so loudly that Clement VII could hear them : " Luther shall be our Pope ! "

Clement had fled to the Angel's Tower, whilst for a whole fortnight the city was given over to the wild licentiousness of a rude soldiery, who no longer recognised any leader. They had become one vast concourse of shameless anarchists. General Lannoy was driven away, and it cost Philibert of Orange no end of trouble before he succeeded in restoring anything like order.

Clement VII relied on the help of Francis I, but that man was like the reed which pierces the hand. And whilst the allies left him in the lurch, he was obliged by hunger to make terms with the Imperial troops of Charles V, in the same year in which, in honour of the Pope, the flames of the torturing fire rose up in Prague and Munich.

It was, indeed, a strange world in which the Emperor Charles V lived.

His ambition was flattered by the thought that the Pope was then compelled to make the ignominious journey to Canossa. On the other hand, he feared that the anger and indignation of the Catholics would not fail to procure him many a bitter enemy, and raising his voice, he expressed his Imperial displeasure at the scandalous conduct of his own troops.

To mete out the full measure, the Emperor commanded public prayers to be offered up in the churches for the deliverance of a Pope, shut up by his army ; these prayers did not, however, prevent him from making good use of the holy father's imprisonment, and to get out of it all that he could.

The ruins of Rome sent a shudder through Europe ; for the Roman Catholics it was a time of sadness and ignominy, whilst the burghers of Geneva said : " It is the beginning of the end."

These brave, self-conscious citizens asked themselves, of what significance it could be to their town that Charles V had treated the Pope so roughly ; and staring at the illustrious Imperial example, they were surprised that they had not yet shaken off the yoke of the weak Bishop, Pierre de la Beaume.

Geneva began to declare for the Reformation. Zwingli, the Swiss Reformer, had seen, as in a vision, the eternal light of the Gospel, shining above the lake of Geneva, and he wrote to his friend, Thomas Hofen, who was getting ready to fulfil a diplomatic function at Geneva : " This mission may, indeed, prove of extraordinary use to the citizens of Geneva, recently received into the confederacy of the cantons."

In these words, Zwingli expressed perfectly the thoughts of Hofen. And whilst the latter fulfilled his political task, he did not delay to make good use of his spare time, and in all simplicity to disseminate the word of the Lord. He found a point of contact in the desire for liberty, which descended from the tops of the Alps into the hearts of these children of the mountains, and the free spirit of the

citizens of Geneva listened willingly to his amiable
words as long as he confined himself within the
limits of neutrality.   Yet when Hofen laid his
finger on the sore, censured excesses, and began to
complain about the crying religious abuses, they
turned their backs to the man, whose new ideas
surprised and troubled them.

Hofen was not a Zwingli ; he was soon depressed ;
he had a feeling such as Jonah had, when the gourd
above his head withered away.   And in the dejection
of his soul he poured out his heart to Zwingli.

With frowning brow Zwingli read the despondent
letter, but the Reformer was far from sharing in
that despondency.   He did everything in his power
to strengthen his weak brother ; and he made an
appeal to the political freedom so longed for by
Geneva, to throw the gate wide open for the Gospel.

According to Zwingli, a people could be governed
only by the Bible or by the sword.   There was no
middle way.   And where there was no holy fear
for the Majesty of God, the cowardly fear of man
would dominate the heart.

In those letters to Thomas Hofen you hear the
rushing of the democratic Swiss blood.

" O my dear Thomas ! " thus wrote Zwingli from
Zurich ; " there is nothing that I desire so much as
to see the doctrine of the Gospel flourishing in
the Republic of Geneva ! Where this doctrine
triumphs there the audacity of tyrants will be suppressed ! "

Hofen felt his heart relieved when he had read this letter. This noble and amiable soul, so quickly depressed, so quickly elated, set to work again with enthusiasm, redoubling his zeal, till a second storm burst upon him, more violent than the first.

The numerous priests and monks of Geneva arranged themselves in close battle array against him. They reviled him in the streets ; they went from house to house warning the people against the heretical infection exhaled by that envoy. The doctrine taught by him was, according to their inward conviction, a cursed doctrine, and the town would become like Sodom and Gomorrah if they listened to this dangerous Berne fox.

Then Hofen was crushed, annihilated ; his task was done, and within a few months he was to travel to that land where all tears are wiped away from our eyes.

During his stay at Geneva as envoy, Hofen undoubtedly often came in contact with Besançon Hugues, the Nestor of the Geneva citizens, who was ready to lay down his life and all that he had for the liberty and independence of his native town. Hugues was a powerful personality, a Roman figure, whose eloquent tongue ruled the assemblies of the people ; a born diplomatist, who knew how to move the stern old men of Berne to tears by his recital of his country's misfortunes, and as Captain-General was one of the most redoubtable defenders of Genevan freedom.

Hofen had undoubtedly placed his hope in this honest, noble patriot ; but Hugues was a good Roman Catholic, and it must have been a bitter thing for the grey old patriot, when, by the force of circumstances, he was placed in the painful position of having to make his choice between the liberty of his town and the belief in the Church of his fathers.

But the choice had to be made ; the seed, watered by Hofen's tears, had sprung up, and next to the old patriots who clung to Rome, a new party, with *freedom and the Reformation* inscribed on their banner, soon gained ground. This party stood strong, by showing that the authority of the Pope and the freedom of Geneva were irreconcilable. And in league with the Government they propelled the ship of state vigorously on in the direction of the reformed waters.

Wonderful !—Whilst a destroying army was forcing its way through the gates of Rome, the Gospel was triumphing at Geneva. And whilst the shameless and riotous conduct of many of the clergy filled the citizens with grief and aversion, the leaders of the new movement cried : " What have we to do with the Prince Bishop de la Baume ? To your tents, O citizens of Geneva ! "

CHAPTER VIII

THE ASHES OF THE MARTYR

THE Pope's throne, however, stood firmer than rash Protestants supposed, and when Johannes Calvin took up his pilgrim's staff to walk to Orléans, persecution entered the streets of Paris.

Nobody had expected this. A sunny peace lay spread out over France ; the Royal Court was transferred to Fontainebleau, so much beloved by Francis I, in order to afford a worthy reception to Hercules II, the young Duke of Ferrara, who was about to marry Renata, the daughter of Louis XII.

Margaret, the new Queen of Navarre, was there too, and the Pope's ambassador, who paid particular attention to her, was so much struck by the harmonious blending of majesty, purity, and loving-kindness that characterised her attitude, that he could not refrain from expressing his unconcealed admiration. She was constrained to take part in the noisy festivities given by her brother ; but amidst all the contamination she kept her garments un defiled and testified to the godliness of the Gospel.

During these festivities there came suddenly like a flash of lightning from the clear sky—the news of the unheard-of scandal, that on Whit-Sunday, May 30th, 1528, in the night, the image of the Virgin Mary, at a corner of the street in the district of St. Antoine, Paris, had been shamefully disfigured.

The festivities were immediately stopped; in this desecration the King saw an attempt upon his kingly majesty, and, furious, flew to Paris, to find out the culprits. He offered a reward of a thousand gold crowns to him or her who could point out the culprit, whilst the police searched every house in the district, without discovering any trace of the criminal.

The capital was in a state of great excitement. Processions were organised to the mournful spot, where the Queen of Heaven had been insulted; five hundred students, with lighted wax candles in their hands, went to the place of disaster; the whole Sorbonne was there; the children of Paris went through the streets in long processions, singing their most beautiful hymns in honour of the Holy Virgin. Thither repaired the princes of the Court. It was quite a pilgrimage. The sound of clarions and trumpets filled the streets, and bare-headed, the burning torch in his hand, the King knelt down to present to the Virgin Mary an image of gilt silver.

This was not sufficient; more had to be done; only by blood could the abominable insult be wiped out. And the Sorbonne, the Parliament, and the King joined hand in hand to root out French

Protestantism.   The red glow of the funeral pyre
again lit up the Place de Grève in Paris, but the
death of a few insignificant and unknown Christians was not sufficient.   Nobler blood must be
shed ; a victim of some repute was longed for ;
the name of Berquin was mentioned.

Erasmus trembled for the fate which threatened
Berquin ; the old Rotterdammer could not for the
life of him understand how any one could court
martyrdom, and he wrote warning letters to his
friend to urge him to flee.

Yet Berquin did not flee, because in his eyes it
would have been a shameful act of cowardice.   His
thoughts were full of victory, and in the strength
of his belief he said : " God helping me, I shall
triumph over the monks, the University, and the
Parliament even."

Things, however, became serious ; the Queen of
Navarre received the ominous news, that Berquin
had been seized and shut up in a strong castle,
whilst she was powerless to save him.

Her brother had turned his face to Rome, and her
mother, who, six years before, had in her enthusiasm
exclaimed : " My son and I are beginning, by the
grace of the Holy Spirit, to know the white, black,
grey, brown, and all the colours of hypocrites ! "
had again joined those many-coloured hypocrites,
in order to persecute God's chosen ones.

Budé, one of Berquin's judges, watched with
bleeding heart the course of the prosecution.   His

whole soul rose up against the murderous plan
that the Sorbonne and the Parliament were con-
cocting against the man who was as dear to him
as his own life, and the thought that he was as
powerless as his friend, who sat there on the criminals'
bench, pained him beyond measure.

He did everything he could to save Berquin.
He visited the accused in prison, sat down by his
side as in the days of old, and was full of sadness
when he perceived that his friend turned a deaf
ear to all his plans to save him.

Then Budé adopted other tactics.

If Berquin could be persuaded to give way a little,
if it were but an inch, a jot, then much had been
gained. It was, he pointed out to Berquin, in the
true interest surely of the good cause which he had
espoused, that by making some concession, he
spared a life that still might be productive of so
much happiness and blessing to others. There
was still such a glorious prospect for him, such an
excellent field of labour, such a noble task !

Budé became more and more pressing ; it was the
voice of friendship, the truest affection, which
whispered into Berquin's ears. And whilst the
Protestants awaited the issue with abated breath,
came the mournful tidings that Berquin had fallen
from the faith.

He had fallen ; his eyes were darkened, and
thinking to serve Christ, he had denied Him.

With relieved heart Budé hastened to the judges

to tell the great news, that Berquin had expressed his readiness to publicly ask God and the King for pardon in the great castle-yard. Yet at the same moment the heart of honest Budé shrank back ; he was frightened at the victory which his eloquent mouth and his friendship had obtained, and in his soul there rose up a mournful thought, that Berquin had served his life at too high a price.

Budé was right. Berquin's peace of mind was gone ; fear, self-reproach, the bitterest remorse took possession of him, and when Budé entered the prison again, Berquin said in a firm voice : " I will retract nothing—I would rather die first ! "

That decided his lot ; Berquin was to die ; the King, who had twice saved him, did not interfere. One April morning,[1] early, the ministers of justice entered the gloomy cell in which Berquin was shut up. He had expected them, and fetched a deep breath when he came out.

The birds were singing on the trees, and the young, fresh lenten green refreshed his eyes. It was noon before the mournful procession reached the Place de Grève. It was black with people, the unusual spectacle of witnessing the head of French Protestantism die, had brought the people together ; a brisk trade was done in letting rooms and windows to those eager to see.

A dung-cart, surrounded by a great number of armed men, conveyed the martyr to the place of

[1] 22 April, 1529.

execution. Berquin had donned his most costly
clothes ; a velvet mantle hung from his shoulders ;
thus arrayed he wished to meet his King, who invited him to the wedding.

He was a model of Christian resignation when
he left the cart, and his face reflected the quiet peace
of a good conscience. Calmly he ascended the fatal
steps of the scaffold, and he turned to the people
to speak about Christ, for whom he was then about
to die, when a wild shout from the hirelings of the
Sorbonne drowned his voice.

The hargman approached ; Berquin bent his
head, and with the rope that was put round his
neck, one of the noblest men of France was throttled
on the stake.

His corpse was cast into the flames, and the little
weak community of Protestantism saw the man
on whom their hope was built, consumed to dust.

Throughout the whole land there was great dejection amongst the Evangelicals, when the sad news
reached their ears. It was a blow at the heart of
Protestantism ; no one had expected that the
nobleman who stood so high in the favour of his
King, would end his life as a criminal at the stake.

Others followed Berquin to death ; the fearful
crept back to the feet of the priests, whilst God's
children comforted themselves with the heavenly
light that even above the gloomiest gallows did not
lose its splendour.

In France there was great sadness ; a long cry

of grief rose up to heaven ; and the Queen of Navarre was the saddest of all.

She was bitterly disappointed ; her ideals had come to nothing, but she put her trust in God and thought of the words : " *And shall not God avenge His own elect, which cry day and night unto Him ?* "

She was comforted, and taking her harp, sang : " O Lord God ! Thy child is passing over the brink of death to come to Thee, his God, his Strength. O Lord God, awake ! And be present everywhere to avenge the death of thine own ! "

The Sorbonne had triumphed. The once defeated Béda sat with a grim laugh of satisfaction again in the exalted seat of the judges, and with Berquin's death the Evangelical belief was reduced to dust.

So at least thought his enemies and rejoiced, but God had ordained otherwise, and from the scattered ashes of the noble martyr was to arise the mighty Reformer of France.

CHAPTER IX

AT THE FEET OF THE LAWYER

FROM Paris to the town of Orléans, with its forty tennis-courts, was a great change for young Calvin. In the sixteenth century Orléans was the most illustrious town of France; Paris was called the capital, but Orléans the heart of the beautiful French country.

It was, indeed, a place of merriment and joy!

There in the shadow of the gigantic gilt bronze cross, erected in honour of the Maid of Orléans, they skipped and danced to the measure of the merry song of hundreds of students, who had flocked here together from the four corners of the globe. Hungarians and Portuguese, Italians and Englishmen here met one another. Moreover, there were numbers of Germans, who from over the mountains had brought with them their language and their Lutheran ideas.

And in this town at this University, at the feet of Pierre de l'Etoile, the king of jurisprudence, sat Calvin with his burning desire for knowledge.

Calvin was much impressed by the acuteness which characterised the great master. De l'Etoile was a sun, by whose brilliant light the lustre of other scientific stars waxed dim. He was of an upright character and amiable disposition, and to the inexorableness of the law he united the tenderness of a mother.

He was a faithful son of his Church, and had vigorously opposed the new ideas which he called heresies. This did not prevent him, however, from conceiving real friendship for the young student, although his evangelical opinions troubled him, and with his large, loving heart he remained Calvin's friend to the end.

Calvin, indeed, at once attracted attention. The sprightliness of his wit, the strength of his memory, and his remarkable style were the sparks of the genius he displayed, whilst his amiability and the gentle, irresistible charm which he exercised, soon gained for him a large circle of friends.

Amongst those friends whom he found on the pleasant banks of the Loire, Melchior Wolmar must be first mentioned. In his house a young, winning boy of ten, named Theodore Beza, attracted Calvin's attention.

Wolmar was wondrously skilled in Greek. And as Calvin had to thank Cordier for his Latin, so he would have to thank Wolmar for that admirable Greek, by which he afterwards became the unexcelled exponent of the Holy Scriptures.

Wolmar was something more than a great Hellenist—he was a true Christian. And to Calvin, who burned to know the truth, Wolmar showed the sum and substance of the Pauline Epistles, viz. *the doctrine of imputed righteousness out of pure grace.*

Yet this heart, thirsting for happiness, had another teacher—that was God. And Calvin began to evince strange and far-reaching ideas, which called vividly to remembrance the heretical opinions in this same town five centuries before.

We mean the eleventh century.

The year 1000 was awaited in breathless anxiety. In desperate fear the months, the weeks, the days were counted that still separated the world from the year 1000, that terrible year, in which the end of all things was to come—the unravelling of the world's history ; the dreaded Last Judgment ; the Terrible Day of the Lord.

Yet the year 1000 had come and gone ; the drooping spirits had revived ; and the millions, who had walked in the shadows of death, trod again the sunny hills of life.

Two and twenty years afterwards, in this very Orléans, to which the Emperor Aurelianus had given his name, strange doctrines were proclaimed, doctrines which were strikingly like the utterances of this young man from Noyon. The proclaimers of these doctrines were then condemned to death, but people asked one another whether after five centuries the rise of these heresies was to be commemorated.

Again Calvin knew not what to do. Hot as a furnace, he was, however, taught in the way of righteousness, and the day was not far off when, with the strength of a Samson, he would break asunder the bonds which had bound his hands. Then he voluntarily renounced the world, in order to possess the highest good, and the world paid the man out by hating him most bitterly.

The mystery of salvation was revealed to him ; he had looked into God's loving heart and was saved.

" O Christ ! " he exclaimed, " Thou hast manifested Thyself to my soul, and henceforth all that blinded my eyes has disappeared. . . . Naked and possessing nothing, I come to Thee."

On his seal he engraved a sacrificed heart, with the following marginal inscription : " O Lord ! as an oblation, I offer Thee my heart, sacrificed for Thee ! "

This was his motto, and he remained true to it all his life.

At the same time, in the Imperial Chapel at Augsburg, the Protestants of Germany handed over to the Emperor the twenty-eight chapters of their Augsburg Confession (June 25th, 1530).

In breathless silence the Confession was read aloud ; and when the reader, the doughty Pontanus, had finished, he said : " Most Gracious Emperor ! This is a confession of faith, which with God's help is proof against the gates of hell ! "

" Sire," added John the Steadfast, Elector of Saxony, " that is also my confession of faith, from which I will not budge one hand-breadth—God do with me what He will ! "

Those were the men who had already quenched their thirst at the eternal fountains before they had been discovered by Calvin. They defied the power of the Emperor, the anathema of the Pope, the anger of the world, because their guilty souls had found forgiveness through the blood of the cross.

And standing on the dazzling mountain pinnacle of faith, whilst angels and devils listened, Luther sang his spirited triumphal psalm, to the glory of God :

> Ein' feste Burg ist unser Gott,
> Ein' gute Wehr und Waffen ;
> Er hilft uns frei aus aller Not,
> Die uns jetzt hat betroffen.
> Der alt' böse Feind,
> Mit Ernst er's jetzt meint ;
> Gross macht und viel List
> Sein grausam' Rüstung ist :
> Auf Erd' ist nicht seins Gleichen.

Yet Calvin did not neglect the study of the law, and made such astonishing progress, that he was no longer regarded as a student, but as a master. One day, Pierre de l'Etoile asked him to give the Professor's lecture, and this young man, who was scarcely twenty years of age, discharged this honourable but difficult task with such clearness and acuteness, that he was looked upon as the worthy successor of l'Etoile. The doctor's title was even offered him, and that he did not accept it was due only to that rare modesty which distinguished him all his life.

The seaman's blood surged in his veins. From Paris he had gone to Orléans, from Orléans to Bourges. There he received the tidings that his father was seriously ill, and he hastened to Noyon to watch by the death-bed of his father.[1]

Did a beam of the eternal light refresh the failing sight of Gérard Cauvin ? We do not know ; the whole scene lies veiled in mournful vagueness. Moreover, the body could not be buried in consecrated ground, as Gérard Cauvin had failed to give a satisfactory answer to the questions put to him by the Church. For the sensitive heart of Calvin it must have been a terrible martyrdom to think that the awful ban of the Church rested on the cold corpse, and much must have gone on in his heart whilst he stayed in the death-room, and his brother Charles was pleading in the Chapter-house for the Christian burial of his father.

Calvin took his father and the laws of Justinian to the grave. His ideal was a quiet little corner in the wide world where he could continue his studies undisturbed and unearth the golden treasures from the Holy Word of the Lord. He was no man for the Bar ; his heart was too tender for the

[1] Gérard Cauvin died 26 May, 1531.

rude attacks of enemies, and whilst he wished to live as a quiet, forgotten citizen, God had ordained that he should die in harness. . . .

His delicateness and sensitiveness were not less great than his tender-heartedness. That went too far, and his friends took advantage of it. His heart was full of affection and gratitude, gratitude for the smallest token of friendship. His friendship was very exacting—it is true—yet was not that exactingness a proof of its sincerity ?

Furthermore, he was almost too particular in the discharge of his duties, in the execution of a commission entrusted to him by a friend.

A whole afternoon was spoilt if he had neglected to bow to an acquaintance, and the forgetting to send a greeting in his letter caused him a sleepless night.

There were two things which frightened him : poverty and riches. Pecuniary difficulties worried him as those little poisonous gnats worry us in summer ; and the fear that he would not be able to meet his obligations made him feverish from anxiety.

When he had left the house of death at Noyon, Calvin had gone to Orléans, via Paris, where the loss of two crowns worried him beyond measure. Those two crowns were to pay a debt with, and not knowing how to get them, he sent in great distress of mind the following letter to a well-known friend :—

" DEAR NICHOLAS,

"It is only necessity that compels me to ask a favour of you—a favour which, I fear, will be inconvenient for you just at present to grant me. But I knew I could speak to you open-heartedly, and as I have a good opinion of your readiness to help, I apply to you.

"My brother, who, as I know, has received the money, which my debtors have sent him, has, with his usual carelessness, disappointed me. I am, therefore, in difficulty and cannot wait a day, even an hour, longer. If you help me you will relieve me from an anxiety, of which you can form no idea, unless you yourself have experienced it. I want two crowns. Cop would have lent them me, if he had not spent all his money in the purchase of furniture for his room. My other friends are too far away, and I should have to wait too long for their answer. Farewell!

"At the end of the week I hope to pay you back the money."

Calvin was nervous and irritable, easily put out and passionate. Yet his heart was characterised by an almost womanly tenderness, and he could with truth say to Viret, who knew him better than any one else : " You know the tenderness or rather the weakness of my heart."

This sounded like a lament, and was it not so ?

CHAPTER X

THE CAPPEL TRAGEDY

WHEN Calvin had followed his father to his last resting-place, Ulrich Zwingli stood with a friend at night in the churchyard of the cathedral at Zürich, looking at the sky.

They were looking to the west of the firmament at a dreadful comet, with an unusually long tail and of a pale yellow colour, which stretched out in a southern direction. Just before it disappeared especially the atmospheric phenomenon made a great impression on them, as it then appeared to glow like a furnace.

Zwingli looked long at the star and seemed to be deep in thought ; then he said : " That ominous comet will light up my way to death."

The number of the forebodings increased. People told one another that above the Brunig two flapping standards had been seen high in the air. At Zug they thought that they had caught sight of a flaming shield in the sky. Loud mysterious peals of thunder were heard. Above the lake of Vierwaldstädter a fleet, manned with armed soldiers, was seen in the air.

Amidst the general dejection, which precedes an impending civil war, Zwingli remained perfectly calm and collected. His mind, it is true, could not shake off the phantom of those forebodings, yet with the far-reaching eye of the Reformer he could see beyond them all, and it comforted his soul to know that the King of Kings would at last accomplish His sacred object.

In the firm conviction of being a soldier of Jesus Christ, he looked with undaunted eye at the black thunder-clouds which were gathering above the lofty summits of the Alps, and was certain of his blessed immortality were the lightning to strike him dead.

Zwingli was a man of the sword and of the Bible. In him rushed the blood of the old crusaders, and he felt but little for Luther's fervent wish, that the strife for truth might be decided without the shedding of blood.

Zwingli's opinion was, that a war, carried on in the strength of the Lord for the most sacred of all beliefs, was good and glorious ; he lived in that conviction, and that conviction drove him to the fatal pear tree at Cappel, where he fell like a hero.

The five Roman Catholic cantons[1] were now quite determined on war. It was a religious war— the bitterest war that is waged on earth.

Zürich was warned of this, yet the majority of the people did not show much alacrity, and hesitating and irresolute, a little army was got together.

---

[1] Uri, Schwitz, Zug, Lucern, and Unterwalden.

At ten o'clock in the morning of October 11th there were only seven hundred men round the standard of Zürich ; the shadows of a terrible disaster fell across the hearts of the brave Zürichers ; there was no order, no discipline, no arrangement, whilst the Job's tidings, that a strong force of the enemy was approaching, multiplied.

In the midst of the terrible confusion Zwingli was asked for, and the council appointed him chaplain of the forces.

Zwingli was ready to go. At eleven in the morning he came out to mount his horse. All eyes were fixed on him ; his face looked as resolute as ever, yet in his eyes there was great sadness.

And it was no wonder—Anna Reinhardt was a part of his life. She was not only a faithful wife, but an unexampled help in his pastoral work ; generous, hospitable, full of love for the sick, a refuge for the poor she never denied ; the home of Zwingli was filled with sunshine by this excellent woman.

When strangers asked who that quick, busy woman could be, the answer was : " That is Dorcas of the Scriptures."

But Zwingli called her his apostolical roe.

The Sunday afternoons were most pleasant. Then the clergymen's wives met at the house of Zwingli, and there they deliberated how they could best serve the Lord and help the poor. If the clergymen were not prevented by duties they joined this circle, and with a loud voice they sang the hymns composed by Zwingli, to the glory of God.

The Reformer thought of all this when he left the threshold of his house.

"We must part," said Zwingli, with choking voice, to his wife Anna, who stood there speechless from grief and her face pale. "God wills it—His will be done! May He be with you . . . with me . . . with us all!"

Then Anna lifted up her tear-dimmed eyes to him and asked with a choking voice : "Husband, shall we meet again ?"

"Wife!" was his answer, "if it please God!"

But Anna knew that a fortnight before he had from the pulpit foretold his speedy death, and the thoughts of death cast their gloom over his open Swiss face.

The Reformer sprang into the saddle and cast a last melancholy look back at the house, where he had enjoyed so much love, consolation, and happiness. Then, with the grieving multitude following him with their eyes, he gave reins to his horse and rode away to the battle and to death.

So he reached the standard of the city of Zürich, but it hung drooping down, and the little army gathered round it in the autumn air, like a mournful funeral procession.

When the troop had crossed the bridge at Adliswil, under which the mountain torrent rushed madly along, the first cannon-shot was heard, about half-way from Cappel.

So the battle had already begun ; their brothers who stood in the vanguard, were in the fight, and as though struck by an electric shock, they hurried on to take part in the strife.

Near the inn, " the Beech-tree," at the top of the mountain Albis, they halted. What an impressive panorama lay there unfolded to the eyes of the Reformer ! He saw the beloved city with its many roofs ; the Zürich lake with its pleasant banks ; the meadows, the vineyards, the fruitful orchards ; and before him, at the foot of the mountain, rose up the grey walls and the spire of the old abbey of Cappel, then the centre of a bitter strife.

" Let us wait here for the reserve ! " said Toning, the captain of the sharpshooters.

" That would be wise if we could hope for an army," replied Lavater, the commander of the troop.

Zwingli's heart beat loud and vigorously. He thought it an unheard-of thing to remain standing there idle, whilst their brothers had such need of their help, and he sprang forward to share like a good shepherd the fate of his sheep.

The grey-headed banneret Schweizer, who bore the standard, said that Zwingli was right. The cannon in the distance was calling them ; it would be an indelible disgrace, if like cowards they remained behind.

So the men of Zürich descended the mountain, and it was three o'clock in the afternoon when Zwingli and his party joined the little troop of the vanguard, just as the Waldstädters were advancing with an overwhelming force.

"Well, Master Ulrich!" said a Zürich citizen, who had never been a friend to Zwingli; "what dost thou say now? They'll dust your jacket nicely for you yonder."

"There are here brave men enough," was the calm reply, "who know as I do that they are in the hands of the Lord, and therefore are not afraid of the odds against them."

The Züricher repented of his harsh words, and replied: "I am ready to lay down my life as well as the others." And the man kept his word.

It was now four o'clock; the autumn day was already drawing to a close, and the thought became stronger that the Waldstädters would postpone the decisive attack till the following morning. But whilst the Zürichers were about to take up new positions, they were suddenly attacked by a murderous fire from the sharpshooters, who had concealed themselves in a little wood, which they had left unoccupied.

It was a moment of terrible confusion, yet Lavater, who knew fear only by name, seized a lance, and, springing before his men, cried out with his lion's voice: "Men of Zürich! fight for the honour of God and for the honour of our masters!"

With his helmet on, his sword by his side, and his halberd in his hand, Zwingli stood there gloomy and silent.

" Master Ulrich ! " cried a citizen, " speak to the men and encourage them ! "

Then the great Reformer spoke of God Who never forsakes His people, and of the lawfulness and justice of their cause, although they should suffer defeat.

His eye saw the great inevitable disaster rapidly approaching, but the Lord God was his refuge.

Trust in God ! He alone can save ! Those were the last words which his fellow-citizens heard from him—they were his testament, which he left to his beloved Zürich.

Then the battle raged. The Waldstädters fought with the courage inspired by victory, the Zürichers, with the desperation of a man who will sell his life at the highest price only.

Hot and fierce was the contest round the great banner of Zürich.

Old Schweizer held it clutched in his wiry hand above the field of the dead, where the brave Zürichers lay felled like cornstalks on the stubble field at harvest-time.

" Stand firm, comrades ! " cried the banneret in a loud voice ; and undaunted he kept his ground till he fell—with the standard so gloriously defended, still in his hand.

Then the enemy gave a triumphant shout, but

the standard did not fall into their hands. The conspicuously heroic courage of a Zürich citizen saved the banner—it was the soothing balsam on the smarting wound.

For the sword of the Waldstädters, who were worked up to madness, did fearful execution ! The flower of Zürich's citizens lay strewn upon the battle-field. Toning, captain of the sharpshooters, for-feited his life ; 7 members of the Lower Court, 19 members of the Supreme Court of Justice, and 482 citizens of Zürich and the environs were all slain.

There lay the father amongst his strong sons ; the rich merchant beside the poor workman ; and the evening breeze blew plaintively over the field of death.

Five-and-twenty Protestant teachers lay there dead amidst their slaughtered flock. Like blood-hounds, the Waldstädters sought for the preachers ; they thirsted for their blood ; the world's history knows of no battle in which so many shepherds and teachers were slain.

Striking and touching was the death of Ulrich Zwingli.

He hastened up to give the consolation of the dying to a citizen, when the latter, bleeding from thirteen wounds, had fallen prone on the ground. A heavy stone struck the Reformer on the head and he fell down senseless. After a time he got up to fall again, wounded in two places. With a great effort he rose up again, only however to succumb as before. And when he got up for the fourth time he received a fierce thrust from a spear.

Then Zwingli could do no more. He lay on his knees, but no longer had the strength to rise, and he saw his life's blood flowing away from his gaping wounds.

" It is nothing," he whispered in a faltering voice ; " they can only kill the body, but the soul they cannot hurt."

Those were his last words. He fell back and lay there with clasped hands, his eyes, over which the film of death was stealing, fixed upon the ever-lasting stars. He lay in a meadow close to the high road under a pear-tree, which was afterwards called Zwingli's pear-tree.

Two plundering soldiers of the Waldstädters found him dying, but did not recognise him. They asked him if he would not have a priest. " And if you are unable to speak," they said, " then commend yourself to the mother of God and call upon the saints."

But Zwingli shook his head and then the soldiers began to curse, whilst one of them turned the Reformer's face to the light of a watch-fire that was burning there. Then he recognised Ulrich Zwingli and was frightened. But a captain, who had served under foreign flags, no sooner heard Zwingli's name than he swayed his broad two-handed sword and killed the Reformer, crying out, " Die, hardened heretic ! "

M. HULDRICUS ZUINGLIUS

[Face page 76

" Thus," writes the chronicler, with affecting brevity, " was Ulrich Zwingli, a faithful teacher of the Church of Zürich, done to death in the midst of his flock, which, like a true shepherd, he had not forsaken till death. He died by the hand of a mercenary, for the confession of the true faith in Christ, the only Redeemer and Mediator, the only Intercessor of the faithful."

A council of war was held over his body. Noble-minded Roman Catholics cried : " Let the dead rest ! Let God be their Judge ! " But their voices were drowned by fierce shouts ; the body was quartered, and the parts thrown into a great fire, whilst the ashes were mingled with those of a swine and scattered to the four corners of the earth.

Zwingli was scarcely forty-eight years old ; it was all over, and with him a great and glorious light in the community of the Lord had gone down.

Anna Zwingli had now become a widow in mourning ; all Zürich went into mourning for its heroes, who had fallen there at Cappel.

But none were more deeply afflicted than Anna Zwingli. Her stepson was dead ; her son-in-law, her brother-in-law, the husband of her so tenderly beloved sister ; her best friends. And she, with her little children, was left behind alone.

It seemed all over with the glory of the Reformation. Zürich had to make a humiliating peace, and popery began to regain its old influence in Switzerland.

" Alas ! " said a teacher in Basle : " Is Zwingli then, whom I so long loved as my right hand, fallen beneath the cruel blows of the enemy ? "

It was the voice of the worthy Oecolampadius, who was consuming himself in the service of the Lord. He had become worn out by the wearisome contest, and in little more than a month after Zwingli's death he followed him to the grave.

" Rejoice ! " he said to his friends, when death was stirring in his veins, " I am now going to the land of everlasting bliss ! "

He was then only forty-five years old. In ideas he stood between Zwingli and Calvin, but his gentle, peace-loving nature was more than once carried away by the turbulent blood of the Reformer of Zürich.

When he was dying he sent for his three children. It was a mournful sight—the eldest was scarcely three years old. He clasped the little children's hands in his and said : " Love God. He will be a Father to you ! "   And then he blessed his little ones.

His death-chamber presented the sublime spectacle of one of the Lord's elect going to his Father. Ten brother-workers were present.

" What news do you bring ? " said the dying man to a friend.

" I have no news," was the answer.

But the dying man had news—he would soon be with his Saviour.

When they were about to open the window to admit more light, he said, laying his hand on his heart : " Here is light enough ! "

That was a different expression to the dying cry of the great German poet Goethe : " More light ! "

When the sun rose in all his glory, his first beams fell on the closing eyes of the John of the Reformation, and mourned by his whole congregation, he passed away to enter into the joy of His Lord (November 21st, 1531).

CHAPTER XI

WANDERINGS

WHILST the sun, red as blood, went down over the smiling valleys of Switzerland, Calvin was writing his first work. And in the spring of 1532 it was published. It was an exposition of Seneca's celebrated work, *Meekness*.

It had made the writer nervous. It gave him no rest ; " the die is cast," he wrote. And the doubt of success, which a writer feels who appears for the first time before the public, caused him no little uneasiness.

The word *Calvinus*, the Latin for Cauvin, appeared on the title-page for the first time. And the Reformer was henceforth to be known under that historic name.

The book was printed at Calvin's expense ; it was a great venture for an author who possessed little, and the worst was, that the printer's bill far exceeded the estimate.

In order to push the book, he had prevailed upon some teachers at Orléans, where he was then staying, to use it when teaching ; to please him, a friend at Bourges promised to speak about it in his lectures. He wrote long letters about it to Daniel, and proposed sending him a hundred copies.

Calvin was often pinched for money. "I must contrive, some way or other, to get back the money that the publication of my book has swallowed up," he wrote to Daniel. "Yet I should be very glad if you would first write to let me know whether my book has been favourably received."

An exposition of a book by a heathen Stoic—how in the world did Calvin get the idea ? It was so thoroughly out of keeping with the burning question of the day ; in writing this book Seneca had dared to make a noble effort to crush the bloodthirsty feelings that began to rise up in the youthful Emperor, Nero. And then, when the French prisons were teeming with Protestants and the flaming faggot fires were burning to ashes the elect of the Lord, Calvin published his exposition of a heathen book !

But yet there is connection. One can scarcely repress the thought, that Calvin was thinking of Francis I as Seneca thought of Nero, and that these theses on gentleness written in elegant Latin with powerful eloquence were an appeal to the heart of the French King to govern with clemency.

The writer of twenty-three felt as Moses did when he saw the cruel oppression of his people ; it was love for his weak fellow-believers that was powerfully awakened in him. In publishing this book he had in view, as appears from his letters, the prosperity of his country which he loved.

With a boldness, which is surprising to us, he expresses, amidst observations on language and antiquity, his thorough disapproval of the political abuses of his time, the lack of good legal administration ; he makes special reference to the principles of absolute government, and reminds the monarch that the greatest safety lies, not in armies and gold, but in faithful friends and the love of subjects.

In this first book even, he takes his firm stand against the tendency of the Stoics' ethics, and this is the more remarkable, as during his whole life he had to defend himself against the imputation of being a thorough Stoic.

" This is the gist of the problem," he says ; " the Stoics reject compassion as a sickness of the soul."

And to this he replies : " No one can be good who is not compassionate. It matters little what the dull sages say in their darkness. In any case, I do not know whether they are wise—all that I know is that they are not men."

To these principles of compassion, sympathy and pity, Calvin remained true, and with all the earnestness of a feeling heart he defended the right of crying eyes at the very time in which he was accused of the greatest hardness of heart.

As a young man of twenty-three he defended the humanness of sorrow, and in the last edition of his chief work, the *Institution*, these words were to be found : " If all tears are to be disapproved of, what then shall we say of the Lord Jesus, from whose body dropped tears of blood ? "

So we see again, that the Calvin of reality had a different heart and a different pulsation to the Calvin of the legend. He was a man of flesh and blood, and had thickly underlined the words of the text : " Blessed are they that mourn, for they shall be comforted."

At the corner of de la Poterne Street is to be seen the gable of a remarkable house with a pretty enclosed balcony, where Calvin after close study loved to rest. The neighbours said that it was no wonder, for the eyes of Françoise Daniel, the daughter of the house, had bewitched him, and kindled another fire in the young man's breast than the fire of knowledge.

Whether that is true or not, who can tell ? So much is said to which no importance can be attached. Whilst Calvin was preparing for his examination as Doctor of Law, there was a merry wedding in the house of the Daniel family, but Françoise was not the bride nor Calvin the bridegroom, though it may well be supposed that he was among the wedding guests.

Five months afterwards Calvin was again in Paris, and the letter which he wrote from the capital to his friend Daniel, spoke of something else than young love and myrtle wreaths.

During Lent, Gerard Roussel, under the powerful

protection of Queen Margaret had preached to a congregation of four or five thousand people, whereupon the Sorbonne had made a vigorous attempt to incite the people against the Evangelicals. Yet it got nicely paid out ; the head authorities of the Sorbonne were imprisoned in their houses, and King Francis got so angry that he banished the fanatical Béda thirty miles from Paris.

The atmosphere was as full of electricity as the air is on a hot summer day, when the thunder-clouds gather in the south ; the excitement increased every day, and one lampoon appeared after the other. The heads of the Sorbonne considered the Queen of Navarre the cause of their trouble. They were furious, and proposed sewing her up in a sack and throwing her into the deepest part of the Seine.

Calvin wrote about all this. He had already become mixed up in the fray, and espoused the cause of the Reformers.

So the morning of All Saints dawned on November 1st, 1533. The Rector, Nicholas Cop, the friend of Calvin, had to deliver the solemn address for that day before the University.

He had requested Calvin to prepare it, and Calvin had replied : " Very well—I will do it."

The text was taken from Matthew v., " Blessed are the poor in spirit."

It was a piece of startling audacity ; never had Roman Catholic France heard anything like it before. It was a manifestation, a demonstration, the voice of Protestantism, the loud echo of Luther's battle-cry of seventeen years before.

It was the voice of Calvin, but the timid student had become the bold Reformer, whose eagle's flight upwards, past the saints and the holy Virgin, astonished everyone.

The unsought-for opportunity had been seized to give civilised and lettered France a fearless explanation of religious principles, which, at the same time, meant an ultimatum, a declaration of war to the Sorbonne.

The Sorbonne at least had regarded it in this light, and trembling from rage, it would not have rested till Cop had been cast into prison, had he not saved himself by flight.

Francis I was then staying at Lyons. And the Protestants, who built their hopes on him, were then to find out that he was the reed of Egypt which pierced the hand that leant upon it.

On the head of Cop a prize was set of three thousand livres ; the persecution burst out ; people said that the King had sworn to destroy Protestantism, root and branch, and Calvin had to make a rope of the sheets to escape with out of the window.

" Calvin, who had fled out of the window," an historian tells us, " made his way with all speed to the suburb of Saint-Victor to the house of a vine-dresser, dressed himself in his coat, threw a linen wallet round him, put a mattock on his shoulder, and then made his way to Noyon."

Political considerations prevented, fortunately, the French King from cooling his passion on the Protestants, as he had intended, and Calvin, who had escaped through a window and narrow streets, was soon seen again in Paris and in broad daylight. But the air was not yet free from storm, although the youth of Noyon was received by Queen Margaret with great honour, and presented even to the King.

Of this, no one was more firmly convinced than Calvin ; again he took his pilgrim's staff in his hand and went to Angoulême, there in peaceful seclusion to continue his studies.

The town of Angoulême is built on a plateau, a sort of rock which suddenly, to a height of more than sixty metres, rises up above the valleys. You still find there the old fortifications, which have been converted into boulevards, whilst the frowning battlements are transformed into smiling parapets.

In this fortress Calvin was to be found ; in a dark, narrow, angular street, where he had taken up his abode with his college friend, Louis du Tillet, pastor and canon.

People asked who the pale young man was, and the pastor answered : " Charles d'Espeville."

But then they were no wiser than before, for who had ever heard of d'Espeville ?

But that did not matter ; it was Calvin's fictitious name and for d'Espeville the house of the kind pastor was a cave of Adullam, where he could prosecute his studies undisturbed.

He had now learned to live from day to day. Experience had taught him to do so. For he had learnt this : if he had looked for rest, dangers had risen up like mountains, and if his soul had shrunk back frightened, the hand of the Lord had prepared for him a peaceful resting-place.

His heart had become quiet like the heart of a child comforted by his mother. The twenty-third Psalm was his portion, and though scarcely twenty-five years old, he seemed already ripe for heaven.

One thing only caused Calvin much grief—his slowness. Yet this slowness consisted in his working at night because he found the days too short. The library of Du Tilly with its three or four thousand volumes was the forge on which this new Vulcan, in the most brilliant French, wrought his religious conviction, and the weaving-room where the great master, in midnight meditations, wove the powerful work of the *Institution*.

As the work advanced, Calvin communicated the results of his inquiry to a few learned men in the neighbourhood. A prior, who bore the strange name of Pope of the Lutherans, belonged to this club, and this amiable " Lutheran Pope " offered his house, outside the gates of Angoulême, as a place of meeting.

"Let us find the truth!" Calvin would say every time that he opened a book.

"Not look for, but find," Calvin used to say. "The truth that we are seeking for is to be found."

At the request of Du Tilly he also wrote sermons and Christian arguments, in order to give the people taste for the true and pure knowledge of salvation in Christ Jesus. And whenever he preached, these significant words generally formed the conclusion of his discourse : "If God is for us, who shall be against us ? "

Yet Charles d'Espeville did not remain under the hospitable roof of the prior of Angoulême ; he turned his face to Nérac, then a distinguished place, and called the haven and refuge of all the comfortless. For there Margaret had taken up her residence. She was again overcome with a feeling of compassion, had made Nérac a free town for Protestant Israel, and, like a cluck-hen, which protects her brood of little ones, had spread her royal wings over the poor exiles, who by terrible sentences had been driven away from sunny France.

She had then made the mournful discovery that her marriage was hopelessly miserable, yet the misery which wrung her heart, made her exactly fitted to become the queen of the wretched. She was good and kind to all. With the learned she could carry on able discussions, for she was learned ; in theology she was at home, and those same fingers, which could execute the finest tapestry work, wrote sweetly flowing verses. She made the best use of her time ; when travelling she wrote pamphlets, and seated in her litter, a court lady held for her the inkstand.

To the Court at Nérac Calvin turned his steps, and there he met Le Fèvre.

Wonderful ! At the very time that the active old man published his excellent French translation of the Bible,[1] and whetted the Reformer's sword with which, in the name of the Lord, it was to achieve great deeds, Calvin appeared there.

The old man, who was already breathing the air of eternity, looked at the youth, laid his hand upon his shoulder, and said with the sacred enthusiasm of a seer : " You will be the instrument by which the kingdom of heaven shall be established in France ! "

Le Fèvre seemed to be immortal ; he was a hundred years old, yet his eyes were not yet dim. And stretching out his arm to the East, he exhorted Calvin to listen to Melanchthon. He thoroughly expressed Le Fèvre's opinions ; his mental affinity with the German Reformer ; Le Fèvre was the French Melanchthon.

Yet this chosen one of God got into Satan's sieve before his little barque had anchored safely in the harbour, and the words of comfort and con-

---

[1] The French translation of the whole Bible was published at Antwerp, April, 1534. At the request of Philip II and the Duke of Alva it was placed on the list of forbidden books.

solation : "All is grace!" once spoken by him to Farel, seemed to have lost their force.

The fears of hell assailed him ; the Almighty stood before him as a wrathful judge, and to Roussel, who exhorted him to take heart and put his trust in Christ, he replied : "We are doomed ; we have concealed the truth, which we ought to have confessed and borne witness to before men."

It was an affecting scene ; none of his friends doubted the sincerity of his piety, but he himself knew it, and saw the abyss before him.

Once he was sitting at the royal table and suddenly burst into tears.

Queen Margaret was much affected, and asked him what it was that made him so sad.

"Madam!" said the old man plaintively, "how can I stand before the judgment-seat of God ? I have in all sincerity preached the gospel of His Son to so many people, who thereby have suffered death whilst I have sought to avoid it, and that at an age when far from fearing it, I ought rather to have longed for it."

Then the Queen comforted the good man, who, for his faith, was an exile at her Court. Again he took heart, heaved a deep breath and said : "I must go to God, for I feel that He is calling me."

Then he turned to the Queen and said : "Madam, I make you my heiress ; my books I bequeath to Gerard Leroux, give my clothes and all that I possess to the poor, and commend the rest to God."

A slight smile passed over the noble face of the Queen, and she replied : " But what do I get then, dear master, of the inheritance ? "

" Madam," replied Le Fèvre with French wittiness, " the care of dividing my goods properly amongst the poor ! "

Then great weariness came upon him.

" Adieu, gentlemen ! " said he to his table-companions. Then he laid himself down to rest, and the Lord closed the tired eyes of His servant.

His friends made no noise for fear of disturbing him in his sleep. But it was the eternal sleep. He had reached the blissful Zion after a pilgrimage of a hundred and one years.

That Calvin was eager to visit his friend Roussel in his abbey at Clairac, can be understood ; in August, 1534, he is said to have gone there, and the stranger is still shown the old round tower with the strong walls covered with ivy, where nearly four centuries ago Roussel and Calvin talked together about the momentous interests of their fatherland.

Calvin had something to say to Roussel, and so he spoke. And about what would he have spoken with greater force and more serious warning than about the false mysticism that he could not tolerate in his friend ?

Roussel has been called Le Fèvre's most faithful pupil, but yet it is true that he deviated from the lines mapped out by his great predecessor, and landed on the churchyard of passiveness.

Nevertheless there ran through his doctrine the golden vein of the Gospel, and whilst he adorned his confession of faith with good works, Roussel showed the remarkable spectacle of a Protestant priest in a Romish frock.

Le Fèvre and Roussel displayed the same characteristics, though the former went farther than the latter. And the death of the hundred and one years old pioneer placed a barrier before the progress of the Reformation.

Le Fèvre was for purifying the temple, on the foundations of which Calvin wanted to erect a new building. Le Fèvre, like Roussel and Queen Margaret, longed for mediation, but they did not serve the Roman Catholic Church. This would have no transactions, no reconciliation, no healing of the breaches ; in the logic of her iron consistencies, she collided with Calvin ; and condemning Le Fèvre's writings to the flames, she was vexed that with the books she could not throw the writer in too. The honour shown to the saints was not sufficient ; the Virgin Mary was to be exalted as the supreme Queen of heaven, and the Pope regarded as the true representative of Christ.

So the Church was bent on war ; what would not bow to her should break. The days of patient waiting were past ; the gates were thrown open, and the battle was to rage along the whole line.

With bleeding hearts Le Fèvre and his adherents had supplicated for the unity of the Church, and mockery and scorn had been their recompense. Now it would be war to the glorious end, and singing their immortal psalms the serried ranks of the Huguenots, with Calvin at the head, came out of the gunpowder smoke.

CHAPTER XII

IN THE FIERY FURNACE OF PERSECUTION

YET the head of the Huguenots was then sitting behind the prison-bars at Noyon, his native town.

What had happened ?

He had gone to Noyon to renounce his clerical appointments ; his chaplaincy and the pastorship at Pont l'Evêque which had been offered him some time before. He was now twenty-five years of age ; the period at which one has either to serve the Church in reality or give up the emoluments connected with it. He felt in his heart compelled to come to the latter decision—certainly a strange feeling to Marx, the apostle of historical materialism, who thought he could explain all the impulses of the soul by the materialistic key.

There at Noyon he was confined in the prison, on account of an unseemly uproar caused in the church on the day before Trinity Sunday.

That tumult was, no doubt, a device, or at least a pretext, to get hold of the dangerous heretic ; for a week Calvin was in prison and then discharged.

Yet two days afterwards, the servants of the law again laid hands on him, and they would certainly

have kept him had not the motives for his imprisonment been disputable.

From Noyon Calvin journeyed to Paris, and there
in the capital he met the restless spirit, Michel
Servet, who had imposed upon himself the task of
rooting out the doctrine of the Trinity, on Protestant
territory.

In Paris the signs pointed to dangers ; nevertheless, Calvin was prepared to risk his life in order to
win Servet for his Saviour.

He suggested an interview ; the place even and
the hour were arranged. Yet Servet stayed away—
a fact the more to be regretted, since Servet died
at the gloomy stake on Champel Hill.

The capital could not hold Calvin ; he longed
for a quieter place, and already saw the dark clouds
gathering, which would obscure the light of France's
sun.

So he then went to Poitiers, accompanied by his
faithful friend, du Tillet, and reached the flat
heaths of Poitou, where many a bloody battle has
been fought.

At Poitiers Calvin unfurled the flag of the Cross ;
he longed to win souls, and spoke with an open
heart about Christ and the great eternity. He
was at once surrounded by a select circle of hearers
and friends, and preached with the burning zeal
of his soul on the great salvation in Christ Jesus.

But the meeting-place was too dangerous, and
to escape the spies, Calvin and his friends went

outside the town and met in a large grot or cave.

That is Calvin's grot, and is so called at the present day. It has now become a place of shelter for the sheep ; then it was a place of refuge for the sheep of Christ. There Calvin preached, and he invoked the Holy Ghost to descend upon the little flock assembled there in Jesus' name.

The Reformer was wont to stand on an elevated spot ; the listeners leant against the rocks. Amidst deep, mysterious stillness the words of life flowed from his lips and he generally ended with an impressive sentence that stirred all hearts.

When he spoke he carried everyone away with him, and the flush of enthusiasm tinged his pale cheeks. Suddenly he was overcome by an irresistible impulse at the thought of man's need. He fell on his knees under those solitary roofs ; the whole assembly followed his example, and heaven seemed to descend into that cave.

Calvin spoke with fire against the mass.

" That is my mass ! " he exclaimed, laying his hand on the opened Bible. Then he bared his head, threw his cap on the table, and raising his eyes heavenwards, said in a touching voice : " O Lord ! if at the Judgment Day Thou wilt punish me because I have spoken against the mass, I shall answer Thee. O God, Thou hast not commanded me to celebrate it. Here is Thy law—here is Thy holy word ! "

From that time a strong desire was awakened
to celebrate the Eucharist according to the Lord's
institution. The many ceremonies, the incense, the
choristers—all that had lost its value ; a plain,
real communion with the Saviour was yearned for,
and the first Lord's Supper was celebrated by the
French Protestants in Calvin's grot.

Yet Calvin could not remain at Poitiers, for the
odour of heresy issued from him, and from the dark
clouds, which his eye had seen, the first lightning
flashes were already darting forth. His fatherland,
whose reformer and benefactor he wished to be,
gave him no resting-place for the sole of his foot,
and he had to cross the frontiers to escape the
French stake.

But in all that was the hand of the Lord, for
Calvin was not destined to become the martyr, but
the reformer of his country, and from Geneva this
powerful patriot sowed in the furrows of his beloved
France the seed soaked in blood and tears.

The most fickle king whom France has ever
known, could not make up his mind how to act
towards his subjects of the Reformation. Policy
was his compass, and the equipoise had leaned first
to one side then to the other. Béda went to prison,
and when the doors were opened for him they were
closed upon Roussel.

Amongst the Protestants themselves there were
two parties, the moderate and the extreme. They
could not agree, and sent an apothecary, a simple-

minded, pious, and sensible Christian, to Switzerland to ask the advice of Farel and other distinguished exiles.

Farel had his answer ready. He drew up a powerful poster written with burning zeal, the preamble of which ran thus :

" Truthful articles respecting the terrible, great, and infamous abuses of the Popish mass, diametrically opposed to the Holy Sacrament of our Lord Jesus Christ, the only Mediator and Redeemer."

The document was printed at Neuchâtel ; the sheets were concealed in bags, which were firmly bound with linen and string, and these clerical dynamite-bombs reached Paris uninjured.

Thoughtful men shook their heads, but their warning was like a word spoken to the deaf, and on the appointed historical night of October 17th to 18th, the dangerous posters were stuck on the walls of Paris and Orleans, and even by a daring hand on the door of the King's bedroom.

Paris seemed as if struck by a fit of apoplexy ; fierce fanaticism awoke, and the furious King hastened to his capital to defend it against the heresy which had entered its gates. Solemn processions were organised. On the heads of the Protestants a price of a hundred crowns was set, and the prisons were filled to overflowing.

Yet these measures were not sufficient to allay the indignation, and the insult committed against the Church could be wiped out only by blood.

The shoemaker Milon, lame and paralysed, enjoyed the high distinction of being delivered up first to the stake (November 13th, 1534).

He could not be accused of having stuck up the posters, for he was unable to walk, but he had been found in possession of them, and for that reason he was condemned to the flames. The jailer lifted up the victim in his arms like a child and put him into the cart which conveyed him to the Place de Grève. So he rode past his home greeting it with a smile, and he was slowly roasted to death in accordance with the demand of the King's advocate.

The rich cloth-merchant, Du Bourg, was a different person. Not as a martyr, but with the proud attitude of a warrior, he strode on between his executioners, the halter round his neck, the torch in his hand. The hand, with which he stuck up the accursed poster, was cut off, but he bore the cruel mutilation with the firm courage of an old Roman. And so he breathed out his heroic soul—amidst the flames, which were kindled on the great fish-market place.

A mason, named Poille, was the third of the martyrs. He spoke of Jesus Christ, for whom he was ready to shed his last drop of blood, which so embittered the executioners that they bored through his tongue and fastened it to his cheeks with an iron pin. But he still spoke—with his eyes, from which shone the heavenly joy of a Stephen ; and amidst a low, smothered cry of fear from God's children, who surrounded the scaffold, Poille was burnt alive.

From this time the death sentences followed quickly one upon the other ; the murderous lust which slumbers in the heart of man awoke, and the terrified Protestants fled to the four quarters of the horizon, like a flock of sheep attacked by wolves.

For Queen Margaret the time had come to unburden her distressed mind by silent tears, and her grief moved the King to release her three friends, Roussel, Courault, and Berthaud, from prison and send them to a monastery. Roussel, the weak reed, bowed his head, remained with the Church and went to his abbey. The terrified Berthaud died a monk, and only the old half-blind lion Courault persisted in his faith. Despising the coarse monk's gown and rosary, he escaped from the thick walls of the monastery and fled to the land of liberty where Farel lived.

Yet with this last favour shown, the King's mercy came to an end. He solemnly declared before a select assembly that he would not hesitate to destroy every heretical member of his family, in order to prevent the others from becoming affected by the same pestilence. Accompanied by his three children, he went bareheaded, with burning candles in his hands, from square to square, rejoicing to see how six of his most faithful subjects were being burnt to death amidst the demoniacal shouts of an excited populace. The Order of the Jesuits was founded, and the man who was destined by God to become the leader of French Protestantism left the country as a refugee.

CHAPTER XIII

THE WHOLE ARMOUR

MEN are getting bad, it is said.

Were they better in former times ?

Two fugitives were making for the French frontiers ; with them they had two servants, who knew their misery, their grief. One of the fugitives —according to a Romish historian it was Calvin— could not suppress his emotion at the thought of France having ejected the Protestants. And notwithstanding this, one of the servants was bad enough to rob the fugitives of the leather bag with all their money, and to gallop off with it. They would then have been in the sorest need, had not the other servant, out of his own pocket, lent them ten crowns. And so at last, downcast and oppressed, they reached Strasburg.

Noble men they were, whom Calvin and Du Tillet met there !

Bucer, who, in the spirit of wisdom and meekness, lectured on the books of the New Testament, must especially be mentioned. Calvin admired the upright heart, the amiable disposition, and the keen intellect, ever busy, of this excellent preacher.

Yet he was rather afraid that Bucer, whom he subsequently called his father, was playing a part which he would too quickly renounce, and concede too much to Rome, in order to preserve peace.

Calvin did not remain long at Strasburg. He feared that the clerical trend in this new Jerusalem might work unfavourably upon the wavering character of his friend, Du Tilly.

It might have done. Moreover, he longed for the quietness of his study, and hoped to find it in Basle.

In this hospitable town, which ten years before had welcomed Farel, he found the resting-place so longed for, in the house of a well-to-do lady ; and thirty years afterwards this excellent woman would tell about the life and studies of the celebrated Reformer.

Here he met Nicholas Cop, his bosom friend, from Paris. How glad must Cop have been to see that pale, never-to-be-forgotten face again in his room. And how much they would have to tell each other !

The tidings from France were sadder and sadder. They heard of the end of the cripple Milon, of Du Bourg, and many others. Calvin knew Du Bourg. How many times he had partaken of that good man's hospitality !

A few months later, an old man, almost blind, hobbled into Calvin's room. It was Courault. And when this faithful witness told Calvin about the persecutions, a deep sigh escaped his breast.

It was really terrible. In the spirit Calvin saw the gloomy strappado, which plunged God's children into the flames, raised again, to cast them anew into the blazing fire, and he cried out : " O with what furious rage are God's enemies filled ! "

Then, however, a strange story was told inside the walls of Basle. King Francis, who had frightened his subjects by his barbarous cruelty, was now to show that his hypocrisy was equal to his hardness of heart. He had amused himself with the charred bodies of his Protestant subjects, but it had suddenly occurred to him that he could not do without the support of the German Protestant princes in his ambitious policy against Charles V, and he made a vigorous effort to justify himself for the murder of his subjects. In a detailed manifesto addressed to the German Protestant princes, the King tried to make them believe that the persecuted were dangerous revolutionists, and to get over the difficulty of lack of proofs, the King made this strange assertion : " I have preferred to bury their peculiar theses in the darkness from which they sprang, rather than to send them to you, who are the light of the world."

It was a cunning trick, for since the Peasant War, the German princes were terribly afraid of the revolutionists, whilst Communism had again broken out under the leadership of the notorious John of

Leiden, who had made the town of Munster the earthly Zion, and paid for his crime on the scaffold.[1]

A cunningly devised plan, that of Francis I. Yet there was one man who watched over the unsullied banner of French Protestantism, and whose soul was set on fire with zeal for God, when his brothers, who were chased like wild beasts of the field, were so shamefully vilified by the King.

Then appeared his *Institutes*. The work was the solemn and impressive protest of a heart moved to tender and sacred pity for those persecuted for their religious belief, and of a conscience trembling with anger and indignation at the shamelessness of a crowned hypocrite.

Yet for a youth, timorous and but little known, it was a bold deed to apply direct to a mighty monarch. The need, however, was urgent ; the flames of the funeral pyre, which consumed the martyr, flew in his face, and it would have been cowardice had he not made use of the only weapon he possessed—the pen—to try this last resource.

The need was urgent. New flames were shooting forth. A godly farmer was brought before the tribunal, dragged to the place of execution on a sledge and burnt alive. A barber at Santerre suffered the same fate, and it was probable that many others would follow.

Yet Calvin espoused their cause ; he put his

---

[1] Munster was taken by the allied princes, and John of Leiden beheaded January 22nd, 1536.

sharpest arrows to his bow and then shot them at
the conscience of the King.

" Sire ! " said he, " you yourself are witness how
greatly our doctrine is slandered every day. Indeed, they tell you that it has no other object than
to destroy all power and authority, to disturb peace,
abolish the laws, to do away with seigniories and
possessions—in short, to bring everything into confusion. And yet you hear only the smallest part
of these slanders. Fearful reports are spread about
it, which, if they were true, would condemn us,
and justly too, to thousands and thousands of
gallows."

It was not his object to secure for the Reformation
a certain right to stand beside the Roman Catholic
Church—he did not supplicate for pardon for the
Reformation. How could he ask for pardon ! It
would be a violation of the truth—the Reformation
brings, indeed, the true light—that shining upon
the path of princes and subjects shall prevent them
from stumbling.

He draws himself up to his full height in a hopeless
attempt to soften the King's heart.

He cries aloud—he shouts in the ears of the
King : " Sire ! consider our case from all points of
view. We are persecuted ; some of us are kept
in prison ; others are flogged ; some again forced
to make a public confession of their guilt ; others
are banished or escape by flight. . . . We are oppressed, insulted, and inhumanly treated ; regarded

as an abomination and a curse—and why ? Because
we place our hope in the living God, and believe that
eternal life consists in the knowledge of the one true
God and Jesus Christ, whom He has sent."

Writing the *Institutes*, he stands upon the lofty
watch-tower, and at those solemn moments his
soul is stirred by the furious struggle between truth
and falsehood, which disturbs the world.   He
sees the calamities ;   the mournful sound of the
death-bell rings in his ears, and the echo of Jeremiah's lamentations is heard in his words as he
writes : " Many seas of disasters overflow the
earth ;   many new pestilences ravage the world ;
all falls to decay.   One must despair of human
affairs, or bring order into them, even by forcible
measures."

And yet men reject the remedy.   " O forsooth !
God's eternal truth must be alone heard in the
Kingdom of God ! "

The letter to Francis I, which forms the introduction to the *Institutes*, contains a series of the
most brilliant sentences that ever flowed from the
pen of the Reformer.   It is pent-up anger that
speaks from them ;   Calvin does not for a moment
forget that the crowned hypocrite is king by the
grace of God, and with undaunted courage he stands
up for the truth.

But he is the son of the sixteenth century, and
defends the truth but not liberty, and while he
does not deny the authorities the right to kill

heretics, he simply demonstrates that his brothers in belief are not heretics.

At the end of the letter he makes a direct appeal to the heart of the King, and finishes his incomparable argument, that was read probably by millions besides the man for whom it was intended, with the following words :

" If the slanders of the malevolent at once stop your case, so that the accused have no opportunity to defend themselves, and, on the other hand, if these turbulent, malicious creatures, without your authority, go on showing their rage, by imprisoning, flogging, and torturing by fire and sword, we shall in sooth, like sheep devoted to the slaughter, be driven to despair ; but yet we shall possess our souls in patience, waiting for the strong hand of the Lord. He doubtless will reveal Himself in His own good time and come armed to deliver the poor from their oppression, as well as to punish the scornful. May the King of Kings confirm, mighty and illustrious King, your throne in righteousness and your rule in fairness ! " [1]

Sharper, more biting language against the officials of the Roman Catholic Church and her sins has but seldom been used by a Reformer, and never was the exaltation of the Church of the sixteenth century defended with such strength of inward conviction, with such thorough knowledge of the Church's past, and with such fire of eloquence, as in this address to the King, Francis I.

[1] From Basle, August 23rd, 1535.

The *Institutes* were written in Latin, that they might be accessible to the whole civilised world. The volume was octavo, and contained little more than five hundred pages, and yet it may be said that the publication of this book indicates a new chapter in the Church History of the West.

The *Institutes* expanded ; Calvin worked nearly all his life at them. The first edition, a book of only six chapters, had increased in the last edition to four books with eighty chapters. Yet the sentences which underwent alteration can be counted ; the substance, the contents, the trend remained the same, and the old man put his seal to what the young man wrote.

The book did not work like the swift, impetuous cavalry attacks which Luther made use of to harass his enemies, but like the slow, irresistible onset of a Macedonian phalanx.

The sales increased from year to year ; the editions followed one upon the other ; the book became for France what Luther's translation of the Bible was for Germany. It was translated into almost all European languages, and no writing of the Reformation period was more vigorously opposed, more fiercely attacked, or more feared by the Roman Catholics than Calvin's *Institutes*.

The contemporaries of Calvin spoke of a gesture which he often made whilst speaking ; how for instance he raised with one hand his black cloth biretta, and with the other pointed upwards.

Sometimes he gave force to that gesture by the words : " All for the honour of God ! " And people had become so accustomed to the expression, that it was understood although unuttered.

All for the honour of God—that expression embraced the whole life of the Reformer, and his *Institutes* were the result of it.

The *Institutes of Christian Religion* are the chief work of Calvin ; as in a golden temple, the great thoughts on the redemption are therein laid down ; the *Institutes* were Calvin himself.

He wrote them in defence of his brothers in Christ, whom he loved ; yet in defending them, he explained and justified the Reformation. He was as scriptural as Zwingli, but Zwingli was exegetical and Calvin dogmatical. Like Zwingli, he had an aversion to traditions, which was not shared by Luther, and whilst Calvin agreed with Luther in the doctrine of the redemption without works, the latter maintained that we are justified by faith, and the former by God, as saving through the sovereignty of godly grace.

The substance of the *Institutes* was Predestination. On that Predestination the Reformed Church of France was founded as upon an impregnable rock, against which the gates of hell should not prevail and the furious attacks of Satan would break like impotent waves.

Whilst France and Germany stood aghast at the unparalleled boldness with which the *Institutes* were

written, and new controversies against Popery
occupied his mind, the writer, with his friend
Du Tillet, was toiling over the snow-covered mountain paths, in order to reach sunny Italy.

What were the thoughts that filled Calvin's
mind when his eyes looked upon the eternal glaciers
in their snow-white garments ? Must not this man,
who had to fight out his great inward battle with
innate sin, have then thought of the words : " Though
your sins be as scarlet, they shall be as white as
snow ! "

The desire of his heart drove him to Italy, to the
place where the Pope ruled ; to the land of arts and
sciences, of heroes and martyrs. There superstition
reigned ; well then, those who were sitting in darkness should know that Christ—and He alone !—is
the hope of a poor sinner.

Calvin's mind was deeply stirred, when from the
last hill he looked down upon the smiling plains of
that Italy where rose the city built on seven hills :
the proud, riotous woman, the great Babylon that
was shedding like water the blood of the Lord's
beloved children !

With that Babylon, with that mighty Goliath, he
went to do battle. For his weapon he had nothing
but a sling, but in that sling lay the word of God
that overthrows the mighty.

Ferrara was the first place they stopped at, and
farther than this Calvin never got.

When Duke Hercules, with his youthful consort,

Renata of France, was celebrating his return to Ferrara (December 1st, 1528), the city had just been grievously visited. The plague had decimated the population ; 20,000 people had been buried in the cemetery ; the shops were closed ; the voice of lamentation was heard in every house, and the lecture-rooms of the University were desolate and forsaken.

Yet the Duke, who was celebrating his joyful return, wished to see joy and not sadness. The wearing of mourning was forbidden ; the church bells had to send forth merry peals, the shops to open, and the lectures at the University to be resumed when he came. And this was done.

In bright festive garments the people went out to welcome the Duke and his consort on the pleasant banks of the Po ; the cannons were fired, from the houses flapped the flags, red, white, and green, and the Duchess Renata was borne in triumph through the gates in a litter.

She was arrayed in a superb dress of gold cloth ; on her head was a glittering crown ; a procession of four-and-twenty pages in crimson surrounded her ; before her went the clergy with the professors of the University, whilst the envoys of France, Venice, and Florence followed.

The historians vie with each other in praising Renata of France on account of her brilliant qualities, the nobility of her soul, the energy and intrepidity of her mind, her clear judgment and her fine sense of justice, as one of the most remarkable women of her time. From her father, the excellent King Louis XII of France, she had inherited her taste for arts and sciences; this taste was strengthened by her intercourse with Queen Margaret of Navarre, whilst as a daughter of France she had brought with her to the Court of Ferrara her undestroyable love for her native country.

Yet her husband was a grandson of Pope Alexander VI; a man who by inclination and policy was a furious opposer of Protestantism. Hercules II excelled others in knightly games, in his hatred against the Reformation, and in the writing of elegant Latin verses. He was a great, strong man; a conspicuous figure at the tournaments; his religion consisted in a fanatical superstition, which did not, however, prevent him from keeping mistresses and bastards.

At Ferrara was the little sensitive poet, Marot, who, on account of the sensational posters, stood number 7 on the list of those suspected; number 22 was Cordier. There were also there many French fugitives, and as Queen Margaret had made Nérac a free place for the persecuted, so Ferrara, under the management of the Duchess Renata, became the cave of Adullam for the oppressed and sad at heart.

In this city, at this Court, appeared two noblemen, one of whom called himself Charles d'Espeville. He was dressed entirely in black velvet, and on his head was a doctor's biretta of the same material.

He wore a broad white collar and a gold ring. He
looked tired—tired from mental exertion ; nevertheless, his face was as noble as it was severe, and
he possessed those distinguished manners which
rendered him fit to move in the cabinets of kings.

Renata introduced her two compatriots to the
Duke as literary men, who had come to visit
glorious Italy, and the Duke, apparently flattered
by their coming, gave them a hearty welcome. For
he was fond of literature and science, and was
not displeased to see the circle of literary men,
who had gathered round his young and intellectual
wife, increasing. It flattered his pride ; it enhanced the lustre of his Court, and there seemed to
him but little that was suspicious in the religious
trend which characterised their meetings.

Yet there had been reasons enough to make the
Duke uneasy, for the air of Italy was filled with
the germs of reformation. In the very shadow of
the Vatican were found men of high culture and
deep study who, as watchmen on the lofty tower,
looked eagerly for the joyful morning which would
raise the Roman Catholic Church from her ignominy,
her misery, her decline, and give her a new, prosperous, and God-glorifying life. A secret correspondence was carried on between Rome and
Wittenberg; under the very eyes of the Pope, as it
were, letters were written to Luther, Zwingli, and
Melanchthon. A society, which before everything
appealed to the testimony of the Holy Scriptures,

was spread over the whole of Italy ; it confessed the doctrine of justification by faith, and had sixty members in the city of Rome.

Yet this movement sided more with Le Fèvre, Roussel, and Erasmus than with Luther and Zwingli. It shrank from a rupture with the Church ; the venerable cathedrals of the Mother Church prevented their eyes from seeing the dazzling mountain-tops of the Reformation ; and they shuddered at the thought of stretching out their hands to seize the crown of the Pope, the anointed of the Lord.

The Capuchin monk, Ochino, was the celebrated speaker of this society. When he appeared in the pulpit the people flocked to hear him ; the largest churches were too small to contain the hearers, who hung upon his words. And when he, the man of self-chastisement, whose thin face told of his continual penance, spoke in the Cathedral of Ferrara with burning eloquence, of the glory of the heavenly Paradise and the all-surpassing love of the Blessed Redeemer, the Duchess was melted to tears of penitence and earnest longing.

Yet behind the brilliant eloquence of this celebrated Capuchin monk lay concealed a lacerated heart. He stood with both feet in the stream, which, thundering down from the heights of the world of thoughts, stirred up the age. He could not remain there ; he must advance or go back ; he had to choose between his Church and the Refor-

mation. And his followers—the Duchess Renata in
the first place—had to make the same great and
difficult decision.

Then Calvin appeared ; he obtained permission
to preach in the private apartments of the Duchess.
From his own lips Renata heard the powerful discourse which, setting aside the regulations of the
Church, pleaded only for the Gospel. He announced absolute, complete justification by faith,
but that demanded also an undivided and total
surrendering to God, to live and die for Him in
perfect self-denial and so to come to that inward
feeling of personal communion of life with God by
which one is conscious, in loving, burning consecra-
tion, of being entirely His, the chosen of His almighty
love. The embodiment of this conception was the
terrible doctrine of election ; it was the profound
expression of that all-penetrating, mysterious in-
dwelling of God in man—for his salvation, his ever-
lasting bliss.

Was the preaching of predestination on the lips
of the youthful Reformer an incitement to meekness ? By no means—he preached obedience to the
Divine will, the severing of bands which bound
one to Baal, the deliverance, the bold deed which
would make one tread, with heroic steps, the path
mapped out by God.

Calvin spoke plainly and to the point ; with a
perspicuity and acumen such as had never before
been heard in Ferrara. He declared that the

priest as mediator is superfluous, as Christ is the
great Mediator ; that the absolution of the minister
can be dispensed with, as God gives it. He rejected
the intercession of the saints, the reconciling power
of the Sacraments, and made an urgent appeal to
personal responsibility. He wanted Christianity in
its entirety—belief with works ; and one's whole
life had to be a Christian life, a growing up to the
stature of Christ.

In Ferrara there were many things of great
interest to Calvin, but his life's vocation was the
preaching of the Gospel, and in the Duchess he
found a soul that was hungering and thirsting after
righteousness. He had many an interview with
Renata ; the Bible formed the chief topic of their
conversation, and the Divine Word was the lamp
that illumined the dark path of the Duchess. She
followed the advice of Calvin to follow that light
steadfastly, and a Roman Catholic writer has said :
" Calvin infected Renata so much with his errors,
that one could never get the poison, which he had
made her drink, out of her heart again."

Yet for the diligent Evangelist of Noyon it was
not sufficient to win a woman, although she wore
a ducal crown. He thought perhaps of something
else—he dreamt, maybe, of conquering the whole
of Ferrara.

Already there was a great movement at the
University, the minds of many were greatly agitated, and it would have been nothing to wonder at

if Calvin had in Ferrara thought possible what was subsequently accomplished at Geneva.

Yet these ideals would burst like soap-bubbles when the Duke showed himself in his true character.

So long as the meetings were confined to weighing and considering, to speculating and comparing, he had remained neutral, but when this strange fanatic from Noyon insisted on one being not only a Christian in name, but also in deed, he became uneasy in mind. And the approval with which Renata listened to the bold preacher confirmed his uneasiness.

It was but a year before that he had gained the ducal crown—and he did not mean to vex the Pope and risk the possession of a dukedom.

With a zealous hand he began to weed out heresy from his dominion ; many men with a leaning for the Gospel received commands to leave his dukedom. And with regard to Calvin, the Duke said with threatening gesture : " That man, that Charles d'Espeville, shall, as soon as he is discovered, appear before the court of justice to answer for his religion."

The Duke's decision struck Renata like a flash of lightning from the clear sky. She felt herself at once deserted by her truest friends, that she would have to remain behind alone with priests who did not understand her and with monks of whom she had a horror.

Calvin, who had been scarcely two months in Ferrara, fled at the very moment that the Inquisition was about to seize him. His departure grieved

Renata deeply, but the bond, which bound her to the Reformer, remained unbroken. She continued to look upon him as a chosen instrument of the Lord ; she was continually in correspondence with Calvin, and this correspondence lasted thirty years, till his death.

When the pen slipped from his trembling hand, he dictated to his brother his last letters, intended for the Duchess. To them he added a medal struck by King Louis XII during his conflict with Pope Julius II, on which was engraved the famous saying : " I will destroy the name of Babylon."

So Calvin then turned his face to the North. The sower had gone out and come back, after having scattered the seed in the furrows. A harvest of blood and tears ripened, and the prediction of the seer of Noyon to one of his spiritual children in Italy would be fulfilled : " He who in this land and at this time will lead a Christian life, let him prepare to die ! "

CHAPTER XIV

BATTLE AND DEFEAT

IT was on an evening in the month of July, 1536, when a stranger arrived at Geneva. He was a young man of seven-and-twenty, of scarcely average height, with a black pointed beard, a high thoughtful forehead, a stern, quick eye, and sharp, regular features.

He came from France. His object had been to reach Strasburg by way of Lorraine, but the roads were full of soldiers, for a new war had broken out between the French King and the German Emperor, and the traveller had taken a circuitous route to the south, in order to reach Strasburg via Geneva.

It was Calvin. After many a long wandering from Ferrara he had at last reached the French capital, but as it was not safe there, he had formed the plan of settling at Strasburg.

It happened that Du Tilly was then at Geneva ; he discovered Calvin and made his discovery known to William Farel.

Farel was agitated when he heard Calvin's name mentioned. He had read the *Institutes*, and in the author of this remarkable book had recognised the keenest intellect and most powerful writer of the age.

He sprang up as though he had received an electric shock ; he was a most impulsive man, and the thought flashed through his mind, that this John Calvin was the man sent by God to help him in his onerous reformatory work within the walls of Geneva.

The meeting between Farel and Calvin under the humble roof of the inn, where Calvin had alighted, deserved to be put on canvas by a painter.

Calvin, shy by nature as he was, stood astonished and hesitating before the impetuous Farel. He had totally different plans ; he longed for a quiet spot, where he might receive instruction instead of giving it. Bucer and Capito attracted him. No, he was not the martial hero to try conclusions with the untamable nature and rebellious spirit of the formidable men of Geneva.

There lay the town stretched out before him ; the noise in the streets reached his ears. The town was full of light, joy, and merriment ; above it was the blue firmament, which was reflected also in the clear mirror of Lake Leman below, whilst the Rhine flowed rapidly past.

Geneva was the cross-point of four high roads ; they led to Savoy and Lyons, Switzerland and the Jura. Everything passed along these roads ; new faces of merchants and travellers were con-

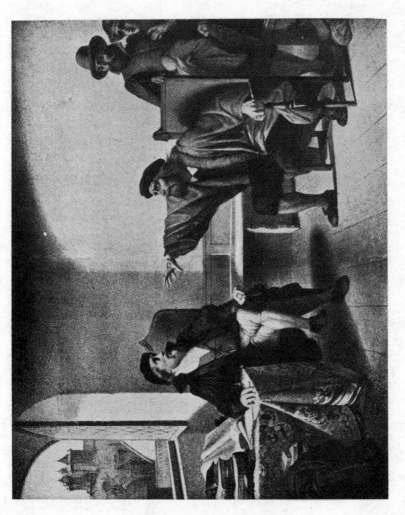

CALVIN AND FAREL (*after Lugardonn*)

[*Face page* 120

stantly to be seen ; the sharp practices of trade prevailed in the great market squares ; it was a town of priors and monks, of knights and barons, and Farel's voice seemed powerless to drown the light-hearted cry of the worldly-minded : " Let us eat and drink, for to-morrow we die ! "

And in this town was Calvin to cast anchor ?

The bare thought sent a shudder through his frame ; for himself he knew no more unfortunate resting-place on the face of the earth than this.

" I am timorous and shy by nature," he exclaimed. " How then shall I be able to fight against those raging waves ? "

But Farel, who never gave up, was not going to give up this time either. He expressed undisguisedly his bitter contempt for the servants of Christ who shrank from the strife ; he reminded him of Jonah, who had the temerity to disobey the Lord's command, and for his disobedience was cast into the sea.

His short form grew taller ; that angular, ugly, sunburnt face with that bristly hair and that red beard was lit up with the glow of a holy zeal.

Like a prophet, he stood before Calvin, and fixing his flaming eyes upon the young man, he cried out with his voice of thunder : " You think of nothing but rest ; you trouble yourself about nothing else than your studies. Well then, in the name of the Almighty I tell you, that unless you give ear to His call, your plans He will not bless.

May God curse your rest—do you hear what I say ? May God curse your studies, if in such urgent need you dare hold back and refuse to give help and support ! "

Calvin had found his man ; he bowed his head ; henceforth his life was to be bound up with that of Geneva !

But who could withstand William Farel ? This iconoclast, this Vaudois could be turned aside by no one. His motto was : " If we can't convince the Roman Catholic heretics, yet we can tell them the truth plainly to their face, as Jesus did to the Pharisees." Erasmus had trembled in his presence. " Never in my life have I seen so bold a man," said the savant of Rotterdam. His strength lay in his manner of acting. During a procession he had snatched the relics from a priest's hand and thrown them into the water. For the Roman Catholics there was no name more detested than that of William Farel. He defied prison and ill-treatment ; covered with wounds, dripping with blood, he appeared before the people to preach the Gospel, and to assure them that the Pope was the first-born son of Satan. Wherever he appeared, strife and disturbance were unavoidable ; the en-thusiasm of the Crusaders, who stormed Jerusalem, was in his heart ; he forced his way into Roman Catholic churches whilst the priest was celebrating Mass, and mounted the pulpit, drowning the uproar with his lion's voice ! Yet this man was humility

itself; he requested that no titles should be put
on his letters, and this bold heart was so sensitive,
that Calvin afterwards wondered more than once,
how greatly that Farel could be affected. Such
was the character of William Farel, who drove the
Protestant plough through the soil of Geneva.

But why had Farel come to Geneva? On a
splendid October day in the year 1532, whilst the
autumn gossamer threads hung in the air, Farel
and his fellow-combatant, Sonnier, had in their
wanderings, discovered in the distance the three
old towers of the cathedral of Geneva. Thither
they turned their steps and visited Olivetanus,
Calvin's nephew.

Olivetanus was greatly rejoiced to see the energetic Farel. He stood in urgent need of help.
Farel appeared to him the right man in the right
place. And whilst Farel immediately began to
preach the Gospel, he pledged his life, that he would
make true his words.

His appearance roused a perfect storm; the
women cried after him and Sonnier: " There go
the dogs, the rascals ! "

Farel wanted to argue, but the priests found it
wiser to fling invectives at their heads, whereupon
Farel, with his usual boldness, answered: " I have
not disturbed the world, nor this town, but you and
yours have disturbed the whole world by your
traditions, your inventions, and your dissolute
lives."

But for the seven hundred priests, who lived at Geneva, this was too much.

" Into the Rhone with him ! " was shouted. He was kicked, trampled on, and would have lost his life had not the authorities interfered. And early the following morning Farel and his companion were conveyed across the lake in a rowing-boat.

A few days afterwards, when the waves of excitement were still high in the town, a strange kind of poster was stuck on the walls.

The passers-by stopped, pointed out to one another the great advertisement, and read the following : " A young man just come to this town will give instruction in the reading and writing of the French language, to all who will, big and little, men and women, even to those who have never been to school. If within a month they cannot read and write he wants no money for his trouble. He is to be found in the Great Boytel-Hall, near the Molard, where the Gold Cross hangs out. He also cures many sicknesses for nothing."

The philanthropic teacher of languages, who came with such alluring proposals, was called Antoine Froment. He was a young man of one-and-twenty, a cowled Gospeller and secret envoy of Farel, who, by stratagem and address, was seeking to win Geneva over to the Gospel.

The new teacher of languages was successful ; people praised his ability, his zeal, and whilst he gave instruction in French he did not delay in giving instruction also in the New Testament. The results were surprising. With the keen insight, peculiar to Farel, he had seen that the fields were ripe for the harvest. Conversions took place ; the number of Protestants increased every day, and at the same time, the same confession of faith as Froment's, was heard from the lips of a Franciscan monk.

On New Year's Day, 1533, the rush to hear the remarkable French teacher of languages was so great, that Froment could not reach his own room. There were crowds of people who tried to get to the steps, the passage, and the stairs, and suddenly the cry was raised : " To Molard Square ! "

Molard Square—the forum of Geneva ! There your ears were deafened by the cries of the hucksters, the din of the market and the fair. There stood the booths, and in the immediate neighbourhood of the well-known inn, the *Golden Rose*, where Servet lodged before he was arrested, the farces, in which the people so delighted, were acted.

To enliven the festivals, firelocks and cannons were discharged ; and whenever quarrelling and discord prevailed in the town, the pugnacious citizens repaired to this square to settle a bloody reckoning with the opponent. Here the Protestants and Catholics glared at each other, pale with rage and excitement, the women with the claw-hammer under their skirts ; and here the prior Werly,

who so zealously defended his church, received on
May 24th, 1533, the fatal sword-thrust that ended
his life and the band which bound Geneva to the
Romish Freiburg.

It was, however, not yet May, but a cold New
Year's Day, and in triumph, Froment was borne
along to the square. He was placed on a seat, and
these people, thirsting after the righteousness of
Christ, cried out : " Preach to us the Word of
God ! "

Then Froment spoke, and the words of his text
were : " Beware of false prophets."

Yet the rage of a fanatical crowd, with armed
priests at their head, came like a tidal wave to vent
itself against him. He had to flee, and took refuge
in the house of an apothecary well disposed to
Protestantism, but the man's windows were
smashed and Froment left the town at the dead
of night.

Yet although Froment had fled, the Gospel
remained. Powerful Protestant Bern supported
the movement and wrote to the Council of Geneva :
" Let truth, your Excellencies, have free course ! "

No one knew what would be the result ; bitterness had reached an unknown height, and the
alarm-bell called the citizens to arms (March 28th,
1533).

The Roman Catholics took a laurel-spray as
their badge ; they organised an army, and whilst
fearful cries of murder and destruction rent the air,

and the loud ringing of the bells filled the streets, they rushed down the heights of St. Peter's to crush the Protestants, who had occupied Molard Square.

The Protestants numbered 2500 men, without the women, old men and children. Their cannons stood ready to fire, and any moment the battle might begin.

Yet the burgomasters tried to calm the minds of the Protestants, whilst the Roman Catholics of Freiburg did the same good work amongst their fellow-believers. The Lord blessed their united efforts ; a compromise was effected, and the Reformation went on quietly with its work within the walls of Geneva.

The warlike Farel entered the city again in triumph, with his inseparable companion, the pulpit, which could be taken to pieces and was fastened together with straps.

Froment followed ; the Reformed Church was founded, and Viret, who in his back bore the deep scar of a lance-thrust dealt him by a priest, baptised for the first time.

Calvin, Farel, Viret—these were afterwards called the trefoil. Two Frenchmen and a Swiss, for Viret was a Swiss. Of these three heroes he was the most distinguished for his meekness ; in a period of strife and dissension he showed the most lovable side of the Reformation ; by the tenderness of his love he had freed himself from the shackles of his age and he once saved the life of a Jesuit, who was on the point of being hanged. He embraced his enemy; he heaped coals of fire on the heads of his opponents, and that they resisted this fire was a proof of the hardness of their skull, not to say of their heart.

In those days the monks made this rhyme :

> " Farel will fight,
> Viret will bite,
> And Froment will rave,
> But us our God will help :
> Let them the devil have ! "

A woman of the inn, where the preachers were staying, confirmed the last line by asserting, that through a chink in their bedroom door she had seen how the devils, in the form of black cats, had sprung about under the table and were fed by the heretics.

But not every one seemed to be certain that the devils would soon fetch them, and a poisoner determined to help them. She was a servant in the house where the preachers were staying, and she bought the poison at an apothecary's and sprinkled it in their soup.

Farel did not eat any of it, he had no appetite. Froment was about to begin when he was called away, as his wife and children had just come. Viret ate of the poisonous soup under the eyes of the servant-girl and became very ill, without, however, dying from the effects. And the servant, who had fled to the cellar of a prior, was sentenced to death.

Then the issue approached with rapid strides. Farel, who expected much from debates, had pressed for an argument with the Roman Catholic divines, and in this argument, which lasted four weeks, Farel came off victorious.

To the beating of a drum the people raged and stormed against the worship of images ; with deafening shouts Farel was conducted to St. Peter's Church, the principal church in Geneva, to preach the word of God,[1] and the Roman Catholic worship was no longer tolerated publicly at Geneva.

The priests could smite their breasts and say : " We are guilty ; we have contributed to the Protestant victory, by our ignorance, our dissolute life, our deep debasement ! " And having carried on the contest to their shame, they left the town as cowards, seeking for consolation and help in the tents of the enemies of Geneva.

The contest against the Bishop de la Baume and his ally, the Duke of Savoy, then became a struggle for life or death.

Baudichon was made captain-general of the Geneva forces ; he had four hundred Volunteers under his immediate command, and these stood ready day and night to prevent an unexpected attack, whilst even a small fleet was equipped to support the defence.

[1] July 23rd, 1535.

Farel stood there in the midst of the anxious multitude like a seer of the Old Testament, and he prophesied victory at the very moment when the bravest citizens expected the capture of their fortress.

For no one could deny that the position was critical ; the strength of the enemy was overwhelmingly great, and the cool, enigmatical attitude of friendly Bern awakened uneasiness.

The men who ruled in Bern were first-class diplomatists ; they said that charity began at home, and thought of the difficult political circumstances in which Bern itself was placed, whilst the terrible disaster at Cappel was not yet forgotten.

Yet all at once when there was great danger of Geneva going over to Francis I to escape falling into the snare of Savoy, the Bern bear made his warcry heard. It sent a chosen body of men, under command of the celebrated General Nägueli, to relieve the distressed town ; the flames of the castles set on fire, in which Geneva had been besieged for two years, were the signs to the town that the deliverers were approaching ; the strong gates of the castle of Chillon opened when Nägueli hammered against them with his stronger fists, and a little Geneva fleet, which had rendered powerful assistance to the men of Bern, brought Bonivard, who had been prior of the Abbey St. Victor and for six long years in the subterranean vaults of

Chillon had sighed for the liberty of Geneva, back to the city in triumph.

The hand which had defeated the Savoy foe was then stretched out to receive a proportionate reward, but Geneva was willing to be the friend but not the vassal of Bern, and the perpetual peace which was made with Bern fully answered the wishes of the Geneva Government.

So after a struggle of thirty years Geneva was placed on the list of the free states. But owing to the disquietude of the times prosperity had sadly retrograded; many houses stood empty; commerce and industry had been seriously affected. Multitudes of strangers streamed through the gates to occupy the empty places, but there was chaff amongst the wheat. Moreover, many Catholic elements had remained behind in the town, whilst licentiousness had become a deeply rooted national sin.

Yet Farel was not discouraged. With a gigantic task before him, which would have made the stoutest heart shrink back, he boldly faced it; day after day his thin long face was seen in the pulpit, exhorting and comforting, reproving and praising, and announcing to the godless that they were quickly ripening for eternal doom.

He thought out a new code of morality, called the monks *shaved robbers*, and with almost scrupulous solicitude took care, as all Reformers do, that the minds of the people should be properly developed by education.

Farel lacked coadjutors. Viret bade him farewell and went to Neuenberg and Lausanne ; Froment backed out. But Farel lacked more, and for the first time in his life the undaunted conqueror of Geneva discovered with tearful eyes his lack of organising talent.

Force his way, storm, pull down the old mouldering building with his sinewy hands—that he could do ! But to build up, to put brick upon brick, to see with a clear eye, whether the wall was in a line with the plummet—that was more than he could do. For this he lacked the calmness and the tact, the clearness and the depth, the creative power. In the midst of victory he felt himself alone and forsaken with his few colleagues, and whilst he was in danger of succumbing to the heavy burden, God made use of the French King, to bring Calvin and Farel together.

For the army of Francis I formed an iron barrier, which prevented Calvin from reaching Strasburg by way of Lorraine ; with a disappointed heart he turned to the south, knocked at the door of a Geneva inn and met Farel.

That was the hand of Divine providence ; Farel saw it with the eagle's eye of a prophet, but the son of Noyon would not see it, till his resisting heart, hungering for rest and quietness, was crushed as it were by William Farel's voice of thunder.

All opposition was frustrated ; Farel, who had triumphed over Geneva, then triumphed over Calvin, and hand in hand they were from that time to found the community of Christ and storm the strongholds of Satan.

To further the cause of the Reformation in the Vaud, says Doumergue, Bern had determined to resort to the means that had there met with such good results and been of such great utility to Farel, i.e. the holding of a great public disputation at Lausanne.

Thither repaired Calvin and Farel, and there they met Viret. With the loud beating of a drum the disputation was announced at the corners of the streets. It lasted a week. Three hundred and thirty-seven priests were invited to this great duel; four hundred and seventy accepted the invitation, but only four could be found to defend their belief.

On Monday, October 31st, in the morning at seven o'clock, Farel opened the disputation with a discourse to the innumerable multitude which had filled the cathedral. In the middle of the church, places were kept open for the speakers, the four scribes, the two presidents, and the five government commissaries of Bern, who were recognisable by their black doublets, the red stripes in their hose, and the fluttering feather in their broad-brimmed hats.

On Friday, after a Roman Catholic divine had come with a cleverly worked-out argument to refute the theses of Farel and Viret, Calvin came forward with an elaborate speech, in which he quoted the principal Fathers to prove the fallacy of the Roman Catholic assertions. He spoke extemporaneously, quoted from his wonderful memory passages from the Fathers, and inflicted a really crushing defeat on his opponents.

In breathless anxiety the people followed his brilliantly lucid argument, and at the end a Franciscan monk sprang up to do homage to the doctrine expounded by Calvin, as the only true doctrine. He asked forgiveness of God, against whom he had so grievously sinned, of the people whom he had misled, and he cast off the garb of his order to go and live as a Christian.

There was a rich harvest for the Evangelical doctrine. The most inveterate opponents became fellow-workers ; others declared themselves won over ; in the three following months more than one hundred and twenty priests and vicars and more than eighty monks embraced Protestantism.

Houses of ill-fame were demolished ; the immoral women were driven from the town, whilst from Bern came the order to remove all images and altars from the churches of Lausanne without tumult, and to abolish the Roman Catholic service.

Without seeking it, without even wishing it, Calvin became the generally acknowledged leader. And at the great Swiss synod, which was held in those days at Bern, and where two hundred and ninety-six parishes were represented, this leader appointed by God, already raised his voice to plead for the amalgamation of the different national churches.

In the beginning no great expectations were entertained of Calvin. He was unknown in the town ; to this was added his timidity, his weak, pale looks—no, expectations were not great.

But the work which he did in conjunction with his colleague Farel soon showed what a gigantic intellect dwelt in this frail earthly temple.

For the organisation of the Church and Church discipline, a memorial was submitted to the authorities for approval ; therein the right of cutting off was assigned to the Church, whilst the authorities might inquire further into the matter afterwards. These articles spoke also of church singing, to put heart into the prayers and awaken zeal.

Besides these articles the Catechism appeared : a short and easy summary of the Christian faith for the young, and a confession of faith which all citizens of Geneva had to swear to. All who refused to take the oath were to be banished—a strange measure, resulting from the unfortunate misconception of the rights of Church and State.

At the appointed hour the Secretary of the town appeared in the chancel of St. Peter's Church to register the oath. Calvin maintained that the people were as ready to take it as the authorities were to impose it. This was true as far as it concerned the inhabitants who had assembled in the church. But many had remained away, and although the majority of the people took the oath, there was still a minority who impatiently looked forward to the day when they would drive Calvin and Farel out of the gates.

In the meantime, however, it was a happy beginning for the Reformers; the churches were regularly attended, and Calvin often looked back afterwards with joy to this period of promising blossom.

The attention of Europe was attracted to the light, which began to beam forth from Geneva; thither from England repaired young men in order to meet Calvin and Farel, and had not the Anabaptists come with their strange doctrines, then, in spite of the innumerable cares and the hot strife, this period might have been reckoned the happiest of Calvin's life.

In the spring of 1537 two Dutchmen applied to the Geneva authorities with the request to hold a disputation with the Geneva preachers.

It seems that these foreigners scarcely mentioned adult baptism, from which they derived their name; circumstances induced them to speak rather on behalf of their heretical opinions concerning the corporality of the soul, the freedom of the flesh, and the abolition of all civil and spiritual order. And these anarchists of the sixteenth century found at Geneva, with its easily moved population, thirsting for freedom and licentiousness, a fruitful soil for their heretical and dangerous opinions.

ST. PETER'S CHURCH [*Face page* 136

The disputation was held; and again Calvin showed what a master he was in defeating his opponents, but the Anabaptists were not divines, nor the hearers either, and in order to prevent the discussion from confusing men's minds the Council put a stop to it. The Anabaptists were expelled the town, so that danger from this quarter was averted. But some of their partisans remained behind in the town, and the storm was already gathering that would crush Calvin and Farel.

After the Anabaptists came Caroli. He was Doctor of Divinity, Prior of the Sorbonne and Canon. He belonged to the first priests who had been won over to the Reformation, but he brought his character with him to the Protestant soil, and showed that the laying aside of the Prior's garb is no proof of a real change of heart.

This man now slung an accusation into Calvin's and Farel's face, which for a moment struck Calvin dumb with astonishment. He was beside himself; his honour as an orthodox teacher, his whole work, everything was at stake. " This Satanic deceiver," thus he wrote to his friend, " has cast a slur upon me which cannot be tolerated."

Caroli had asserted that Calvin denied the doctrine of the Holy Trinity—that was the accusation.

Calvin asked for a synod to settle the question; he therefore went immediately to Lausanne, and did not even mind a journey to Bern.

The synod was held, and never did Calvin contend with such vehemence as he did against this man. In his written defence he called Caroli an impudent liar, an apostate, a scoundrel, who richly deserved hanging, and Viret besought him in vain to moderate these sharp expressions.

But it must be added, that Caroli was, indeed, a man of thoroughly bad character, a dissolute wretch, who on more than one occasion had imposed upon Calvin, and had the blood of two holy martyrs on his conscience.

Then Calvin's passionateness, the fire that burnt in his inmost soul, were manifested, and he literally crushed Caroli under the weight of his proofs.

Calvin and his friends went out free ; that they had denied the Holy Trinity had been nothing but a slander, and Farel gave Caroli the *coup de grâce* by unmasking him to the whole assembly.

So then at the highest Church Congress Calvin's honour was vindicated, but it is not easy to hush the voice of slander, and the authorities at Bern continued to be suspicious of the restless French stranger.

The disquietude spread even to Basle, Zürich, and Strasburg. Bucer wrote to Melanchthon about the matter in such a way that he could not but help thinking that the Church of Geneva had gone over to the Arians, and the names of Servet and Calvin were coupled together. For the Reformer it was like a blow in his face, and by the inexorableness with which he afterwards acted towards Servet, he wished expressly to show that he had never had anything to do with this heretical Spaniard.

There were other disquieting phenomena. The cunning Bonivard, who had a sharp nose for finding out which way the wind lay, joined the enemies of Calvin and Farel.

The great Council came to an end,[1] so that their opponents got into office, and although these men had not forgotten the heroic courage which Farel had displayed during the heavy siege, yet he and Calvin were urged to be moderate above all things. It was reported that the two reformers wished to found a new Popedom at Geneva ; against Calvin's front door blows were dealt with the butt-end of muskets ; in the evening crowds of people jeered before his windows, crying out : " Into the Rhone with the traitors ! "

But they stood like rocks in the midst of the surge.

Blind Couraud was taken into custody, and his colleagues went to the Council to protest against this violation of liberty.

It was in vain. They were forbidden to mount the pulpit on the following Easter Sunday, but they did so nevertheless, surrounded by their friends and their enemies, whilst knives were drawn.

The storm-clouds kept gathering more and more ominously over the heads of the two Reformers ; among the Council of the *Two Hundred*, the question

[1] February 3rd, 1538.

arose, what one had to do with those two disturbers of the peace, and with a great majority of voices it was decided to banish Calvin and Farel from the town within three days.

Then Calvin gave the following famous answer : " Let it be so ! If we had served men, then we should have been badly rewarded, but we serve a great Master, who will reward us ! "

So they went, leaving a place which, situated on the frontiers of the French and German world, seemed fore-ordained for a far-embracing, international field of reformation labour. One would have said that Calvin and Geneva were fitted the one for the other ; it had appeared that this little corner of land on Lake Leman was to become the fruitful field for the development of Calvin's far-reaching reformation thoughts.

But had not that been a chimera ? Did not Geneva drive her reformer away from the land like a leper ?

" Come ! " said Farel in a resolute tone, " it is well ! Let us go in God's name ! "

So they went, leaving a great work behind them. But their hearts were strengthened in God.

CHAPTER XV

FAREL went to Neuchâtel, Calvin to Basle, where the plague had entered.

A nephew of Farel's was smitten by it. Calvin nursed the man and another. And yet it was afterwards said that Calvin fled away on account of the plague.

When Farel's nephew died Calvin paid the doctor's bill and the burial expenses. Yet it was afterwards asserted that Calvin held his purse-strings tight.

In Strasburg, however, they knew him better ; he received urgent invitations to serve the Church there ; and as he had remained at Geneva against his will, so he then went against his will, but with the blind obedience of a brave soldier, to Strasburg, and said to Bucer : " Here I am."

Bucer, the reformer of Strasburg, was a strange phenomenon.

He was short of stature like Zacchæus, but of powerful intellect, with a great head on a muscular neck. Bucer was organiser, orator, exegete, divine, the model of a father, and a staunch advocate for the marriage of priests.

He usually had a bitterly small income : the half
of what a day labourer now earns.   Yet his hospitality was proverbial ; no poor man was sent away
by him, whilst his uprightness was above all suspicion.

He durst without scruple tell his friends the
truth.   At a glance he saw the weak side of the
Geneva fugitive.

" You are an irritable man," he said to Calvin,
and Calvin accepted the remark with the meekness
of a Christian.

There were other excellent men in Strasburg, with
whom Calvin was to become acquainted.

There was Capito, the man of the clerical aristocracy ; Jacob Sturm, a son of the Patricians,
the friend of the Landgrave of Hesse, and the best
statesman whom Strasburg ever had ; John Sturm,
the printer, who gave a model school to Strasburg :
a man distinguished for piety and knowledge ; the
preacher Zell, as amiable in character as he was
indomitable in courage.

With these excellent men Calvin came into contact, and had daily intercourse, after the storm of
adversity had driven him from Geneva.

As soon as he arrived at Strasburg, he went to
Capito's ; he lodged with Bucer ; he held con-
ferences at the house of Zell ; John Sturm and
Jacob Sturm saw him frequently at their houses.

So Calvin settled at Strasburg.   And in order to
get the right of citizenship, he had himself enrolled
on the guild of tailors.

Three long years Calvin stayed at Strasburg. It was the practical school where he was formed to become subsequently crowned the King of French Protestantism. There was no more excellent training school to be found for Calvin ; the Swiss called Strasburg the Antioch of the Reformation ; it was a second Wittenberg on the frontiers of France, a watch-tower, from the pinnacles of which the course could be seen of the strife that was disturbing men's minds and making the earth tremble.

Here in the old German Hanse-town Calvin could find out the faults which he had committed at Geneva, and exercise the tact to avoid them in the future ; his sphere extended far beyond the borders of the surrounding lands ; his knowledge had deepened, and he was made proficient to become the celebrated law-giver of Protestant Sparta.

Blind Couraud, who had been banished with Calvin and Farel, had in the meantime reached the end of his hard life, and his blind eyes then saw Christ, whom he had so faithfully served.

With Du Tilly things had turned out quite differently. He had gone back to Rome, to which he had once turned his back, and he wrote long letters to Calvin, to persuade him to do the same.

He belonged to the class of the three friends of Job, who were poor comforters, and he asked the Reformer whether, in the adversities and misfortunes which he had experienced, the chastising and wrathful hand of the Lord was not to be seen. His old friendship for Calvin was not yet dead, but it wanted to drive him to a corner, where an abyss yawned before his feet, and to the money which Du Tilly offered to Calvin in his financial difficulties, a condition was attached which the latter would not have accepted, even if he had had to die of hunger.

In Geneva Calvin had been pastor and political leader. In Strasburg his work was confined to the office of shepherd and teacher. He preached four times a week, and proclaimed the Gospel outside his French Church, to the Anabaptists, with success and blessing.

He made serious efforts to maintain discipline, substituted clerical inquiry for confession, and showed himself in stormy weather the resolute helmsman who held the rudder firmly to guard Christ's little ship against shipwreck.

He was animated by an all-prevailing desire to promote and confirm the peace of the churches. He gladly overlooked minor points of difference, in order to preserve unity, and his soul longed for brotherly love and harmony.

The work of the Reformer grew heavier ; he was overwhelmed with labour. To his four sermons a week were added three lectures, for which, as professor, he enjoyed a salary of fifty-two guilders a year ; he had to fight many a battle with the heretics, who, from all parts, poured into the hospitable Strasburg, and in lengthy dissertations he gave his decided opinion about marriage.

This was indeed necessary, for eleven years before no one less than Luther had in his sermons on the book of Genesis, asked the question : " Must a man have more than one wife ? " and given the answer : " It is not forbidden ; I could not now forbid it, but I will not recommend it."

The opinion of Melanchthon and other reformers was to the same effect, but Calvin thought differently. And his deeper insight into the Scriptures induced him, on the authority of those Scriptures, to condemn all polygamy as sin.

Now it is very probable that Bucer, who was such an enthusiastic lover of home, said more than once : " Calvin, why don't you look out for a wife yourself ? "

And in sooth, marriage plans began to flit through the learned brain of the Reformer. He wrote about it to his bosom friend Farel, and enumerated the virtues which he expected in his future wife.

These were no small matter. He mentioned modesty, willingness to help, simplicity, economy, meekness ; beauty of face was a matter of minor importance, but, on the other hand, he hoped that she would look well after his health.

A few months afterwards he could have made a brilliant marriage with a rich young lady of title. But there were two things which made Calvin look serious ; the young lady seemed to be proud of her position, and was unacquainted with the French language.

Calvin wished expressly that she should learn the French language, whilst with his habitual hastiness he already asked Farel to marry him.

But after all nothing came of it ; the little ship suffered shipwreck before it reached the harbour, and instead of an invitation to get ready for the journey, Farel, to his great astonishment, received a letter from Calvin containing the following communication : " I shall not enter into this marriage, or God must deprive me of my reason ! "

In the meantime he was in the greatest pecuniary difficulties, and in order to secure himself against pinching want, he was obliged to take boarders. But these pupils were, as a rule, as poor as himself, and in these straitened circumstances Calvin learned the struggle for life.

Yet he did not give up his marriage plans, and in Idelette von Bure he found the woman, who was ready to marry him for better or for worse.

Idelette was a widow with two children ; fortune she did not possess, but gentleness, piety, and captivating amiability formed the dowry which she brought with her.

For Calvin it was enough, and seven long years they lived happily together.[1]

Idelette's beautiful face made one think of Calvin's mother ; she was still young and dark-

---

[1] They were married in the beginning of August, 1540.

IDELETTE VON BURE, WIFE OF CALVIN   [*Face page* 146

eyed. The happiness was great for the poor wanderer, who had never known what it was to possess a roof of his own ; it was indeed too great, and God quickly tempered their joy, as Calvin expressed it, lest they should overstep the bounds. He fell ill ; Idelette fell ill too, and the Lord showed the two young people how frail all earthly happiness is.

Idelette was the model of a Christian wife ; the lovable side of the Reformer ; the soothing hand, which healed the wounds inflicted by his sharp reforming sword.

She visited the poor, watched by the bedside of the sick, threw her doors wide open to strangers, and accompanied her husband in the few walks which he took. She comforted him when he was altogether disheartened ; she rejoiced like a child when a cheerful smile lit up the serious face of the Reformer, and lay on her knees in the sitting-room when the sound of tumult was heard in the streets and cries of murder were raised against the Protestant preachers.

Idelette has been described as a shy, submissive wife, but she proved that she was a resolute, energetic woman, who inspired even the dying with courage.

The marriage was blessed with a child. It was a son. But it was a premature confinement, and in the perplexity of his fear Calvin wrote to Viret : " God have pity on us ! " [1]

[1] July 28th, 1542.

The mother got well again, but the child died when it was about a fortnight old. And then it was not fear, but deep sadness which caused Calvin to write : " God has indeed dealt us a heavy blow by the death of our son, but He is our Father and knows what is good for His children."

Calvin never had any more children. And a Jesuit was only too ready to cry out : " Do you see ? That is the curse which rests upon Calvin ; such a scandalous man was not allowed to have children." But Calvin answered, that in Christendom he could count his spiritual children by tens of thousands. . . .

The visible form of this Christendom was the Church. And it is really interesting to see how Calvin arranged the services in this Church at Strasburg.

On Sunday mornings the Confession of sins followed the Exhortation, as is the custom in French churches at the present day. After this, the minister spoke a few words of Scripture to comfort the conscience, and then the congregation began to sing the first five commandments. A short prayer from the minister followed, and then the congregation sang the other five commandments. Then came the sermon—a long prayer—a psalm, chanted by the congregation—the Benediction.

Calvin adapted himself at Strasburg, as he did in Geneva, to the forms of worship that were customary there. In Geneva the Lord's Supper was celebrated three times a year, on festivals, and although Calvin was an advocate for the monthly celebration, he nevertheless gave way, when he saw that it was impossible to bring the congregation over to his way of thinking.

Calvin believed in absolution, although he gave it another name. After the public confession of sins, he considered it desirable to pronounce a solemn promise of forgiveness of sin, in order to comfort the depressed in heart. And that he did not do so arose simply from the desire not to hurt the weak. Calvin, moreover, felt strongly the desirability of administering the Lord's Supper to the sick, but in Geneva this was not the custom, and as it would have been regarded as a strange innovation, he left things as they were.

He attached much importance to kneeling in prayer ; on his knees he had gained his victories, and his heart expanded when the singing of the Psalms pealed through the arched roofs of the church.

The Reformation brought Church-singing, and Calvin loved the Psalms. At first he had sought for other songs, but had not found them, and the Psalms with their sorrowful heart-cries and their unshaken confidence in God were indeed wonderfully adapted for the militant and suffering Church of the sixteenth century.

Luther wanted to retain the Latin in the Church, but Calvin, whose desire was to reach the whole

nation, shook his head and said : " In the Church
the language of the people, and nothing else ! "

He needed thus translated Psalms, and the poet
Marot, whom we met at Nérac and at the Court
of Queen Margaret, afterwards supplied these needs.

With the Psalms, the Church of Calvin grew up.
The martyrs sang them at the stake ; they have
resounded in prisons and on the battle-fields ; the
body-guard of Condé sang them.

They have gone far over the frontier of France.
The Gueux sang them ; the Roundheads of Crom-
well sang them ; they have re-echoed in the great
forests of Poland.   They have gone beyond the
frontiers of Europe ; they have been heard in the
hinterlanden of Africa ; they have sounded above
the roar of the ocean, and this mighty choir was
led by Calvin, the father of psalmody.

CHAPTER XVI

A FRENCH VOICE AT A GERMAN SYNOD

THE French Emigrant Church at Strasburg, at the head of which stood Calvin, grew rapilly. It flourished and became a model for the other parishes, and from a distance of five or six miles the converted Anabaptists brought their children to be baptised.

Nevertheless cares continued to harass the Reformer, and side by side with spiritual needs, poverty began menacingly to raise her head. His books did not bring in anything like what he had expected ; his publishers complained bitterly about the slow sale, and he had to borrow money to pay his rent. In the midst of the most profound studies, fearful cares oppressed him ; they gave him no sleep, no rest. And whilst his brain was busy with world-reforming plans, he thought of the crown which, when he was better off, he had lent to the Vaudois brothers and then needed so badly.

But, on the other hand, it was a gloriously luminous point, that there at Strasburg he was freer and more independent than he had been at Geneva, where he constantly came into conflict with the worldly power, whilst a rich spiritual blessing was a kingly recompense for his pinching poverty.

At Strasburg Calvin came into contact with the great German world ; one day Idelette had to pack his boxes, and he set out with his friend Bucer to the Diet of Frankfort, there, where the heart of the German people beat, to make serious studies of the German Empire, to meet the celebrated Melanchthon, and to beg the protection of the German princes for his persecuted co-religionists in France.

German Protestantism was then at the zenith of its power. In the north and south populous provinces had renounced the Roman Catholic faith ; in vain had the Emperor's statesmen tried to oppose triumphant Protestantism ; and the sharp eyes of Calvin, whose eagle glance nothing escaped, had noticed the confusion and dejection in the camp of the Roman Catholics.

Then the die had to be cast which was to decide the lot of Germany and Christian Europe. Like a general, Calvin watched the allied forces drawn up in battle array ; he sifted the reliable from the wavering states and made calculations as to the future attitude of the electors. In his long letters to Farel he explained, with great acuteness, how the foreign complications of the Emperor Charles V would further the efforts of their Protestant co-religionists ; he thought long and deeply over the stirfe in Gelderland, and on the sudden death of the

Prince of Saxony, he cherished the hope of bringing the whole dukedom over to Protestantism.

Although in his heart convinced of the power of the Gospel, he maintained that God works indirectly, and whilst his French blood distrusted Charles V, he advocated an alliance between Francis I and the Protestant princes of Germany. In spite of his democratic nature his eye was fixed on the Queen, who ruled the world, and the political mind of Francis I rejoiced that the flames of his fires had never reached this formidable heretic.

Frankfort, Worms, Regensburg saw Calvin ; with restless zeal he worked to win all Germany over to the Gospel ; and he wrote about Germany in language such as the German nation had seldom heard since the death of Ulrich Hutten. Melanchthon leaned on the giant of Noyon, but Calvin felt the cares of the strong man, who had to be responsible for everything. He saw a sad delay in the triumphant course of the Gospel ; he was surprised at the indulgence of the Wittenberg Reformer and angry with Bucer, who when at Worms wanted to mediate to a dangerous extent, although he was convinced of the good faith of both.

Wherever Calvin spoke he excited the surprise of the learned by the depth of his knowledge. But he cared not one iota about personal fame ; and when the landgrave, Philip of Hesse, invited him to dinner and showed him every honour, he bitterly vexed the stern Puritan by his second marriage.

Calvin was indeed shocked at the terrible lack of Church discipline in Germany; in his eyes the German clergy lacked the independence, which as soldiers of Christ they should have had; in the Lutheran doctrine he saw remains of Judaism, whilst the lukewarmness of the German Protestant princes grieved him greatly.

This lack of congenialness of spirit was mutual. People called him the noisy, fanatical Frenchman, and his great reputation for learning was evenly balanced by the aversion which was entertained for the iron consequences of this stranger. Greatly depressed, he returned home, although his confidence in the ultimate triumphs of the Gospel remained unshaken, and he reached Strasburg at the very moment that the prophecy pronounced by him respecting Geneva was on the eve of being fulfilled.

Calvin had profited by a short triumph of his enemies at Geneva. The catastrophe of 1538 was a triumph. The Lord's Supper was to be celebrated with unleavened bread, as Bern, against Calvin's protest, had persisted in celebrating it, and the new preachers who had sold the right of the first-born had become the pliant, submissive servants of the authorities. But this revolution had brought the religious liberty of the Reformed churches and the political liberty of the town into danger; the Roman Catholics lifted up their heads; the Mass was again spoken of, and the former Bishop of

Geneva, the unlucky De la Beaume, wished to make an effort to win back lost ground.

A meeting was held at Lyons which was called a conference, but which in reality was a conspiracy against the independence of Geneva. And the sharp-witted Cardinal Sadolet was instructed to write to the citizens of Geneva.

The letter was received and handed over to the Council. It was in order. The Council acknowledged in friendly terms the receipt of the letter, and would answer it in due course.

The hearts of the Catholics beat faster when they learnt that a learned priest had written a Romish defence against Protestant doings, and two days after Sadolet's letter was received, several citizens durst appear before the Council with the request that the oath which was required of confession of faith might be withdrawn. But after this Roman Catholic assertion of strength, followed the Protestant reaction. Sadolet had to be answered ; the Geneva clergy had neither talent nor mind for such an undertaking. The Bern bear [1] was heavy and slow—what else was to be done than request the exile of Strasburg to reply ?

In six days Calvin was ready with his polemic. It was an iron hammer with which the argument of Sadolet was smashed ; and many of Calvin's former opponents exclaimed : " Blind that we were —how could we be parties to the banishing of this excellent teacher ! "

[1] The Bernese have a bear on their arms.

Broils in the town strengthened the desire for Calvin's return ; Johannes Philippe, one of the foremost citizens of the town, was, for high treason, led to the scaffold ; France and Bern both threatened the independence of Geneva, whilst within the walls anarchy raised her head, and the different parties stood ready to tear each other to pieces.

There was no longer any choice ; the staunchest patriots turned their eyes to Strasburg, and cried out imploringly : " Come over and help us ! "

CHAPTER XVII

ON THE TOP OF THE MOUNTAIN

CALVIN would not go.

Again and again he thus poured out his heart to Farel : " When I remember how unhappy I was there at Geneva, my whole body trembles and revolts whenever there is a talk about my being called back."

Like a martyr he had held out at Geneva till the people drove him away. And delighted that the heavy yoke was lifted from his shoulders, the Reformer shrank from venturing again into that warring abyss.

Like mountains the difficulties rose up before him ; *he was wondrously perplexed*, as he expressed it ; he feared the influence of Bern, whilst, on the other hand, he understood perfectly well that without the moral support of the Bernese, it would be difficult for him to maintain his ground in the unsettled city of Geneva.

Nevertheless his sincere love for the Church of Geneva was not yet dead, and the more his eye saw of the endless difficulties which awaited him at Lake Leman, the more he hesitated to make a decision himself. He did not trust his own judgment and called in the advice of his coadjutors, whilst he, choosing a middle course, expressed himself ready to reorganise the Church at Geneva without remaining there for good.

Then the impetuous Farel appeared before the footlights. Once by his passionate language he had seen Calvin defenceless at his feet, and that was to happen again.

For eighteen long months Calvin held out, afraid to come to a decision. Farel heaped the bitterest reproaches on his head. He asked him whether he wished to wait till the stones of Geneva called him ; he reproached him for the haste with which he had left the city, and his tardiness in returning to that city.

Under these violent attacks, Calvin, with a self-denial which is the more striking in one of his irritable and passionate nature, offered up his heart. In extreme anguish of soul, he made the device chosen by him, a heart offering itself to the Lord, a reality ; and he did not consult with flesh and blood when he turned his steps to the city which had expelled him from her gates.

Calvin was disarmed ; he capitulated ; and Farel led his captive to Geneva.

In the beginning of September, 1541, Calvin set out from Strasburg. His way led partly through the same districts which he had once travelled as a pitiful refugee. Now it was a triumphal journey.

Amidst the cheering of the population he returned in joyful triumph ; he excused himself to the multitude for his delay in coming, but they were too glad to make any complaint. They had got him back again—that was the happy event of the day ! And they would keep him till death should part them. . . . Where were Calvin's enemies ? The four burgomasters who had worked together so zealously to banish him ?

Two of them had fled because they had tried to create an uproar, and their death sentence lay already signed ; the third escaped from the walls through a window, but was so much injured by his fall that he soon expired, whilst the fourth was led to the scaffold and beheaded by the executioner of Geneva.

That was the fate of the four magistrates, who, in the days of their prosperity, had poured out upon Calvin the vials of their mockery and scorn. And then Calvin's friends remembered the prophetic words which he had written on parting : " Let us humble ourselves and not resist when God humbles us. In the meanwhile we will wait for His time, for quickly shall fade away the crown of pride of the drunkards of Ephraim ! "

" What a turn through God's appointing ! " exclaimed the Prussian King William I on the battle-field of Sedan reeking with blood. Those same words Calvin might have uttered more than three centuries ago.

Driven away with scorn, he now returned with the greatest honour to the place, which Farel, in the name of the King of Kings, had indicated to him ; and the same people who had once cried "Crucify him!" now shouted Hosanna.

The Council had provided for the bringing over of his family. The town-herald, who had spent three-and-twenty days in fetching Calvin from Strasburg, received fifty guilders for his trouble ; for Mrs. Calvin's journey, seven guilders and four-pence were disbursed, which was far too little, whilst for the furnishing of the house assigned to Calvin, a hundred and twenty guilders and two pence were paid.

The love and esteem for Calvin's person assumed a naïve, almost childish character. One of the councillors had discovered, not without commisera-tion, that his gown was shabby, and immediately orders were given to a tailor to make him a new one. The minutes of the Council record the gown—eight gold crowns were paid for it. Moreover, St. Peter's Church, at the request of Calvin, was provided with new seats, whilst against one of the pillars a brand new pulpit was placed.

The question of salary gave the Council much trouble, and at last it was fixed at five hundred guilders, two measures of corn, and two casks of wine.

There was much discussion about those five hundred guilders! Some said it was too little ;

others declared that Calvin could put by a nice little sum every year.

In reality Calvin got as much as a burgomaster, and twice as much as any other clergyman. But those functionaries were men who could put their arms up to the elbow in gold ducats, whereas the clergy were often in want.

Indeed Calvin had a modest income, but, considering what she had before, Idelette was suddenly enabled to live in comparative luxury ; but that they did not do so reflects credit both on Calvin and his wife. For anxious in the poverty which had so bitterly harassed them, they were not less with the five hundred guilders which were paid to them every year. Their hospitality soon far surpassed the liberality of the town, and Calvin—a great honour indeed !—left no treasures.

How wonderful are the ways of God !

It was true that Calvin and Farel, when they left Geneva, had asked to be restored to their honour both in Bern and in Switzerland without being able to obtain a hearing. Their humiliation had been complete ; their truest friends had deserted them ; and not till the inflicted wounds began to heal, till German hospitality had welcomed him to Strasburg, and he had experienced the pleasure of regular and undisturbed labour, did Geneva call him back.

But then his longing for Geneva was gone ; he had seen the abyss which there yawned, and it was his fervent hope that the wish he once had to return to Geneva, might never be fulfilled.

Then, however, it was just the time for him, who by a wonderful concurrence of circumstances had smoothed the paths for his return.

In these events Calvin felt and recognised the hand of his God, of his Father, and this timid, modest man, this child of Noyon, was appointed His instrument for realising in this little corner of the earth the programme laid down in the *Christian Institutes*, and to found there a community which should shine and glisten like a city on a mountain in the glow of the morning sun.

With the terrible earnestness of a prophet, Calvin appeared in Geneva, and the solemn pealing of the great bell of St. Peter's summoned the penitent children of the city to listen to the preacher.

The great church was filled to overflowing ; there was a special celebration of the Lord's Supper ; and one day a week was set apart for penitence and prayer.

Calvin worked with the strength of a Hercules. The first weeks of his new labour in Geneva belong to the most laborious of his laborious life.

The zeal with which the congregation of Geneva clung to the shepherd of their souls, has seldom been equalled in Protestant Churches. Not the little Council of five-and-twenty, not the great Council of two hundred, nor the General Council of voters ruled Geneva in those days. Calvin ruled ; his will was law ; he was the uncrowned King of the Republic. And the words that he had once spoken in the unshaken confidence of faith had been fulfilled : " Marching under the banner of Christ, we can return from the battle only as conquerors."

Calvin had learned much in those three years of his banishment. He had learned the prudence which characterised Joseph at the Court of Pharaoh, and he subdued the passion which may rightly be called his chief characteristic sin. He kept a sharp eye on the zealots of his own party, and showed a spirit of reconciliation that surprised them. They had fully expected that he would at least in his first sermon sharply attack his former opponents, but with a tact that commands our admiration he made not the slightest allusion to them. He had not come as the vengeful head of a party, for he had read in his Bible that vengeance belongeth to the Lord, but as a true shepherd of souls, whose sacred avocation it was, to lead all sheep to the true sheepfold, that is Christ.

He had to speak but a single word to deprive the former teachers of their appointments, but with wise moderation he refrained from uttering that word, and this attitude must have made a great and deep impression on the majority of the people.

Meanwhile the times were serious. In the East glistened the crooked sword of the Turks, and the plague, that terrible scourge of the Middle Ages, rode on her pale horse into the towns of Western Europe.

With deep sadness, Calvin heard that that excellent man, Capito, had succumbed at Strasburg to the complaint, and that Bucer had seen his wife and six children laid in their graves before he was himself attacked by the fell disease.

Geneva was not spared ; the angel of death stretched his hand over the city, and the death-bell was heard and the black biers seen in all the streets. Fear lay on every face ; many fled ; commerce and industry were at a standstill, and the courts of justice were closed.

The Council adopted stringent measures. All foreigners had to leave the city within three days on pain of the rack ; nobody, who had the plague, was to go through the town before ten o'clock in the evening and after three in the morning without a flag-bearer ; the militia festival was postponed ; cats and dogs which might transmit the germs of the plague were killed, and the plague-stricken who were not looked after in the hospital received a hint to choose as their dwelling-place the huts in the direction of Champel Hill outside the town.

The clergyman, Peter Blanchet, offered to act as spiritual consoler to the sufferers in the hospital. He went as he had done the year before. But this time the doors of the hospital were only to open to let the dead body of the hero pass through, and the Council found themselves in the difficult position, whom to choose in his stead.

Many of the clergy showed their reluctance ;

THE COUNCIL OF GENEVA (*after Labouchere*)

[*Face page* 164

the report was spread that one of them had used the expression, " better sit with the devil than in the hospital."

Calvin and his colleagues appeared before the Council, and the Council decided that Calvin, on account of the Church services, could not be missed. Therefore from among the other preachers a choice had to be made, but they had serious objections, for they thought of their wife and children, and candidly confessed that they had not the courage to risk their life in that terrible pest-house. Only one clergyman offered to undertake the deadly office, if the lot should fall upon him, and the Council accepted his proposal for the time.

The Council had weighty reasons for sparing Calvin. The Government does not place the general who has to direct the battle at the head of the attacking force. But the question may be asked, what the Reformer would have done had the lot fallen upon him.

The question had already been answered by Calvin by his attitude at Strasburg, when, of his own accord, he had nursed two men suffering from the plague, and, moreover, by his remarkable letter to Viret,[1] in which the following lines occur : " The plague is already beginning to rage here more violently. Few of those affected by it recover. One of us has to be appointed to help the sick. When Peter Blanchet offered himself, we willingly let him

[1] October 1st, 1542.

go. If anything happens to him, I fear, after him, to have to incur the same danger. For we belong to all the members of the flock, and cannot hold back from those who, more than others, need our help."

This is Calvin as he lived and always was ! No bragging, no vain boasting—he willingly let Blanchet go, because he saw the dark cloud of death above the terrible hospital.

But though his flesh shrank back and his soul trembled with fear, yet he would go if duty called him ; under the law of that iron discipline which becomes a soldier of Jesus Christ. And he would have shut himself up in the hospital with the plague-sick, to die with them. . . . In all this he had but one object in view. Luther had said : " War with Rome to the death ! " Calvin's watchword was : " Order and discipline ! "

And he girded himself in order to resume the great reformation work, that had once suffered shipwreck.

CHAPTER XVIII

THE GENERAL IN THE MIDST OF HIS HEROES

ORDER and discipline !

No, to these something else was added. Calvin's watchword was : " Liberty, order, and discipline ! "

" Pretty liberty ! " cried a woman from the populace ; " once we were compelled to go to Mass ; now we are dragged to hear the sermon ! "

But that woman did not understand Calvin's object. He meant the liberty to serve God according to the Gospel.

The people had to go to church—that is true. But the laws made by Calvin, and which at the present day seem to us like the despairing act of a tottering and decaying Church, God made use of to make the dew of the Holy Spirit descend on the hard Geneva furrows. Citizens who cared little about religion and went grumbling to church, were to become the pillars of the Church, which they had once despised, and the vigorous and muscular physiognomies began already to depict a future, when Geneva would be called the Pella of sorely tried French Protestantism.

The ideal of a Christian Republic one began to

think possible, and even before the authorities approved of the ordinances submitted by Calvin, he, like a second Savonarola, requested the Council to inscribe the monogram of Christ, the letters I H S, on the public buildings, the coins, and the flag of Geneva.

Not the cross of the Roman Catholic Church that had supplanted the true cross, but Christ, the Redeemer of souls and of nations, it should be.

The Council acceded to that wish, and the monogram of Christ should henceforth be imprinted on the forehead of Protestant Rome.

Calvin went on the premise, that God is the Ruler of all, and that every other government can only exist by reason of His authority. His standpoint was, that all kinds of government can be good, although for Geneva he considered the republican form the most desirable ; and on those foundations, laid by him, arose in the Netherlands and England, in Scotland and North America, the temple of liberty.

In the beginning, says the historian P. Henry, there were five pastors and three assistants, whose regular duty it was, *inter alia*, to hold public Bible readings every Friday. They had also to visit the sick and superintend the education of the young. Moreover, they formed, together with twelve elders, two of whom belonged to the Little Council, four to the Council of Sixty, and six to the Council of the Two Hundred, the Church Council, which met every Thursday, and whose chief occupation was to look after the conduct of the citizens. They had the right to call to account all who had transgressed the existing laws of order and discipline. This moral court of justice had an officer at its disposal to summon the offenders and bring them before it. For a first offence there was a serious admonition, for repeated offences a refusal of the Lord's Supper. If, however, the crime committed were of such a nature, that according to the laws of the State a fine or bodily punishment had to be imposed, then notice of this was given to the Government to take the necessary proceedings.

These laws breathe the spirit of the sixteenth century; the Church and State were firmly and closely interwoven; the idea was, that the Church embraced all citizens.

A stern spirit had got the upper hand of the merry, licentious life of Geneva. Gambling and wine-houses disappeared; dancing was forbidden; adultery, first punished with six days' imprisonment and a fine, was subsequently, at the express desire of the general assembly of the people, punished with death.

Only at five places, set apart for the purpose, might men amuse themselves with bowls; the wearing of showy dress was not tolerated; moderation in eating and drinking was prescribed, whilst the elders of this Protestant Sparta went from house to house once a year to convince themselves that the laws and ordinances were carried out.

The preachers themselves went out to induce the citizens to go to church ; Calvin more than once made such an excursion on Sunday. But staunch advocate as Calvin was for forcing the people to hear, he was altogether averse to long preaching.

He could not stand it ; it worried him, that Farel kept the people so long in church, and he considered it more effective to edify them by short sermons than to weary them with long ones.

It was in those days that Geneva lost one of her most excellent citizens by the death of Ami Porral, who, in 1532, converted to Protestantism, contributed incalculably much to the triumph of that religion within the walls of his native city.

In the great peril of 1536, when Geneva, threatened by Savoy, the Bishop, and France, was on the verge of the precipice, he did more than anyone else to secure the help of Bern. No one in the little Republic had seen better than he, how the independence of Geneva was strengthened by the Reformation, and he was in truth Calvin's right hand.

The death of this patriot was beautiful and affecting. Calvin stood by his bed and spoke of the only consolation in life and death.

" I am as sure of that truth," replied Porral, " as though it were brought me by an angel."

Whilst the golden gates of the heavenly Jerusalem were opening to receive him he would no longer hear of enemies. He sent for them to his death-bed to make friends of them, and his lips whispered words of peace, love, and reconciliation.

At two o'clock in the afternoon Idelette appeared. He still recognised her kindly face. She spoke words of comfort, as a sister to a brother.

Then he cried in the words of Simeon : " Lord, now lettest Thou Thy servant depart in peace, according to Thy word : for mine eyes have seen Thy salvation."

" And shortly afterwards," says Calvin, " he gave his pious soul into the hands of the Lord."[1]

A new chronicler was wanted for the town and the choice fell upon Bonivard, the Erasmus of the Geneva Reformation, who was then fifty-one years old.[2]

He accepted the appointment, and two years afterwards married.

Calvin thought the marriage very comical. Bonivard was a widower and had fixed his choice upon a widow, who had two husbands in the grave already. Calvin wrote to Viret about it and told him that he had laughed immensely.

But the new couple did not laugh. They soon got to high words ; Bonivard found out that his spouse was nothing like his first wife, and she in her turn bitterly bewailed being married to such a man. On a certain day she went off, and as she would not return, she was put in prison on bread and water, to teach her the duties of a wife.

[1] June, 1542.   [2] The end of 1542.

The woman died and Bonivard married for the third time—a widow. It was quite an undertaking for the woman, for Bonivard was not a man of order ; he knew nothing about economy, and his debts would have ruined him, if the Government had not come to his assistance again and again.

When his third wife died, Bonivard, in his seventieth year, married for the fourth time ; against his wish, but at the urgent request of the Church Council, as he had made promises of marriage. And the end was that the chronicler of Geneva was cut off as member of the Church.

So the people cried Hosanna to the Reformer, but there is only one step between adoration and revilement, and Calvin had already experienced how quickly the mind of the people can change.

There was something else : Luther could rely upon the vigorous support of powerful patrons ; the noble elector of Saxony and the pushing Land-grave of Hesse would have drawn the sword for him, if necessary. With Calvin it was different ; he had to depend on the favour of the people, which shifts like the sand on the seashore, whilst in secret a small but obstinate party schemed and drudged to throw him out of the saddle.

Moreover, what was Geneva, even though it offered him help ? It lay on the junction of three roads, where three powerful Roman Catholic states met ; it was a town of scarcely sixteen thousand inhabitants, with weak ramparts and weak walls, badly protected against a hostile attack. Calvin had to seek help from a higher source, from above, and from above he sought it. And his fervent prayer and the strong faith of his flock formed the firm, invisible wall against which all the force of the enemy would break powerless.

The glory that emanated from little Geneva shone forth as far as Poland. Geneva became the great central point, where the mightiest intellects met.

John Knox was there ; Marnix of St. Aldegonde, the author of the immortal Wilhelmus song ; Cranmer, the reformer of England—three names which imply three revolutions.

Under the genial direction of Calvin, Geneva became the university, where the heroes and martyrs of Protestantism were educated. Here was their cradle ; the Calvinistic view of life with its unshaken doctrine of predestination instilled steel into their blood. From this little insignificant spot of the world they went forth into the high road of life. No river, no sea, no mountain could stop them ; they possessed the blind obedience of the Jesuit, without the gloomy heretical hatred which animated them. They ventured into England, where, under the rule of Henry VIII, no man's life was safe ; into Spain, France, and Italy, where the scaffold awaited them. They were bound to the strangling pole, and there to die ; the flames of the funeral pyre beat into their faces ; they were cast into dungeons, where the light of the sun and the moon never shone.

They were a chosen band destined by their blood to win nations to the Gospel. And this chosen band, although it died every day, was immortal, for the gaps in the ranks were filled up again and again by new heroes and martyrs, who, with sustained enthusiasm, fought and died for Christ.

Calvin was their teacher, their leader, their anointed king. He gave them his blessing when they went forth to battle, and without a muscle of his face moving, he heard of their sufferings and death. Only occasionally did he lose the iron self-control which becomes a general; then grief, dejection, sadness came upon him with the force of a mountain torrent, and in the bitterness of his soul he cried out: "They are led as sheep to the slaughter!"

So, many heroes and martyrs went forth from the city, but many exiles returned, who, on account of their belief, had fled from the land of their forefathers.

Amongst them were grey-headed old men, weak women, little children. Amid the biting cold of winter they wandered along the precipices of the high mountains, badly clad, benumbed, losing their way in the confusion of the snow-covered footpaths, perishing from hunger and cold.

Now and then they looked back, distracted by the fear that they heard the cry of their persecutors, and then they stumbled on, the poor oppressed flock of Christ, till suddenly, on the left of the last bend in the road, they discovered, afar off, a low cloud—the mountain pass.

Then the fugitives felt a strong, cold current of air, and Mount Blanc rose up before them, the mighty giant in his white, majestic snow-mantle.

A few steps more—and something glistened before their eyes—it was Lake Leman.

Then they quickened their pace ; their weary eyes shone bright again, and along the rough slope, which amid a sea of fir trees went ever downwards, their trembling eyes sought the horizon.

Suddenly they stood still ; they stretched out their arms—and there ! before them ! rose the lofty towers of St. Peter's Church. . . . That was Geneva ! —the Pella of tortured Protestantism !—the town of Calvin !

The wanderers embraced one another, cries of joy, choked by tears, were raised, and greatly moved, they sang :

> The Lord I love, He's ever true to me ;
> He hears my voice, my plaints.   Where'er I pray
> He bends His ear ; I cry to Him alway ;
> He gives me help, from dangers all sets free.

During a period of scarcely ten years, Geneva, which had less inhabitants than Zutphen, has now received and housed four thousand refugees.

It was a heavy task that required great pecuniary

sacrifices, and yet was accomplished with wonderful devotion.

Let us not forget—that the poorest part of the emigration came from France. Without shelter, without clothes, driven away from their native land by the fury of persecution, they reached Geneva. They were shipwrecked men, who had been cast upon the shore of Geneva. And they brought nothing with them but distress, misery, hunger, and the wounds inflicted by furious, religious hatred.

New fugitives kept arriving ; they spread about to make room for the next ; it was an endless procession of spectres with lean jaws and eyes far sunk in their sockets—it was a procession of poor wretches, martyrs of the Reformation.

The Geneva houses were not large. Moreover, every family formed a little state in the state ; and to their Puritanical austerity, the Geneva Protestants added a certain prudent reticence towards the unknown stranger.

But these characteristics were dissipated at the heartrending sight of the fugitives going through the streets deprived of everything. And with irresistible strength came another characteristic, compassion, pity for these poor creatures.

Beds were got ready—five, six in one room. Some houses had five-and-twenty beds. Quite a revolution took place in the regular course of housekeeping, and the good Geneva housewife, who up till then had done everything with the regularity of clockwork, showed her approval. She vied with her husband in works of Christian hospitality, and for the persecuted unlocked the holy of holies, where her children were not allowed to enter.

She cut up her clothes to help her sisters, she robbed her linen-press to protect the half-naked children from cold ; she herself went without many things to feed them all ; she refreshed the exhausted strangers with wine and herself drank water. O women of Geneva ! O daughter of Calvin ! Blessed shall your memory be till the end of time !

CHAPTER XIX

"AS FOR MAN, HIS DAYS ARE AS GRASS"

LUTHER could reckon on the support of influential patrons, but he no longer needed that support. And whilst gloomy and ominous sighs filled the air, he was to leave the scene of battle, where he had fought with so much honour and courage.

In his sermons, letters, and conversation, the old fire and energy of this heroic heart were still apparent, but a longing for the heavenly country was unmistakable. With trembling heart he also foresaw a religious war, and then thought of an old prophecy, according to which the lands of Germany were to be harassed with a terrible religious war.

His last sermon, preached at Wittenberg, was the farewell of a dying man. Every one felt it ; every heart was moved. And from Wittenberg he went to Eisleben, his birthplace, there to die.

Properly speaking, he was ill only once in his life ; that illness lasted but a day, and it carried Luther away to eternity.

In the evening he complained that his chest troubled him so, and thought that it meant death. Three times, shortly after each other, he said :

" Father, into Thy hands I commend my spirit !
Thou hast redeemed me, O God of truth ! "

Then he was still ; the films of death were fast
closing over his eyes.

Once more he awoke from his stupefaction. Then
Dr. Jonas turned to him and asked the question :
" Reverend father, dare you die in the doctrine
which you have preached ? "

" Yes," replied Luther, with an astonishingly
clear voice, so that all present could distinctly
hear it.

That was his last word on earth. And he fell
asleep that night[1] between two and three o'clock,
about sixty-two years of age.

As a benefactor to nations, he was conveyed to
Wittenberg amidst the ringing of all the church
bells, solemn dirges, and the lamentations of the
population.

The young counts of Mansfield and fifty noblemen with their retinue, formed the procession of
honour ; in the evening Halle was reached ; the
people had poured out of the gates ; all the clergy
and the members of the Council had assembled at
the gate. The body was placed in the vestry ; the
church was crowded with people, who, with weeping voices, sang the funeral psalm.

The following morning the body was conveyed
over Bitterfield and Kemberg to Wittenberg.
Catherine von Bora, Luther's wife, and her three

[1] February 18th, 1546.

sons, followed directly behind the hearse ; the earthly remains were, according to the wish of the deeply afflicted Elector of Saxony, John Frederick, to rest near the pulpit of the Wittenberg Schloss Church, from which the great Reformer had so often preached his soul-stirring sermons.

Melanchthon made a funeral speech ; Bugenhagen too, spoke a few suitable words. And when he, overcome by sadness, burst into tears and exclaimed : " Who will be our shepherd now, who our teacher ? We are forsaken, left orphans ! " all the people burst out into one mournful cry of grief.

Luther and Calvin—two Reformers ! But what a difference ! Luther was bold, undaunted—the man of feeling ; Calvin was sharp-witted, deeply sensitive—the man of logic. What the one lacked, the other possessed ; they were Elijah and Elisha ; and it was the Lord's gracious ordaining that Calvin should be the successor of Luther.

With what reverence did Calvin look up to the doctor of Wittenberg. " We say it frankly," he thus expressed himself, " that we consider Luther a great apostle of Christ, through whose mission and work the Gospel has, in our time, been brought back to almost its original purity."

He declared with all the earnestness of his soul that Luther had had to contend with no less difficulties than the Apostles had themselves, for he had to overthrow the Papal colossus, a power which

CATHERINE DE BORE

[*Face page* 180

had struck fatal roots firmly and deeply in the national life of the Christian West.

The angel of death, which had cut off the life of the German Reformer, appeared a year later at the immoral Court of Francis I, to summon the King before the Judgment Seat of God.

His throne was, to the topmost steps, bespattered with the sacred blood of the martyrs.

It was a year and a half since fourteen men, who would not deny their belief in Christ, were hanged and burnt on fourteen gallows placed in a wide circle on the great market-square of Meaux.

With their tongues, mutilated by the executioner, they praised God's grace and comforted one another with their last breath.

More horribly did the hirelings of Francis I act towards the Vaudois. The inhabitants of the town of Cabrieres, who, trusting to the solemn promises made in the name of the King, had willingly opened their gates to the French soldiers, fell under the sword-cuts of these soldiers, who had changed into executioners.

To extort confessions from the innocent, their feet were thrust into boots filled with burning lime. A barn full of straw, to which forty defenceless women had fled, was set on fire and the poor victims who tried to escape were caught on the pikes.

By hundreds the wretched Vaudois wandered about in the forests, there to die of hunger, or to be captured and dragged to the gallows.

The cries of distress uttered by the Swiss and German co-religionists reached the ears of Francis I, but he replied in a hard-hearted tone, that they should be sensible enough not to meddle with matters which did not concern them.

And this was the mournful end of a King's life, that was devoted to knightly pomp, thirst for fame and scandalous excesses.

Father of science, this man has been called ; in the martyrology of the Reformed Churches he has another name.   And he died unlamented.[1]

Francis I departed this life, but the sword that persecuted the French Protestants was not sheathed. The stream of fugitives that crossed the French frontiers went on, and among the wanderers who reached Geneva was a young man, who, by his tall, impressive stature, his distinguished manners and noble appearance, immediately attracted attention.

The pedestrians stood still and looked back at the Burgundian as he passed into Cannon Street and knocked at Calvin's front door.

The Reformer had seen this man several times before—fifteen years before in Wallmar's dwelling. And he gave Theodore Beza a hearty welcome.

Beza had gone through much in those fifteen years.   This merry, life-loving poet, this brilliant, fêted *littérateur* could say with truth, that God had snatched him as a brand from the fire, that

[1] March 31st, 1547.

henceforth he might devote his life to the service of the King of Kings.

But Satan had paid him out for leaving his service.

His future was blighted ; the Parliament in Paris stood ready to burn the runaway heretic in effigy, and like a beggar, without money, without protectors, without prospects, he arrived at Geneva.

What was he to do ? He did not know ; Calvin, whom he asked for advice, did not know either ; and his family refused all help.

For a time Beza thought, with the pecuniary assistance of a friend at Geneva, of starting a book-printing business. Geneva had no printing office ; the plan seemed a good one, and business men were consulted about it.

But the Lord frustrated the plan, for He had already provided for the sorely tried Beza. Lausanne called him as professor to her University, and he was soon to shine there as a brilliant star in the scientific sky.

Before Beza left, his marriage with Claude Benosse was solemnised.[1] Merrily rang the bells of St. Peter's Church ; Calvin performed the cere-mony, and the congregation sang the comforting Psalm :

> He that has God his guardian made
> Shall under the Almighty's shade
> Secure and undisturbed abide.

[1] October, 1548.

CHAPTER XX

THE LOFTY WAVES OF ADVERSITY

Was it really true what the congregation sang to kneeling Beza and his bride ?

There were weak believers who began to doubt it. They looked towards France and trembled ; then towards Germany and uttered a cry of fear.

For German Protestantism was in danger. The signals of distress went up. And by the cowardice of one, the shortsightedness of another, and the treachery of Duke Maurits of Saxony, it was hurled from the acme of its power to the verge of the precipice.

Calvin, who was deeply pained by the cruel fate of his compatriots, was again much affected by the adversities of his German co-religionists. He trembled for the life of his dear friends, Bucer and Melanchthon. And this man, by nature so bashful and timid, was, now that the German oak had been blown down by the storm, to become by God's will, the leader, upon whom the eyes of all the sad at heart were fixed.

Even before the war against the Schmal-Kaldic League burst out, Calvin had chosen the firm standpoint from which he regarded the German religious war. And his soul was full of bitterness at the false card which Maurits of Saxony intended to play.

"There is at present a rumour," he wrote, "at which I am not so much surprised as grieved, namely, that Maurits will co-operate with the Emperor, in order to ruin his nephew, John Frederick of Saxony, and his father-in-law, Philip of Hesse, and at last himself too, which is certainly not his intention. If that is true then the devil must already have got him entirely in his power. In the meantime I hope that our Antiochus, who at present makes us so afraid, will soon be put to such straits, that he will have no more time to think of the gout in his hands and feet. His accomplice, Sardanapalus, may God visit in the same way, for they have both equally deserved it at our hands!"

By Antiochus Calvin meant the German Emperor Charles V; by Sardanapalus, King Henry II of France, the son and bloodthirsty successor of Francis I.

It was as clear as day, that the warlike preparations of the German Antiochus were for the destruction of the Protestant Schmal-Kaldic League, but the Elector of Saxony could not see it. Moreover, the Elector was slow by nature; he was fond of procrastination, and kept hoping for a peaceful solution of the disputes.

At Mühlberg his army was attacked by the Imperialists. He was then in Mühlberg Church listening attentively to the sermon. His orderlies brought him the news that the Imperialists were crossing the river which protected his army, but he would not believe it, and remained in the church till the service was over. This dilatoriness cost him his army and his own liberty. His army was routed, and after a brave resistance he himself was taken prisoner.

For Duke Alva and the other Imperial generals, it was a source of inward joy to see the captive head of the German Protestants, and the warlike Bishop of Kildesheim, who in full armour had taken part in the battle, declared afterwards, that he would not have missed the sight for hundreds of ducats.

Charles V made use of his triumph to set a terrifying example, and pronounced the unheard-of sentence that the Elector, John Frederick, should be beheaded for rebellion.

The Elector was playing at chess when the death sentence was read to him. With admirable resignation he laid the fatal document down beside him, and looking at the Duke of Brunswick, who was playing with him, said calmly : " Cousin, pay attention to your game ! You are in check ! "

The Imperial flags were seen flying in all the Protestant districts ; Wittenberg, the centre of German Protestantism, surrendered, and Charles V appeared with his forces at the grave of the great Reformer.

In reverent silence the Emperor stood at Luther's grave. But the grim Duke of Alva could not restrain his bitterness, and cried out in a mocking tone : " The bones of that arch-heretic should be dug up and burned to ashes."

From his lofty watch-tower Calvin viewed the disasters of his co-religionists. Like the old prophets of Israel, he could have covered his head with ashes and girded his loins with sackcloth. The fierce triumphant cries of the enemy cut like knives into his soul ; he beat his breast and said : " It is on account of our many sins, and because we do not give God the honour due to Him, that Satan has such power over us. Therefore we must humble ourselves before God, and implore His grace."

The hand of the Lord rested heavily on Calvin, and coupled with the general disasters there was sadness and suffering at home.

Idelette had spoken words of consolation to the noble Burgomaster, Ami Porral, when he lay at the point of death, and now she herself lay stretched on her death-bed.

Calvin had feared this. In the midst of his onerous duties, the anxious fear had more than once taken possession of him, that all was not well with his wife.

The premature confinement of the child, that she was allowed to keep only for a fortnight, had impaired Idelette's health. It is true, it seemed as if she would get better, but appearances were altogether deceptive. The sickness returned with greater strength, and in 1545 Idelette was on the verge of the grave.

Yet once more there seemed a ray of hope.

" My wife is improving," Calvin wrote to Viret ; " but her cough is still bad."

Yes—that cough—that was the mischief ! Consumption—that was the sword of Damocles that hung threateningly over the Geneva vicarage.

Idelette kept up bravely ; she never spoke about her ailments ; if her husband looked at her with the anxious eyes of love, she smiled at his unnecessary anxiety.

It would not do for him to know the truth, for that would destroy his domestic joy. But Calvin was not to be deceived, and when the busy housewife, exhausted and worn out, had no longer the strength to leave her bed, he knew that the end was near.

The faithful doctor redoubled his energy to save this precious life, but the oil was spent, the lamp went out, and Idelette went to the house where there are many mansions.

It was a beautiful spring day [1] when Idelette died ; the birds were singing and the trees were clothed in soft, green verdure. Calvin remained in the sick chamber. His clerical brothers had

----

[1] March 29th, 1549.

been there and had offered up their prayers together.

She lay there, her faith in God never wavering. Not with the night boat, but in full sail, she was about to enter the eternal haven. She seemed already to have left this earth—her soul drank in the air of heaven.

Calvin sat there, crushed as it were, by the bedside of his wife, and those seven years of married life, which the deepest mutual love had made a pleasant oasis in the midst of the great sandy desert, passed like a vision before his mind's eye.

Now that this faithful helpmate was being taken from him, Calvin saw more clearly and distinctly than ever what a blow the Almighty was dealing him. And amidst these painful meditations, whilst his heart was filled with sadness, he heard Idelette's dying strains : " O glorious resurrection ! "

Lifting her kindly eyes upwards, she murmured : " O God of Abraham and of all our fathers—never has one of the faithful, who trusted in Thee, been deceived."

At six o'clock Calvin had to leave her to attend to his duties.

He seemed to be an old man, walking through the streets. He saw nothing, he thought of nothing else than his dying wife.

At seven o'clock Idelette began to lose consciousness. And perceiving this, she said with astonishing presence of mind : " Let us pray—all pray for me."

Then Calvin came home again. He bent down over the beloved face ; then he saw that she was near the heavenly Father's house. She could not speak, but he saw clearly that she still recognised him. He spoke to her of Christ, the great Conqueror of death, and of the hope of eternal life.

Then, however, his feeling overcame him, and he sought the quietest corner of the house, threw himself on his knees and called upon God for strength.

At eight o'clock the wife of the great Reformer breathed her last. It was not dying—it was a peaceful falling asleep ; as of a child that falls asleep in the arms of its father.

" Is she dead or sleeping ? " thought they who stood by, but Calvin knew, and with his face buried in his hands he sat down in sadness at the death-bed of his so dearly-beloved wife, who with him had borne the heat of the day and the cold of night.

The son and daughter of Idelette's first marriage were also there. Idelette had never spoken about their future when she should be taken away, so as not to trouble her husband. But three days before her death Calvin had referred to the subject, and to comfort her said that he would continue to be a father to the children.

" I have already commended them to God's care," was her reply.

" That does not prevent me from looking after them," said Calvin.

Great, striking, and affecting was the confidence

that Idelette placed in her husband. This confidence was the reason why she had not spoken to him about her children. And when one of her neighbours, with the kindest intention, had urged her to do so, she had replied : " That they may live a good and holy life—that is the chief thing. I do not need to urge upon my husband the necessity of bringing them up in the true doctrine and in the fear of the Lord. If they are good, then I know that he of his own accord will be a father to them. And if they are not, then they are not worthy of my asking anything for them ! "

When these simple and noble words were afterwards reported to Calvin he exclaimed with sorrowful admiration : " This greatness of soul will have more effect upon me than hundreds of entreaties ! "

Idelette dead ! The sun of his day and the kindly star of his long nights set—O, it was like a heavy blow upon his heart !

Not till that lovely face was stamped with the image of death did he know how dearly he had loved her.

Many of the reformers married again. Bucer himself was a strong advocate for this. And Viret, that great child, once wrote with charming *naïveté :* " I am not very fond of widows, but as it is difficult to get all we want, we must not be too particular."

And so Viret married. But Calvin never thought of marrying again ; he himself was opposed to it, although he had married a widow.

The image of his wife was too deeply imprinted in his soul ; a piece of his heart was borne away with it to the dark, gloomy pit of the Geneva churchyard, in which the earthly remains of his beloved wife were laid, and only the thought of an eternal reunion on the other side of the grave could comfort his deeply afflicted soul.

" The admirable providence of God separates us in this world to unite us again in His heavenly kingdom "—those were his own words.

CHAPTER XXI

THE GERMAN EMPEROR'S PRIDE BROUGHT DOWN

STRENGTHENED by God and knowing that his children are purified by suffering, Calvin set to work resolutely, without looking back. The more his brethren were persecuted, the more he longed for the unity of all children of God. Through Melanchthon he hoped to unite the German Church with the Protestants in the South, to bring Geneva in close connection with Switzerland, and to unite the Protestants of France under one banner by the same creed. His ideal was one indivisible Protestant Church, divided neither by mountains nor seas, extending to England and Scotland, to Sweden and Poland. He first betook himself to Neuchâtel and Zürich to put an end to the suspicion prevailing there, to erase the distressing page of the Marburg Conference, where Luther's vehemence had prevented any compromise, and to explain as clearly as possible to the Swiss, that in the Sacraments the body and the blood of the Lord are really imparted to us in the spiritual and not in the bodily sense.

Calvin now had great and blessed influence on all

Protestantism. While he had already shown before, that he was not narrow-minded by signing the Augsburg Confession, he now drew the firm lines of unity. The sun at Geneva shone in unbroken splendour ; it had become the greatest attraction of European Protestantism, and the greatest men of this eventful time stood in connection with Calvin. We mention Petrus Martyr, the son of Florence, whom Calvin, on account of his erudition, called the wonder of Italy ; the theologian Bullinger, living in Zürich and having become a Zwingli the Second by his sincerity, activity, and zeal ; Lasky, the bold, undaunted Pole; Renata of Ferrara, who glittered in the Italian sky like a bright star. In the heat of persecution the cry of " Close your ranks " had been heard in France. Many nobles had joined in a strong phalanx of Huguenots under the command of the heroic Joanna of Albret, the daughter of Margaret and the mother of him who has been called the greatest king of France. In the North new life began to stir, Sweden and Denmark gave the example ; in Poland the sun was rising. In Germany there was some relief, and the Protestants had reason to exclaim in joy : " The Lord bends the hearts of kings like brooks." Strange things had happened. The Evangelicals had trembled before Maurice of Saxony, and lo ! this powerful man, the grandfather of Prince Maurice, became their deliverer. He laid siege to Magdeburg, but on entering the vanquished fortress he suddenly

remembered that the inhabitants of Magdeburg
were his brothers in the Faith. He addressed the
burghers, who had gathered in the market-place,
as their friend ; he shook hands with the members
of the Council and promised to treat them leniently.
He did more. He formed a treaty with two Protestant princes, concentrated his army, and with his
long, ruddy beard waving in the wind, he pushed
on as swiftly as a mountain-stream, through the
narrow passes, to surprise the Emperor.

Granville had once shrugged his shoulders at
Maurice of Saxony ; the Emperor had taken him
only for an ordinary German prince, who was
tipsy four times a week. However, Maurice had
learned at the Imperial Court how to deceive the
innocent ; he had made dangerous progress in
that hazardous school, and the pupil was finally to
crush the great master, who deceived the whole
world. The Emperor at Innsbruck was quite absorbed in the deliberations of the Council of Trent,
and prepared to extirpate the Protestant religion
with its ideas of political freedom, when the tidings
reached him that Maurice was approaching in forced
marches. He grew pale at the tidings, and he, who
had dreamed of uniting the countries of Charlemagne
under one sceptre, put on the worn-out apparel of
an old woman to escape in this disguise. The road
to Flanders, however, had been blocked when his
army was defeated, and late in the evening of
May 19th, 1551, amidst showers and thunder-

storms, the Emperor fled from Innsbruck to escape his former ally.   He could not ride, as he was suffering from gout, and in a litter, as harassed as an outlaw, Charles V took the way to the East, while the torches of his attendants lighted the hardly passable path.   Maurice of Saxony let him escape ; he said that he had no cage fit for such a bird, and amused himself by starting him as one does wild game. Hardly had the Emperor left the town, when the shrewd Chancellor Granville informed the imprisoned Elector, John Frederick, that his captivity had come to an end by Imperial command, while he was only required to promise that he would follow the Imperial Court voluntarily until further orders.   When the Elector opened the door the next morning, the Spanish guard had disappeared.   He was at liberty. God had broken his chains.

Though the slowness of his military exploits had shown him to be an indifferent general, his constancy during imprisonment proved his excellence as a Christian.   No efforts had been spared to induce him to sign the Interim, forming a proposal for the adjustment of religious peace !   No threats could frighten him to sign a paper offensive to his evangelical faith.   The ignoble revenge of the Emperor did not hurt him either.   His Court chaplain had been removed ;   Luther's writings and a costly Bible, printed on parchment and decorated with illustrations, had been taken away, but all these vexations had not disturbed his admirable peace of mind—he who had been vanquished at Mühlberg had retreated into an invincible fortress : in the entrenchments of a clear conscience.

Now he was free, but he kept his promise as a prince and a Christian. He hastened to follow the Emperor along untrodden paths, and the Emperor was deeply affected on meeting John Frederick again. He promised the Elector Imperial favour and mercy and then continued his flight as far as the centre of Carinthia. It was a weary, distressing flight ; with the inexorable enemy at their heels the fugitives had to pull down the bridges behind them to delay their approach. All the splendour of the Imperial dignity was gone ; within twenty-five days the glory of twenty-five years was demolished and nothing was left to Charles V of all his magnificence but the gout, from which he suffered more than ever. A Roman Catholic Council was held at Trent, but the members dispersed in great fright on hearing the trumpets of the Protestant army ; the panic spread among the most faithful paladins of the Emperor, and left by all, he realised the frailty of all human power. The Protestants had seized Innsbruck, a meeting of German princes was held at Passau, and the famous treaty signed there secured the German Protestants religious liberty and equal rights with the Roman Catholics. For two generations this treaty effected religious peace ; then the Thirty Years War broke out, by which Germany was devastated.

CHAPTER XXII

CHARLES V aimed at a universal empire; Calvin's ideals were higher, he aimed at a Christian state: Christian in its divisions and its laws, considering itself responsible to God for the actions of all its subjects.

Laws are to be obeyed—that was the inexorable rule on which Calvin based everything. When applying laws he always took care, with great impartiality, that the rich did not come off scot-free, while the poor were punished. One of the first punished by the Government as a law-breaker was a councillor of Geneva; another was a burgher of high standing. An obstinate gambler got the confiscated cards hung round his neck, and was tied to the pillory for an hour in sight of the people. The organiser of a dissolute masquerade was obliged to implore forgiveness on his bare knees in St. Peter's; a perjurer was hoisted on a ladder with his right hand tied up, and put in the pillory for hours. On account of his having dressed somebody's hair indecently, a ladies' hairdresser was put in prison for two days; parents, who evaded the law of compulsory education and kept their children at home, were fined. Adultery was punished; adulterers were led through the streets like criminals. Afterwards several punishments were made more severe; at a general meeting of the people it was resolved, that adultery required capital punishment. At the same time it was in the Geneva of the Reformation, that those men were living who had driven Calvin triumphantly out of the town, and who were to oppose him now the more violently, as the Evangelical leaven was doing its work more thoroughly. They were the Libertines. While Calvin had pitched his camp in Geneva as a centre for the great spiritual fight to be fought from the Apennines to the northern fjords and from the Atlantic Ocean to the Russian steppes, he was to be harassed most forcibly by his sworn enemies in this very camp, as he was before his banishment. The camp taken by him was over a volcano, and every day, every hour the eruption could take place, destroying himself and his congregation. In this critical fight earnest and pious men of severe morals and fixed national aspirations were on his side. They stood shoulder to shoulder, realising that their only strength was unity. And thus they defied the fierce attacks of their enemies, hoping in God. In 1546 the general strife broke out, when a manufacturer of playing-cards, who had sustained some loss, one night gave vent to his bitterness against Calvin. He called him a Protestant bishop worse than his predecessor ; the councillors who supported him were traitors, and Calvin's religion simply deceit and tyranny. The Council condemned Ameaux, but Calvin thought he had been judged too leniently, and so the Council of Two Hundred condemned the manufacturer of playing-cards to implore forgiveness, torch in hand. In the camp of the Libertines this severe sentence roused much indignation ; they disturbed the divine service when Calvin preached, and the authorities were compelled to have the gallows erected, in order to frighten them. The next year blood was shed. Gruet, formerly a canon and now one of the Libertine chiefs, threw off his mask and spoke words of great blasphemy against Christ. His house was searched and a number of blasphemous writings as well as a dangerous correspondence of high treason fell into the hands of the Government.

His guilt had been proved, Gruet had attacked religion and wanted to betray the town to the Duke of Savoy. His fate was not dubious, he paid for his crime with his life.

The case of Perrin, the Governor of Geneva, was still more painful to Calvin personally, for Perrin had been his faithful friend for a long time. Perrin's wife had been to a ball prohibited by the Council ; the Church Council heard of it, and Calvin was not satisfied until the lady, though she belonged to the highest rank, was sentenced to some days' imprisonment. Perrin, who had also been to the ball, fled, but a letter written by Calvin caused him to be arrested.   This was a letter full of touching tenderness, in which Calvin appealed to their old friendship, besought him to sacrifice his pride to the welfare of the Republic, and to submit to the decision of the authorities.   This was too much for Perrin ;   he returned, willingly submitted to the decision of the authorities and underwent a slight punishment.   Thus this thunderstorm passed by. They were reconciled.   And Calvin thanked God. This was in May, 1546.   In the month of June of the next year, Perrin got the very important commission of forming a treaty of commerce with the French Government.   During his absence, his wife, with her venomous tongue, had again given rise to complaints, and on his return in the autumn, Perrin heard that she had been banished to Bern territory with her father, a man whose morals were very bad. Perrin flew into a passion.   He brought back his wife, rushed into the council-room, and striking his fist on the table declared that he had rendered too many services to the town of Geneva to be insulted so grievously in his nearest relations.   To Calvin this appeal to a high municipal position was intolerable.   " If you will not submit to the yoke of Christ at all," he said, " go and build a town somewhere in which you can live at your pleasure ; but as long as you are here, you shall not escape the laws ; and though there were in your dwelling as many diadems as heads, God will surely know how to prevail." In all these disastrous quarrels this was his fixed rule. From the elevated, inviolable tower of his religious conviction he beheld the petty doings of mortals who tried to thwart him, the servant of the Almighty King. They were a troop of fools, not able to move without the will of their heavenly Father. This conviction turned the Reformer's blood into steel, and he wrote with a smile round his clearly-cut mouth : " The grievances undergone here are exaggerated abroad. In Lyons I was reported to have died in more than twenty ways. It is true that Satan here has means enough to ignite the fire, but the flame vanished like flax."

Meanwhile Perrin had played with fire. When he referred to his services rendered, the severe councillors wondered if these services were indeed so great. He had formed an advantageous treaty of commerce, but the most singular negotiations were reported to have been entered into on his own authority with a foreign power. No less a thing was alleged than garrisoning Geneva with a corps of French artillery. This was meant for a defence of the town, as Perrin asserted, but the Government maintained that in this way Geneva was entirely at the mercy of France. It could not be proved, that Perrin had committed treason ; but, to say the least, he had acted with the greatest thoughtlessness, and the Council dismissed him from an office which he evidently was no longer able to fulfil properly. However, in the bosom of the Council itself opinion was divided on this point ; there was a strong minority, protesting fiercely, and the waves of the people's passion arose in the streets and squares. The Council of Two Hundred degenerated into a Polish Council and wild cries of hatred for Calvin were uttered. Then Calvin, who was at a meeting with his colleagues, rose to throw himself amidst the wildly excited people, in spite of the most pressing warnings. He may have been slightly paler than usual, but he never hesitated. With folded arms he defied the rioters thirsting for his blood ; then he passed the threshold of the town hall. The shouts and cries increased, daggers flew from their sheaths, while Calvin went to the centre of the hall resolutely and immovably. Then silence ensued, and amidst this ominous silence he called out : " If you desire my blood—here it is ! If you want to banish me—I will go. And you may try once more to save the town without the Gospel ! " Like hissing arrows these words left his lips ; this man with his clearly cut face had become the conscience of Geneva. He was in their power. If they liked, he should not leave the hall alive. But there was nobody who laid hands on him, they durst not ; his powerful eyes awed them. By respectfully making way for him, they acknowledged his superiority. Three days afterwards Calvin reminded them of the approach of Christmas and that they should celebrate the Lord's Supper together. As for himself he bore no grudge and was willing to be reconciled to Perrin. At that moment he was sincere ; many of his adherents may have been so too. For the moment there was peace again. But it was only apparent peace. The old hatred arose again, and Calvin was abused most shamefully. The Libertines would not let him walk about unmolested ; they hissed him when he passed, changed his name into that of Cain and called their dogs Calvin to insult him. Hardly a year after peace had apparently been restored, Calvin was compelled to complain of Perrin and some other burghers, who purposely absented themselves from the communion service. Once more he earnestly tried to bring about a reconciliation, in order that the communion at Whitsuntide might not be desecrated by spite and enmity. The Council thanked him for his good intentions, but the Libertines secretly had intrigued so successfully that Perrin had been appointed first burgomaster a month afterwards. Filibert Berthelier knew this. He was the son of the famous martyr who had died for his country in 1521, and used his advantageous position to abuse the Church Council, which had summoned him, in the most disgraceful manner. Put under Church discipline on account of several shameful deeds, committed some days before the Communion service in September, Berthelier appealed to the Council. The sentence was annulled by the Council, where Berthelier's and Perrin's friends held the reins. They seized the opportunity

to triumph over the Church, and declared that
Berthelier was free to attend the communion, if in
this he followed the dictates of his conscience. In
this way the Council had shown its position definitely,
but Calvin had also done so. He preferred death
rather than allow Berthelier to attend the communion. Sunday came. The town was in fearful
suspense. The rumour was spread that the Council
had secretly given Berthelier a hint to stay away
from church, but that he had made up his mind to
go with a number of friends. The bells were ringing.
The people were already hastening to church.
Gradually the large building, the arches of which
were supported by twelve heavy pillars, was filling.
The burgomasters, the Council, and twelve men
of the armed body-guard now entered in the colours
of the town, grey and black. They took their usual
seats as on every Sunday. It was time—Calvin
ascended the pulpit. His glance went over the
crowd. The building was full ; only some late
comers pushed in hurriedly. There was the communion cup, and yonder, near a pillar, his eyes
descried—among a defying troop of Libertines—
Berthelier's shameless face. They had come to
attend the communion service. . . . Calvin was
silent ; the last drop of blood had left his face ;
immovable like a pillar stood the iron legislator of
Geneva. Then his lips opened to deliver the usual
short sermon ; he read the liturgy and said amidst
breathless silence, in a slow firm voice : " As long

as God permits me to stay here, I shall show the
constancy He has granted me, whatever may happen.
And I shall follow the line of conduct, which my
Master has made perfectly clear to me." He descended from the pulpit and consecrated the bread
and the wine. Then the Libertines rose, left their
seats and approached the communion-table. . . . It
was a moment of suspense. There stood Calvin. He
stretched his hands over the sacred symbols, his
stature seemed to rise and his eyes flamed, when he
exclaimed : "These hands you may cut off, these
limbs crush, here is my blood—shed it. You shall
never compel me to give what is holy to the godless !" The Libertines hesitated. Was it the awe-
inspiring attitude of the servant of the Lord or the
threatening murmur of the people that made them
hesitate ? They stopped ; then they left the church.
And never has a more exciting communion service
been held at St. Peter's in Geneva. In the afternoon
Calvin preached again. His sermon was a vale-
dictory address to his beloved congregation, for
every moment he expected the order of banishment. He had chosen as his text the farewell
words of the apostle St. Paul to the Ephesians :
"And now, brethren, I commend you to God and
to the word of His grace."

The whole congregation was moved, there were
tears in the preacher's voice ; their hearts were
touched. Leaving the church, Calvin went home
to await the order of banishment. However, the

order did not come ; the Council durst not sign the warrant, and the people of Geneva were attached to Calvin more closely than ever. It was a matter of surprise that a small party, a fraction, had ventured to raise such tumult and revolt ; in spite of the respected names borne by some of its members they did not at all represent the people of Geneva, and Calvin, whose seat had been endangered, was strengthened by the fierce fight. Calvin's victory meant Farel's triumph. Farel had come to Geneva, and alluding to their pantheistic ideas, he had called the Libertines atheists. When he returned to Neuchâtel, his place of abode, he was called to account by the Geneva Council, and refusing to be retained by the magistrates of Neuchâtel he returned to Geneva at once. He was recognised in the street by some turbulent Libertines, who surrounded him and cried : " Into the Rhone with the rascal ! " The undaunted hero laughed at their threats, and, rescued by his brothers in the faith, Farel was led in triumph to Calvin's house. His cause had become their cause ; they repaired to the town hall in great numbers, called Farel their father, and would not suffer him to be designated as a false minister. The Council let the matter drop ; the people had taken the responsibility and the accusers stole away ashamed. The arrival of Farel, however, had been connected with a dismal and terrible event, which has been written about to this very day.

CHAPTER XXIII

THE GENEVA STAKE

NINETEEN years before, Calvin had been willing to risk his life to have a conversation with Michel Servet, and now—in 1553—Servet came to the town of Calvin to end his life at the stake. He was a Spaniard, like Ignatius Loyola ; a gloomy man with a strange adventurous mind, a student of geography and geometry, of medicine and theology, who revealed his learning in a flow of words, without ever having been able to get his degree. There was something intrepid in this man, but if his intrepidity became too dangerous for him, he did not mind getting out of difficulties by a series of untruths. His system was based on the pantheistic doctrine of the Anabaptists, and while he defended the right of astrology he attacked the doctrine of the Trinity with the same zeal. Twenty-three years before, people had already been excited by Servet's zealotry. Gentle Œcolampadius was alarmed at his doctrines, and Zwingli had advised Œcolampadius to do everything in his power to oppose this detestable blasphemy. It is true, that Servet dared speak words, which were intended as a shameless attack on

Christianity, and that he wrote things which make us shudder. Well—in the confusion of his ideas and the unrestrained pride of his heart this man sadly imagined that the Reformers stopped half-way in their work, while he considered himself ordained to restore Christianity to its former splendour. However, in Calvin's eyes the denial of the Holy Trinity and his pantheistic ideas meant the disorganisation and destruction of Christianity, which Servet pretended to defend, and Calvin, in whose strong memory the attack on his own orthodoxy had made an indelible impression, felt the more need to adopt firm and rigorous measures against the dreams of the Spanish heretic. What spirit can have induced Servet to take the fatal road leading to the Geneva dungeon ? He had just escaped from imprisonment at Vienna, where a Roman Catholic court had sat in judgment upon his heretical opinions, and the way to Italy lay open before him. He could have avoided Geneva. And when he entered the town, yet why did he stay a whole month ? Probably he counted upon the help of the Libertines and the strong support of Perrin, who was still burgomaster ; the rumour that Calvin's fall was expected will have reached him, and in his rashness, which characterised this man, he no doubt imagined himself to be the successor of the famous Reformer. Amidst the most violent disturbances, while the sword of Damocles was hanging over Calvin's head, Servet appeared in

Geneva. Calvin was most distressed. Had not he enough to struggle with ? He requested the Government to imprison Servet, and one of the magistrates gave the order. But according to the Geneva laws nobody could be imprisoned on a mere accusation, unless the accuser was also imprisoned. This was a law of the Medes and Persians, and Calvin would undoubtedly have been compelled to change the pulpit for the dungeon, had not his secretary offered himself as a substitute. Imprisonment, it is true, was nothing dishonourable in itself. In those days one was imprisoned as easily as one gets a warrant nowadays. On some days the prisons were like our waiting-rooms—so crowded were they. Hardly anybody escaped the dungeon, society ladies, members of the Council, men holding the highest posts, like Perrin, all had to enter it. In a ponderous deed of accusation of thirty-eight articles Calvin explained his objections to the doctrines of Michel Servet ; the accused answered, defended himself, and boldly challenged Calvin to a public debate, relying on the good-will of some councillors. He would not speak, but he would let the Holy Scripture and the patriarchs speak. And they would destroy Calvin's doctrines.

Calvin wished for nothing better ; his democratic blood made him rejoice at the prospect of fighting out the quarrel in church and in the presence of all the people. He made up his mind not to accept the decisions of a hostile majority—not he ! However, the congregation would participate in the violent struggle, which their leader had to fight, to be edified and strengthened in the doctrine leading to godliness. Hard, fierce and bitter was the struggle. Angels and devils fought for the soul of Geneva ; the heights of heaven opened over the town and the depths of hell under it. And from this infernal abyss, where God is cursed and hated, arose the blasphemous words uttered by Servet, gnashing his teeth : " The Holy Trinity is a three-headed hellhound."

The Council, afraid of possible disturbances, gave no permission for a public meeting ; new sessions took place, while Servet, who had an ally in the jailer, beheld with eagle's eyes the violent religious-political struggle in the bosom of the Geneva Republic. The written memoir required of him in the beginning of September was evidently drawn up under the impression of a considerable decrease of Calvin's power. Servet saw his papers increase in power in proportion as those of Calvin decreased ; the accused began to be an accuser, and he collected the stones with which to crush Calvin.

He said in his memoir to the thirty - eight articles :

" Calvin is a liar, a blasphemer, and who dares assert that a murderer and a criminal accuser is a true minister of the Church ? You, Calvin, do not know, what you say ; you are a villain, if you continue to judge of what you do not understand—do you intend to deafen the ears of the judges by your barking ? "

Calvin appeared before the Court himself to dispute with Servet. He attacked the pantheistic doctrines of the Spaniard. " Suppose," he said to Servet, " that somebody stamped his foot on this stone floor and said that he was stamping on your God. Should not you be horrified to hear the majesty of God subjected to such blasphemy ? " No, Servet did not feel this horror. " I feel no doubt whatever," answered the man, " that this bench, this sideboard, and everything that exists forms the substance of God." " According to you the devil himself is God ! " cried Calvin. And Servet answered with a laugh : " Do you doubt it ? " Here they were, the monstrous ideas which had struck the Reformer already eight years before in a correspondence with Servet, and which made him write to Viret as follows : " Servet proposes to come here, if I want him to. But I will not pledge my word, for, if he came, I should not suffer him to leave Geneva alive however little my influence might be." The authenticity of this letter has been doubted ; afterwards it was considered indisputable, in any case it clearly shows Calvin's point of view, which he never relinquished. He was most anxious that Servet should be punished ; if the denier of the Holy Trinity should come off scot-free it meant for him the destruction of the work to which he had devoted his life. Now that he was alone, and

the kind, comfort-speaking lips of Idelette were
closed for ever, there were moments in his life when
his strong mind was on the point of sinking into
the slough of despair ; then he seized his pen to
pour out his heart to Farel and Bullinger ; in these
moments of gloomy doubt he even thought of leaving
the camp and ending his days in some remote place.
Bullinger urged him not to give way to this dejection
and complete the ruin of the town, trusted to him,
by leaving it to its fate in a fit of despair. Farel
came over himself to strengthen his beloved brother
in his hard struggle. He declared he should deserve
the most hideous death, if he caused anyone to forsake the most holy faith, and that Servet deserved
the same punishment. It was the Roman Catholic
idea which possessed Farel and Calvin and all the
Reformers, none excepted. Servet was of the same
opinion. On a letter to the Council he declared
he was ready to die, were he unable to crush Calvin.
However, he requested that Calvin might be arrested
too and beheaded in his place if he had revealed
Calvin's errors. Servet wondered why the magistrates were so long in pronouncing the sentence. He
had said his last word—why should they defer the
sentence ? He called Calvin his only enemy, a
sorcerer, who ought to be driven from Geneva, and
claimed Calvin's fortune as compensation for the
possessions he had lost through him. Three weeks
more passed without Servet's receiving an official
answer. And then he understood that his prospects

were dark. The arrogant tone of his sayings was no longer heard ; he became meek and submissive, and his letters showed his distress. Meanwhile the decision had taken place, but outside Geneva. The Council had sent the papers of the lawsuit to Bern, Zürich, Bazel, and Schaffhausen, and the answers came in on September 18th. Each answer was double : one from the Council and one from the Church Council of the place, so there were eight answers. They were definite and unanimous ; Servet must die ! that was their harsh and inexorable demand. The Bern Council, whose advice was highly prized by Geneva, was not satisfied with capital punishment only, but demanded the stake, contrary to Calvin's wish to save Servet from the horrors of such a terrible death. Thus Protestant Switzerland had passed judgment, and the Geneva Council could only uphold this sentence. Acquittal would have been an insult to Church and State, whose opinion had been asked, and treason to the Reformation, the honour and safety of which were at stake. Many members of the Council had hitherto considered the lawsuit only as one between a Spaniard, whose monstrous doctrines disturbed them, and a Frenchman, whom they hated. However, this Frenchman was supported by four powerful Protestant Churches, and it was no longer dubious which side the scales would turn. Then Perrin sprang to his feet to save Servet. He demanded acquittal, but the Council refused, for this acquittal would have caused Calvin's banishment. Then he requested the case to be brought before the Council of Two Hundred, less influenced by the advice of the four churches, and counting among its members many enemies of Calvin. This request was also refused ; then Servet's doom was irrevocable, and in spite of the strong attempts of Calvin and his colleagues to save the unfortunate man from the terrible death by fire, Servet was condemned to the stake.

Farel was in his company in the morning of October 27th as his spiritual supporter, when the bailiff announced to Servet that this was his last day. He was left in ignorance about the stake, but the thought of having to die was sufficient to overwhelm him for a moment. Farel wished Calvin to meet the unfortunate man once more, and Calvin came with two councillors and friends.

Servet begged Calvin's forgiveness, and Calvin answered : " I hereby declare that I have never desired to take revenge on you for any personal insult."

When he had been led to the town hall, Servet heard that he was to die at the stake. It was a terrible moment. He besought that he might die by the sword, but it was in vain. And Farel accompanied him to the stake. Farel asked him if he did not wish to commend himself to the prayers of the spectators, and Servet answered in the affirmative.

However, Farel considered it his chief duty to convince the heretic of his errors even in his last moments.

At half an hour's distance from Geneva lies the hill of Champel. This hill is reached by a pleasant road, on the right two shady avenues, known under the name of the large and the small Philosopher's path from time immemorial. The Dutch theologian Arminius, who studied in Geneva, devised and completed his theological system here.

To this hill they repaired. From its summit could be had a magnificent view of the river Arve, streaming past in capricious curves, of the bright valley with its vineyards, the autumn foliage of which was glittering in the October sun, while the wide horizon seemed to be supported by the green tops of the Jura Mountains. Here Servet was to die. He knelt down to pray. Farel once more insisted upon Servet's renouncing his errors and so vehemently as to seem painful to us, but he refused so firmly that all the spectators were impressed. " Invoke the eternal Son of God ! " urged Farel, but he exclaimed : " Jesus, Thou Son of the eternal God ! " It was only a change of words—that was all. Yet this change was the yawning gulf of their difference. Servet did not acknowledge the eternity of the Son of God. His writings were tied to his body ; a wreath of straw and green leaves, sprinkled with sulphur, crowned his head. The fire was smouldering ; the wood was wet ; bitter and long was the death-struggle. And from the dense smoke came the voice of the dying man : " Jesus, Thou Son of the eternal God ! have mercy upon me ! " Even now, after three and a half centuries, this stake has not yet been extinguished ; the flames are bursting forth, and in the glow of these ruddy flames stands out the image of Calvin. However, this stake was not Calvin's wish ; he had protested, and the Government erected the stake in order to show that it had the power of rejecting Calvin's request for mercy.

Yet Calvin desired Servet's death ; all the blue water of Lake Leman cannot wash away this fact ; the wings of this profound philosopher were tied by ideas, which we have learned to consider as errors. On the three hundred and fifty years' commemoration of the day on which Michel Servet ascended the stake, a number of ardent admirers of the great Reformer Calvin were gathered in Geneva to unveil a remarkable monument, consecrated to penance and remorse. The monument, made of a block of granite, bears two inscriptions. One is :

" On the 27th of October 1553 died at the stake at Champel

MICHAEL SERVET

from Villeneuve, Arragon,
born on the 29th of September 1511."

And the other inscription is :

> " We, the respectful and thankful sons of
> Calvin, the Great Reformer, condemning
> an error, which was the error of the age
> in which Calvin lived, and valuing above
> all things Liberty of Conscience according
> to the true doctrines of the Reformation
> and the Gospel, erected this monument of
> penance on the 27th of October 1903."

It is strange—neither in Geneva nor in any
other place in the wide world has there been an
available spot for a statue in commemoration of
Calvin, but to one of his most determined adversaries a monument has been erected. Its purpose
is not the glorification of Servet, but at the same
time he has been distinguished, which is hardly
compatible with the anti-Christian and blasphemous
ideas which he defended.   And we feel entitled
to ask if it is right to mention an error of Calvin's
age without making mention of the errors of Michel
Servet.   Yet it is quite right that the error, which
caused Servet to die at the stake, was an error of the
age in which Calvin lived.   The bearers of the most
venerable names in the Protestant world rejoiced
at the tidings of Servet's sentence of death.   Beza
was now satisfied, so were Haller, Sulzer, Musculus ;
gentle Melanchthon wrote : " The Government was
right to put the blasphemer to death."   It was the
Roman Catholic leaven in the Protestant dough :

in the Protestant as well as in the Roman Catholic circles it was the general idea that every heresy, spread among the people, should be punished by death. The reformed churches had another special reason to adopt rigorous measures. It was a well-known fact that Anabaptists, Libertines, and Rationalists, all preachers of false doctrines like Servet, found and obtained followers in the Reformed circles. In this way the Protestants got a bad reputation; they were said to be tainted, infected with revolutionary ideas, and without the slightest doubt this opinion would have been confirmed, if Servet, who had been condemned to death by the Roman Catholic court of justice in Vienna, had got off scot-free in Geneva. It is true, he could not have been acquitted without violation of the principle which prevailed in the civil and religious world of Christianity : the principle that the public authorities ought to exterminate all idolatry and all heretics. This principle, exalted to a dogma, is centuries old. It is much older than Calvin and Calvinism, it existed even eleven centuries before Calvin ; and the well-known Father Augustine was its creator. For fourteen centuries up till the days of the great French Revolution, this dogma swayed its inexorable sceptre and dominated the mind. It was laid down in the Emperor Justinian's statute-book, brought forward again by the jurists of the fifteenth century, and adopted as a public right by all the European

Christian countries in the sixteenth century. However, the cruelty of the Roman Catholic Inquisition is not to be found in Protestantism. While the Roman Catholic Church declared that all heretics deserved death, Calvin and the Protestant Churches wanted only those to be punished who made public propaganda for their heretical opinions. This does not alter the fact that the principle in question prevailed for fourteen centuries, and that the thirty-sixth article of the famous thirty-seven Articles of Faith expressly mentions the extermination of all idolatry as the task of public authorities. In the different Protestant creeds this principle has been embodied. It is expressed in different ways ; the tone is either milder or severer, but in reality there is no difference. The Second Helvetian Confession and the Westminster Confession, which go farthest, have spread most. As a matter of fact the question of the persecution of heretics in the Protestant world was not finally settled till the eighteenth century and in consequence of the Revolution. However, the abolition of this persecution was not the consequence of the revolutionary principle, for this rigid dogma had to give way to the idea of the Reformation, which has liberty of conscience for its motto, and does not suffer any man to have power over the conscience of another. Did not the Protestants of the seventeenth century fight for liberty of conscience ? Who can deny this ? They fought and suffered for this sacred principle, but while they respected liberty of conscience, they called liberty of worship into question. That was not all ; they did not dare grant liberty of speech. This was the error, it was the error of the age, and Calvin, the father of the French Reformation, was the son of his age.

CHAPTER XXIV

STRUGGLE AND VICTORY

In the autumn of the year 1553 Calvin had maintained his ground at St. Peter's in Geneva by his splendid courage at the celebration of the Lord's Supper ; peace and quiet would have prevailed within the walls of Geneva if Filibert Berthelier and his followers had wished it. The Church Council requested him to acknowledge the serious and rightful grievances against him and, confessing himself guilty, to return to Christ. But Berthelier could not be induced to do this ; his obdurate patrician mind objected to stooping to people whom he considered as intruders, and the weatherwise forecast a hurricane. Alas ! it was so. It began with rows at inns, noisy, improper songs in the street, irregularities, and provoking violations of the regulations. Some ringleaders were arrested, but it was no good. Their friends visited them and turned the jail into a ballroom. The cause of the Libertines was brought before the people. They began to wonder how it was possible that Frenchmen, foreigners in Geneva, held the reins, and if it were not high time to stem the tide of foreigners. What was that Farel but a foreigner ? And Calvin, who

222

was at the head of the town, or at least imagined himself to be so, had not even been admitted to the freedom of the town. They complained that a lot of shabby people, the scum of Europe, crowded into the town, and that the famous Geneva of old would go to rack and ruin, if the national conscience of the children of Geneva did not sweep this miserable lot from the streets. This was, of course, malicious exaggeration. To be sure, there was chaff amongst the wheat. But more wheat than chaff, and Calvin did his utmost to free Geneva from impure elements. The noblest inhabitants of France flocked to it. Geneva was their place of refuge, their Pella, the cave of Adullam for all the oppressed. It even became their country, as their old country rejected them, and it may be questioned whether history shows another example of such a speedy and complete fusion of nationalities. They found no favour in the eyes of the Libertines, as they were allies of Calvin, whereas their praises would have been sung if they had assisted in unhorsing him. However, they refused to do so, for Calvin was their leader, their protector, their father—his name had been engraved on their minds, never to be erased. They knew Calvin as a child knows its father, and Calvin knew them ; but the Libertines did not know them, as their hatred blinded their eyes. Without any emotion, quite insensible and unmoved, without a shade of pity or compassion, they passed these fugitives. That was not all. If the fugitives were poor, they were reproached with taking the bread out of the mouth of the poor in Geneva ; if they tried to find work, the employers were set against them ; if they came with money, they were scorned like traitors, who had come to Geneva to bribe its burghers. Sneers and jeers were lavished on these refugees, and this wrung Calvin's heart. "They shamefully despise the exiles of Christ!" he exclaimed in his bitter indignation. He seemed to have triumphed, but then the demon powers reappeared like a black tidal wave, threatening to wash away his life's work. He was accused, in consequence of his doctrines, of considering God as the author of sin. Castellio, the ambitious rebel, who had been banished from Geneva for calumny, harassed the Reformer from Basel with his fiercest Pelagian arrows, as Albert Pighius, the well-known Roman Catholic theologian and violent defender of free-will, had done in former times from Kampen in Holland, while Bolsec, the former Carmelite monk, spread nonsensical ideas about the doctrine of Predestination. There were moments of great despair, in which Calvin cried out, like Elijah on Mount Horeb : "It is enough, receive my soul, that I may die!" The Reformer uttered such-like words, and, tortured by his enemies, vexed and teased like a horse by a swarm of hornets, he envied more than once his brethren who went to the stake calmly and triumphantly as if they were entering a banqueting-hall. To be burnt by the Papists, that was only a short pain, and then the end. What could bind him to this life of sorrow ? Idelette had been the star shining on his sombre life and making it bright by her loveliness. But Idelette was in her grave, and he had been left at his solitary post. It was a miracle that he did not lose his mind and had not to be locked up in a madhouse.

"One thing makes me persevere in my hard struggle," he wrote to an intimate friend, "that I shall soon be released by death."

If he appeared in the street he was hissed at. When he heard his name called out and looked round, people said : "We only mean our dog !" Calvin's name was given to dogs to make him despicable in the eyes of the public, and when he passed the Libertines, they said : "Cain ! how are you, Cain ? "

One day, fatigued with preaching, he came from the upper town ; on the bridge he met three persons, who molested him and evidently wanted to knock him down. The day before, Perrin's wife had succeeded in running over another preacher, and this man nearly lost his life. This was the lot of Calvin who was called the King of Geneva, and who, when at work in the evening, was startled by knocks at the windows and the door, by shameful cries of derision. This was not all. Half-drunken creatures held mock-processions with burning candles, through the town, bawling disgraceful parodies on the psalms and quite laughing at the idea of being arrested. They caused riots, startled quiet burghers, and declared that the end of the Calvinistic tyranny had come. Perrin, who had once awakened such great expectations, seemed to be incited by the evil one. He proposed depriving the emigrants of all arms except their daggers, and this was acceded to. However, the next year he proposed taking away their daggers ; a grievous insult, which Perrin made the more grievous by declaring, that these foreigners had plotted to betray the town into the hands of the French king, Henry II. He pretended to have heard this on good authority. The king himself had said it in a letter, written to the Council of Bern. The fugitives were astounded at this monstrous accusation ; but in the Council of Two Hundred, Burgomaster Lambert rose up full of indignation, as their defender and protector of their reputation. Lambert could venture to say more than the others, for his brother had perished as a hero at the stake of Chambéry. " Mr. Perrin ! " he said, " don't you feel how absurd your accusation is ? Are you such a fool as not to understand that the emigrants despise the man who murders their brethren and who will not spare them, if he lays hands on them ? Besides I greatly wonder why you should come with this accusation. You used to be less anxious about the safety of this town ; seven years ago you did not mind helping to provide it with a French garrison ! "

The burgomaster had more to say. He stated that the town had everything to gain and nothing to lose, if these true, honest burghers were admitted to the freedom of the town. They had admitted not more than fifty during the last five years; he strongly advised the Council to be more liberal on this point. The burgomaster's speech was successful; during the first months of 1555 sixty emigrants were admitted to the freedom of the town. At the same time the Council understood that the discipline, exerted by the Church, ought to remain in their hands. And they were convinced of this by a speech, made for them by Calvin, who, with the Holy Scriptures in his hand, clearly showed that public authorities had no more right to meddle with Church matters than the Church had to meddle with the rights of the State. The change of front in the Council acted like oil on the Libertine fire. It was especially the preachers whom they hated. The enemy did not understand what was the use of all this preaching and Bible-reading and confirmation classes—what good came of them? Two preachers were more than enough for Geneva, and the others had better be dismissed. Some riots took place; rebellious fishermen and skippers armed themselves and appeared in the town hall to let the Council hear their threats—within four days three demonstrations took place before the town hall. This was the crisis; and Calvin wrote to Farel: " Remember this poor town in your prayers ! "

One peaceful evening in May, the leaders of the Libertines put their heads together. Perrin and Berthelier were present at the meeting; they had a good glass of wine, and Perrin had the honour to be put at the head of the rebellion.

Berthelier was not so muddled as to be blind to the risk he ran if they should fail. He was not so sure of the victory, and would rather have gone home to bed. However, it was difficult to go back now; he had already gone too far. The cup was handed round once more, and then he firmly put himself at the head of a crowd of people, who were to save Geneva from the hands of the foreigners. " Away with the French ! " was their motto. The burghers, sitting on the doorsteps under the sloping roofs, fled into their houses and bolted their doors, but the burgomaster, who was at the head of the watch that night, met the agitators calmly and warned them to go home. Go home—they had something else to do ! Perrin snatched away the staff, the symbol of the official's authority; the watch was pushed aside and the cry of murder: " Kill them, kill them ! " resounded in the streets. However, the bold enterprise came to a miserable end. The sons of Geneva, whose help had been called in, did not move, as they would have nothing to do with these ringleaders; the watch was reinforced, they scoured the streets and arrested whomever they could catch. The next morning the town had resumed its usual appearance, the rebellion had been nothing but a farce, and the shopkeeper laughed at it behind the counter when serving his customers. However, the Council did not laugh. For them it was painfully true, that they had to punish the rioters according to the strictest laws, and they wanted to show that the authorities, according to St. Paul, did not wear the sword in vain.

The sentence for Filibert Berthelier was as follows :

" We burgomasters and councils of Geneva make known, that on the 6th of June, 1555, the present sentence pronounced upon Filibert Berthelier and his accomplices has been publicly announced by sound of trumpets, and this on account of their detestable, shameful plot against the existing Church and against the town, as well as against the order and peace of the burghers. The above-mentioned Filibert Berthelier, one of the conspirators and an enemy of the town and its peace, has been condemned to be taken to Champel and there beheaded. His body to be quartered and exhibited in four places in the vicinity of the town, as a warning to others who might commit a similar crime in the future.

" Thus signed by us."

Berthelier and Perrin, who were both condemned to death, had fled meanwhile, and Berthelier's brother, together with two other demagogues, had to pay the piper. They mounted the gloomy scaffold, the executioner's sword glittered, and their heads fell as sacrifices for the agitations of a party which had fought to the death against Calvin for eighteen years. Thus Calvin had gained the victory. Calvin the Reformer! Calvin the Victor! No, Calvin's ghost would arise from his grave, if we called him Victor. He never sought his own honour, his greatest honour was to serve; he had reached the zenith of his joy, when Geneva was the awe-inspiring scene of Christ the Victor.

And Calvin, who had compared himself with David without fear, in the introduction to his commentary on the Psalms, had now got rid of all his enemies.

CHAPTER XXV

THE TRIUMPH OF THE GOSPEL

REST ? That was a word not to be found in Calvin's vocabulary. For forty years he wore the harness, and he was to die in it. For him rest only meant change of battle-ground ; if the centre was attacked less forcibly, he rushed to the threatened side-wings ; and to France, which had driven him from its threshold like a leper, he particularly devoted his cares and prayers. Persecutions were again taking place in Protestant France ; the smoke of the stake was rising to the blue sunny sky ; the sufferings and death of the " five prisoners of Lyons," as they are called in the chronicles of the martyrs, filled the hearts of the Evangelicals with grief and melancholy joy. They were five youths, students at Lausanne, well known to Calvin, Beza, and Viret, who betook themselves to the south of France to sow the seed of the Gospel, followed by the prayers of the congregation. They were treacherously arrested in Lyons, brought before the judges and condemned. The sentence caused great dismay in Switzerland ; the Bern Government offered its mediation ; Calvin did his utmost to save the five proclaimers of the word of the Lord. However, it was in vain ; the sentence of death was signed, and Calvin, who could not save their lives, now, in his letters, gave them strength to face death. He wrote, with tears in his eyes : " Your fetters have become famous, the tidings of your death will resound far and wide, in spite of Satan, and to the glory of our Lord." In this way he wrote ; firmly though deeply moved, constant in his courage and faith, himself prepared to sacrifice his body to God in the fire at the stake. In the lovely month of May, when everything breathes peace and quiet, the five martyrs, in ash-coloured clothes and bound with strong ropes, mounted the dungcart which was to convey them to the place of execution. It was a curious procession ; the executioners with their rigid faces, the clangorous soldiers, the priests in their black garments, pointing to the condemned and calling out to the people : " That is right—firewood for hell ! " while the martyrs, not forsaken by the Saviour, resolutely sang this psalm : " I will honour the Lord with all my heart ! " They mounted the stake full of courage ; the youngest first, while Martial Alba, the oldest, came last. He embraced his comrades, one by one, saying : " Farewell, brother ! " And they consoled each other by saying that their sufferings would soon be over. The fire was lit, and from the flames their voices were heard exclaiming : " Courage, brethren, courage ! " Then the columns of smoke rose up ;

the flames sparkled, and it was over. From his dungeon in Rouen, Richard Le Fèvre wrote to Calvin : " I am writing this to tell you that at Whitsuntide I hope to have entered the kingdom of heaven, and to be seated at the banquet of the Son of God, if I am not called before by our beloved Master."

However, Le Fèvre was mistaken. At Whitsuntide he was still on earth. It was not before July 7th, 1553, that the stake was prepared to convey the soul of this holy martyr to heaven on the wings of the flames. While black thunderstorms threatened to come down in France, the sky had cleared on the other side of the Channel. Henry VIII had been gathered to his fathers in Westminster Abbey in 1546, and with him had sunk into the grave a religion which could only be confused with the real work of the Reformation through bad faith or through narrow-mindedness. Edward VI was only nine years of age when the king died ; the Duke of Somerset took up the reins of power as regent, and issued a proclamation containing the application of the true, pure Christian doctrines to the whole nation. England was closely connected with Geneva in those days through Calvin, who dedicated his exposition of the first Epistle to Timothy to the Duke. In this serious crisis the Duke asked Calvin's advice, and Calvin wrote the remarkable letter, in which he set forth his opinions as to the course which the Reformation in England ought to adopt. It was a far-reaching programme of action laid before the Duke by the Reformer ; he proposed to turn England into a Geneva on a large scale, and he wished to see public authority used as a sword to gain the victory for the Gospel. It was this idea which had brought Servet to the stake and which suffered no heresy ; which wondered if crimes committed against men should be punished and greater crimes against God should be left unpunished ; it was the law of Justinian come into force again. The Regent agreed with the programme and would have had it made into a constitutional law without any delay, if political interests and religious hate had not caused him to fall into disgrace. It is true, the Duke's honour was restored, but he was to fall a victim to shameful intrigues a second time. Then the moment came when he had to work out another programme of Calvin's by resolutely climbing the steps of the scaffold. Without any hesitation he fulfilled this task, and dying as a martyr, he was mourned for by a young king, in whose name he was murdered. Edward VI had noble principles and a warm heart, and his excellent abilities gave rise to the greatest expectations. He had broad views ; in every respect he had freed himself from the fatal ideas of justice which had prevailed for eleven centuries, and it was only after a long and persistent refusal that he had been induced to sign the death-warrant of a woman, who had denied the incarnation of the Son of God. The young king was burning with holy zeal for the Reformation, and his accession was quite a relief after the rule of a king, who had his wives beheaded in order to marry others, and who respected neither divine nor human laws in his kingdom, but only the law of his own will. Edward VI was fourteen when the Reformer of Geneva dedicated two of his works to him : the exposition of Isaiah and that of the Epistles. This dedication had nothing to do with flattery. Nothing was more repugnant to Calvin than slavish homage even to a crowned king. Calvin knew that these Commentaries were well adapted to the quick understanding and the shrewd intelligence of the king, and that they were suitable food for a prince who hungered after righteousness. Were not his tutors themselves astonished at the progress made by their royal pupil ? Had not he a burning desire for knowledge ? Did not he make a Reformation plan himself at that time—all unaided—in the form of a dialogue, showing his practical as well as his gifted genius ? Des Gallars, a clergyman, handed the two dedications of Calvin to King Edward in London. They were accompanied by a letter, written by Calvin, in which he referred to what, in his opinion, ought to be done to complete the blessed work of the Reformation in England. The tone of this letter was simple—he spoke to a king by the grace of God, but between the lines one could read the tenderness of a friend, of a spiritual father, and Edward received this letter as a respectful greeting from a spiritual king.

As a token of his veneration Edward sent Calvin a costly present, and Calvin, in whose thoughts England was uppermost, answered with a short exposition of the eighty-seventh Psalm. His homage to the king consisted in a warning not to forget the kingdom of heaven, his love in a reminder, that a true Christian is above a crowned king. Then combining king and Christian he continued : " Sire ! It is an invaluable blessing that God has called you to be a Christian king ! "

Not only with the king, but also with him who was the king's right-hand—Archbishop Cranmer —Calvin kept up an earnest and far-reaching correspondence. The hand of the tyrant, called Henry VIII, had rested like lead on the shoulders of Cranmer, but the hope of seeing the English people one day refreshed by the living waters of the true Reformation had never left him. With this young, energetic king by his side he dreamt, in his enthusiasm, of a mighty union combining all the Protestant Churches. " Close your ranks," was the watchword heard from Rome, and Cranmer wondered if the time had not come for the Protestants to do the same. The Roman Catholics had their Council of Trent—why were no means devised to hold a Protestant Council as a stronghold against the other ?

With the vehemence of a Protestant of the sixteenth century he wrote about this ideal to Calvin. And charmed with the grandeur of this plan, with

which he entirely agreed, Calvin replied that he
should not mind crossing ten oceans, if need be, to
attend such a glorious Protestant meeting. Edward VI! Calvin's heart began to beat when he
heard his name. Never did he find a king more
eager to build the walls of Zion and pull down the
kingdom of Satan. But what Calvin experienced
a hundred, nay a thousand times, happened again
—his hope was nipped in the bud. When the young
king ascended the throne he was already doomed
to an early death, phthisis undermined his precious
life, and he was not yet sixteen years old when he
entered the kingdom of heaven, about which Calvin
had written to him with so much eloquence. " This
is the end of Protestantism ! " said the Roman
Catholics in England in exultation, and Mary the
Bloody, who succeeded her half-brother, did everything in her power to realise this prophecy. Queen
Mary's childhood had been without any joy. Educated in the strict ceremonies of the Roman Catholic
faith by her mother, she had from infancy hated the
Protestant heresies, and her father, Henry VIII, who
had driven her mother from the throne so unjustly.
Thirsting for revenge she ascended the throne. It
is true she had promised not to make any change
in religious matters ; but no sooner did she hold
the reins of power than this promise was forgotten.
She prohibited the vernacular in divine service ; she
dismissed all married priests and left them to their
fate with wife and children, bereft of everything.

Cranmer was thrown into a damp dungeon, and so great was his fear of the queen, that he denied his faith to save his life. But though he forsook his Saviour—Christ did not forsake him. With a bleeding heart he bewailed his fall ; he recanted, and, led to the stake, he held his right hand in the flame first, because this hand had signed the abjuration. A long cry of anguish arose, England was plunged into sorrow, and the heart of the English people was greatly embittered. Yet the queen was inexorable, she had sworn that she would destroy Protestantism root and branch, and in her zeal she was so indomitable, that even the Pope and Charles V were alarmed at her ardour. The tables were turned. Edward VI had prepared in his country a hospitable Pella for the French brothers in the faith, driven from their country by the Roman Catholic fury, now England was turned into a shambles, and a number of English fugitives betook themselves to Geneva, there to find shelter till the storm was over.

In this way the bond between England and the town of Geneva became stronger and closer than ever. The name of the great Reformer sanctioned it, the Church of England got its Calvinistic stamp, and with Queen Elizabeth, who succeeded Mary the Bloody, the persecutions came to an end. To this queen Calvin dedicated his exposition of the prophet Isaiah, but the queen never accepted the dedication. Had the Reformer vexed her ? Was she annoyed at what he had once said : " Women-rulers are less desirable " ? Indeed, she was, and Queen Elizabeth never forgot these words. How splendidly did she refute them in her long, magnificent reign ! When her mother, Anne Boleyn, showed her when a baby to Henry VIII, he angrily stamped his foot on the ground and cried with a scornful laugh : " A daughter ! What is a daughter to me ! " Yet his daughter was worth ten sons, and this queen became the founder of England's greatness. What Calvin had said about women-rulers, John Knox repeated in his sharp way and thus incurred the hatred of two queens. One has already been mentioned, the other was Mary Queen of Scots. It is said of this Scottish queen, that nobody could behold her without admiration or love, and that nobody could read the history of her life and death without grief and sorrow. She, the daughter of the rough mountains of the North, grew up at the wanton Court of France and was educated in the strict Roman Catholic faith. She was as frivolous as she was charming, noble-hearted, but at the same time capricious and hot-tempered.

John Knox was her powerful opponent. He had proclaimed the word of the Lord at St. Andrews, when this fortress was surrendered to the French. He was sent to the gallows and sighed in slavery for two years ; then he regained his liberty. Knox was the spiritual son of Calvin, and the living link between Scotland and Geneva. He was already fifty when he made Calvin's acquaintance and came

under his influence. He went farther than Calvin ;
he made heroes, not martyrs, of the Church, and
traversed Scotland like a Protestant crusader, Bible
in hand and sword girded on. The queen trembled
before this powerful man. He told her frankly,
that Christians have a right to rebel, if they are
hindered in their religious ceremonies. This was
a thesis never defended, but always refused by
Calvin, but Queen Mary did not know the Bible so
well as Calvin, and she had to give way to the
Scottish Reformer, who compared persecutors to
madmen requiring a strait-waistcoat, that they
might not trouble anyone. He wished that she
might one day become the Deborah of Scotland,
but this was a figure of speech she did not understand, and bitter tears of vexation streamed from
her eyes, as all her threats fell powerless before his
granite forehead. Knox was a man of steel ; hard,
inexorable, the harnessed " beggar " among the
warlike Scots. More than once he went to Geneva ;
there he saw the triumph of the Gospel after the
fall of the Libertines, and exclaimed in exultation :
" Since the days of the Apostles the earth has not
beheld such scenes ! " It was a wonderful fate that
brought the daughter of wealth and cultivation face
to face with this Elias of the Reformation. She had
been hospitably received by the stubborn Scots,
though they were averse to her faith, and they
would have remained faithful to her, if her frivolity
and the wanton dancing at her Court had not

Scotorum primum te Ecclesia, CNOXE, docentem
Audiit auspiciis estque reducta tuis;
Nam te cælestis pietas super omnia traxit
Atque reformatæ Religionis amor.

JOHN KNOX

[*Face page* 240

roused the indignation of the Puritans. Knox made the churches resound with his severe sermons, and he inserted in the prayers of the service these words : " Enlighten, O Lord, the heart of the Queen—I beseech Thee ! " Knox did not spare anybody ; he was an iconoclast, an opponent of the nobility, hard, rough, and upright in his virtues as well as in his faults a giant, kneeling before God but rising like an eagle before man. On his tombstone has been rightly written : " Here lies the man who never bowed to the face of man." Ardent preachers from the south of France brought Calvinism to the Netherlands—we have been taught so—history-books tell us so. However, a famous historian has discovered that these ardent preachers only existed in the imagination of historians, and that, on the contrary, there would be something to say for the supposition, that Dutch preachers went to preach Calvinism in some places of France. The Dutch had an aversion to France, and this national trait also appeared among the Dutch Protestants. France was their sworn enemy, with whom their people had fought so many a hard fight, and though Condé and Coligny wished to annex their country in order to secure them liberty of conscience, they flatly refused to accept this proposal. This suspicion of everything coming from France was so deep-rooted that Franciscus Junius, a clergyman in Antwerp, who had come from France, was strongly suspected, in spite of his excellent gifts and noble character, as the congregation in their teacher only saw the French-man, and it took them a long time to forget his nationality. That Calvin took a great interest in the religious movement in the Netherlands need not be mentioned, and that he made the acquaint-ance of a great many Netherlanders is without doubt. He must have met Petrus Dathenus, when this remarkable man was preaching in Frankfort ; the brothers Marnix attended Calvin's lectures in Geneva, a great many Anabaptists and Libertines, who lived in great numbers in the Netherlands for a long time, became acquainted with Calvin's doctrines. The Reformer did not speak Dutch, but neither did the German Emperor, Charles V, who could not understand his own subjects, and had to call in the aid of his Chancellor, Granville, to translate the German correspondence into French. French was heard far beyond the French frontiers ; it was Calvin's native tongue, while he had a perfect command of Latin, the universal language of scholars and educated burghers. Farel did not like the Southern Netherlanders, he called them unsteady and unreliable, but Calvin knew them better, and in his work, *On Vexations*, he highly praised the courageous contempt of death shown by the martyrs of Flanders and Artois. No French preachers, but Calvin himself, influenced the Dutch people. This influence was not sought for by Calvin ; his work had soon got known here.

What by the grace of God distinguished him

particularly : the absolute acknowledgment of the Sovereignty of God, the implicit obedience to the Holy Scriptures, the profundity of faith, the clearness of his doctrines and their unlimited application to life—all this specially appealed to the Dutch. The characteristic quality of the Dutch Reformation, as far as this can be mentioned, is not the religious superficiality of Humanism, not the sober intellectuality of Zwinglianism, not the inertia of Church conservatism, neither the licentiousness of Anabaptism or Libertinism, but, above all, the doctrine embodied in Calvinism, in the profound comprehensive sense of the word. In various ways and by various means, God at the same time brought together and united his Church in the Netherlands and his minister in Geneva.

CHAPTER XXVI

DOUBTLESS Calvin's attention was drawn to the Netherlands and to Brussels in October of the year 1555. In the lively capital of Brabant, the States General of the seventeen Provinces had assembled ; the Emperor Charles V was there, so was his son, Philip II, the sombre king with his sickly face, whose name is written with bloody letters in Dutch history. It was a brilliant meeting in the Palace at Brussels. There were the chief magistrates in their robes and chains of office ; the knights of the Golden Fleece in their glittering armoury, the flower of Dutch nobility. The Emperor had visibly aged, the peace of Passau had turned his light hair into snowy white. He had to lean on a wooden crutch for support ; his hands, ankles, and knees were stiff with gout ; this man of fifty-five looked like an old, decrepit man—only from his dark blue eyes there flashed at times both pride and majesty. The royal personages : the Emperor, his sister, the Governess Mary, and Philip II, were seated under the canopy. Then the Emperor rose slowly, leaning on the shoulder of a young man, who afterwards got the name of the Taciturn. Leaning on the shoulder of Prince William of Orange, Charles V gave a short survey of the thirty-eight years of his reign. He described his campaigns, nine in Germany, six in Spain, seven in Italy, four in France, ten in the Netherlands, two in England, and two in Africa. He mentioned eleven sea-voyages, his victories and peace negotiations, and tried to convince his audience of his arduous endeavours to promote the welfare of his subjects and the defence of the Roman Catholic faith. The Netherlanders had experienced that he had defended the Roman Catholic faith. Most severely had he treated the Reformation in these provinces. He had intended to exterminate the heresies by his sharp placards, he had threatened to behead the men, to bury the women alive, if they did not return to the pale of the mother-church. Luther's and Calvin's writings were forbidden on pain of death, and the placards became more and more severe. But had this availed ? Had not the sacred fire, purging the hearts of the martyrs, proved stronger than the fire consuming their bodies ? Psalms had ascended from the flames, and the blood of the martyrs had become the seed of the Church. Charles V had instituted the Inquisition ; the martyr, Jan Bakker, was the first of the long series of martyrs, estimated at 50,000 in these provinces. However, Charles V was not what Philip II became, a bloodthirsty zealot. His politics influenced his religion. Among his regiments some were Protestant ; they had their own preachers, who followed the Imperial Standard to the Netherlands, and, unpunished, spread a faith which, if believed in by the Netherlanders, threatened them with death. The Emperor was more opposed to Calvinism with its ideal of liberty than to the Protestantism of the German princes ; and he had a number of stakes erected in the Netherlands at the same time that the German religious liberty was secured by the peace of Passau. The Roman Catholics in the Netherlands greatly wondered at his inexplicable resignation to this peace, and they could not make out the man, who, if he had been an ardent supporter of the Pope, would have risked his last soldier to annul the peace of Passau. As has been stated before, he was not a zealot, and his stadtholdership influenced his religion. Indeed, he had not forgotten that his army had once plundered Rome, and that he had even ventured to attack the Pope. Therefore, his hatred of Calvinism was as much political as religious ; he considered Calvinists as people, in whose blood ran the desire for political liberty, and he had tried to crush both heresies at one blow. But was Charles V then like Philip II ? Did he take a cruel delight in torturing subjects, whose way of serving God was different from his ? Let us be impartial and not forget that the Emperor lived in a time when religious liberty was considered a monstrous folly, and that he had sworn to defend the Roman Catholic religion. He had not only promised to do this, but sworn it. Besides he was reminded not only by the clergy, but also by many nobles, that an Emperor by the grace of God was bound to keep the oath sworn to defend the Church of God. He was also aware of the terrible scenes resulting from the sinful degeneration of the Reformation. At the Imperial Court the errors of the Anabaptists were well known. The Anabaptists, as numerous as mushrooms in the Netherlands, were turbulent and restless by nature ; the revolutionary blood ran through their veins, and they frightened the quiet burgher, while they put the Reformation in a most unfavourable light. The notorious Jan Beukelszoon, of Leiden, maintained that he could do more than cutting, which he had learned as tailor. He called himself King of Zion, and became one of the ringleaders of the sect, who considered themselves as the chosen people of the Lord, who were to bring the millennium on earth. They betook themselves to Munster to give loose reins to their passions and carnal appetites, till the town was taken by storm, a terrible judgment passed, and Jan of Leiden was pinched to death with red-hot tongs. These facts, however, did not prevent Charles V from treating the Protestants in the Netherlands most mercilessly. Chivalrousness was unknown to this chevalier ; mercy was ignored by this Christian Emperor. He was a mean, untrustworthy, cunning man ; he deceived his enemies by taking advantage of their trust in his promises ;

he had the unfortunate Elector, John Frederick of
Saxony, led about like a bear with a chain, and there
were but few moments in his life in which his human
feelings prevailed. He was bent on extending his
territory and spent millions on increasing the
splendour of his realm.

However, in small things he was most thrifty ;
the soldier who brought him the sword and the iron
gloves of Francis I, was sent off with a hundred
crowns, while a sum of ten thousand crowns would
not, indeed, have been too great for such a capture.
The three soldiers who swam across the Elbe with a
sword between their teeth to procure him the boats
for the victory of Mühlberg, were rewarded with a
jacket and four crowns—that was all. No, not all
—they each got a pair of stockings besides. At that
price Charles V bought a whole electorate, and he
smiled with pleasure like a merchant driving a good
bargain. This battle of Mühlberg was not a thing
to be smiled at by the Dutch Calvinists. Like Calvin,
they turned away with disgust from Maurice of
Saxony, who betrayed the cause of Protestantism
by taking the side of the Emperor. They were not
reconciled to him before he had made another
change of front, humiliated the Emperor and saved
German Protestantism. It was even prohibited to
mention the peace of Passau in the Netherlands,
where it was looked upon as high treason. It is
the more to be wondered at, that the Emperor met
with so much affection and sympathy in these

provinces. On the other hand, it must be remembered that he had a special gift of making himself agreeable. He who went to Africa, because Europe was too small for his ambition, also rode to the ring with the Flemish nobles, shot at the popinjay with the cross-bow at Antwerp, drank beer with the Flemish peasants, and amused them with Flemish jokes. These things the States General remembered, when he abdicated. Besides they were moved by his helplessness, and the Emperor himself, affected by this sad and solemn moment, spoke in an unusually touching way.

Then he turned to his son. He pointed out to the young prince that the brilliant realm, over which he was to sway his sceptre, would abundantly pay the debt of gratitude, if his reign should be distinguished by a wise and loving care of his subjects. Prosperity would approve of his abdication, if his son proved himself worthy of his goodness, and this would happen, if he kept the laws and defended the Roman Catholic faith. Finally, he addressed the States General. He admonished them to be loyal to their new monarch and to maintain their union ; he besought them to forgive all his errors and offences, assuring them that he would remember their obedience and affection in every prayer to the Supreme Being, to Whom he was going to devote the rest of his life. Never had the Emperor spoken in such a touching way. He was weeping, all were deeply moved, from all corners of the large hall sobs were heard. At this solemn moment the Netherlanders forgave their monarch his crimes; the broken privileges, the placards, the strangling poles, and the fires of the martyrs—all were forgiven. Had not he killed their bodies to save their souls ? At this last supreme moment they thought that they heard the beating of a father's heart in his voice. Philip threw himself at the Emperor's feet ; the Emperor wept, so did his son. These tears were real, they were the last ever shed by Philip. While Charles, the persecutor, departed to bury himself within the sombre walls of a Spanish cloister, Philip, the executor, came forward to burn out in the Netherlands the Calvinistic heresies as a wasp's nest is burnt out. The threatening thunder-clouds gathered on the horizon ; the reports which reached Cannon Street at Geneva became most ominous, and the first flashes of lightning announced like flaming heralds, the terrible Eighty Years' War.

CHAPTER XXVII

THE GREAT MASTER

WHAT are we, when we think of Calvin's work and energy ? He was very weak, spat blood, and suffered from unbearable headaches. He suffered more than most people ; fevers undermined his strength ; a harsh letter, a bitter word, could shock his very soul. In spite of this he surpassed all his contemporaries in working-power ; he turned the night into day to finish his gigantic tasks ; he dragged himself to the pulpit, even though excruciating rheumatic pains racked his body ; and sinking down in a chair, exhausted and dead-tired, he still complained of laziness and indolence. A gigantic task was resting on his shoulders in Geneva. He was a preacher, a teacher, and a pastor, as well as the attorney-general of the Protestants ; his house was an information-office ; it was the great centre of attraction for foreigners, who were considered as guests. He was unsalaried Minister of the Interior, while the very hand, which wrote to kings and electors, directed words of consolation to a humble labourer, persecuted for his faith, and the powerful author of the Institution managed to find time, in spite of his endless troubles, to procure good posts for God-fearing servants and to help young people in getting married. Everybody depended on him ; he was everybody's adviser ; the Marquis of Vico, who lived in St. Peter's Square, knew everything about it.

Galeas Caraccioli, Marquis of Vico—everybody in Geneva knew him. Foreigners, fugitives, wanderers coming from the South, asked for him, and they were told : " Oh, the Marquis of Vico, the reformed Elder of the Italian colony—he lives there ! " He was reformed Elder, and his uncle was Pope in Rome—similar relations occurred more than once, in a time when the Reformation inexorably separated the son from his father, the husband from his wife. In the gloomy dungeons, on the instruments of torture, on the scaffolds, much was suffered, but this breaking up of families severing the tenderest ties of love was worse. It was exceedingly deplorable ; from the sixteenth century, the century of the Reformation, a sharp cry of pain resounds through all ages. The Marquis of Vico, the celebrated man, belonging to a family counting twelve principalities in its two branches, drank the bitter cup to the last drop. Like a long, glorious summer's day, life lay before the marquis when he married an enormously rich duke's daughter, at the age of twenty. He seemed to be fortune's favourite, the Emperor Charles V appointed him Chancellor ; honour, respect, fame greeted him everywhere, his wife and children were the glory of his marriage, and many a one envied the knight, as brave as he was amiable. Then one day a Spaniard came sowing the first seeds of discord in this happy household, to proclaim frankly with the resoluteness of a Luther and the ingeniousness of a Calvin, the doctrine of vindication through faith only. Ochino, the Capuchin, followed, while Petrus Martyr, the great theologian, developed the same ideas in his lectures. Before the marquis had been married five years, the seed of the Gospel took root in his soul. On a journey to Germany afterwards his conversion was completed, and he returned to Italy to say for ever farewell to his family, who refused to renounce the Roman Catholic faith, in which they had been brought up. He staggered as if intoxicated under the heavy burden, which his weak shoulders had to bear. That he would have to leave his sunny country, his posts of honour, his palace, a glorious future, was hard ; but, what was the lack of all this compared with the loss of an old father, whose pride he was, to the loss of a wife, whose soul was united with his by strong, fervent love, to the loss of the nine children, who were as dear to him as the apples of his eyes !

His wife met him with the baby in her arms. His heart seemed to fail him, but he departed. The marquis came to Geneva on a summer's day. The Reformation had inexorably got hold of him, and there he was—a poor, wretched man, who had left

his joy in life behind in the sunny South. . . . Did
the reformers receive him with sympathy and compassion ?   Did they offer the lonely man the cup
of brotherly consolation ?   The answer may be
read in the dry returns of the Geneva Town Council.
It says in the registers that the marquis was admitted on condition that he would behave in submission to the others, and that they would keep an
eye on his movements.   No consolation awaited him
but suspicion, they were not quite sure that he was
not a spy, and so the former Chancellor of Charles V
was put under supervision of the police.   Where
could the wretched man pour out his heart ?   Where
else than in the cave of Adullam opening into Cannon
Street ?   So the marquis came to Calvin, and here
he found consolation.   Calvin was his friend, his
protector, and did not think it beneath him to
declare that his own faith had been strengthened by
the striking example of this Italian.   Meanwhile the
departure of the marquis from Naples had roused
great agitation in his native town.   His father
immediately sent after him, and a member of the
family found the lost man in Geneva and sent word
to Naples that the marquis was living in a lowly,
simple dwelling.   Everything that this messenger,
a cousin of the marquis, could do to make him return
he did.   With tears in his eyes he described the state
of despair, into which the marquis had plunged his
family : the grief of his old father and the despair
of his wife.   The fugitive was deeply moved, but

he persevered in his decision to live in liberty of
conscience, and his cousin had to go back without
having effected his purpose. Then his father
summoned him to Mantua, informing him that he
had found for him a place of refuge on Venetian
territory, where he could freely profess his faith.
The marquis hesitated; but the consideration,
that the proposal was a favour from the Roman
Catholic Church, induced him to decline. Then his
wife requested to see him, and the marquis came
to Vico to embrace those who were dearest to him
on earth, after a seven years' absence. They saw
each other to say farewell for ever; this they knew,
for his wife was as firmly resolved to remain faithful
to the Roman Catholic Church as he was to cling
to his Evangelical faith. The hands of this husband
and wife were clasped, they looked into each other's
eyes full of woe and love, and yet they were separated
by a terrible abyss. To take leave of his old father
was hard, but to take leave of his wife and children
was harder. They would not let him go, they
followed him into the hall, and his wife implored him
to have pity on her for love's sake. All were weeping: the cousin who had seen him in Geneva, and
the marquis himself. A pretty girl of twelve clasped
his knees and sobbed: "Father—do stay with us!"
All the little hands kept him back, it was a scene to
melt stones into tears. Yet the marquis departed
without looking back, his heart torn with the
bitterest grief. When he had returned to Geneva,

he made up his mind to be divorced from his wife. Then both would be free—he and his wife.

It was Calvin again who had to give advice, and Calvin sat down to write to the marchioness. He shrank from advising a divorce, and tried to find a way to secure liberty of conscience for the marquis and at the same time the happiness of domestic peace. This way he found by proposing to the marchioness to come and live in a free and neutral place, where they could each serve the Lord according to their conscience. Thus the matter would be solved in the most satisfactory manner. It seemed a little like the proposal which the marquis had declined, but this was not really the case, for now he would claim as a right what was formerly allowed him as a favour. However, the confessors of the marchioness were harder hearted than Calvin; under their strong influence she declined, and a divorce was the mournful solution. The marquis married again. Michel Cop conducted the wedding service at St. Peter's. The marquis set up his household according to his modest means; his clothes were plain and simple. Yet he was constantly visited in his lowly dwelling by the most substantial citizens, not as an indigent man, but as a prince in the audience-hall of his palace. He no longer bore the title of marquis, yet he was saluted with the respect due to his former rank, and the people of Geneva called him the marquis. Never was a more faithful reformed Elder. He not only

strengthened Calvin in his belief, but the whole
congregation in theirs ; he was a true overseer ;
he constantly paid pastoral visitations. He visited
the poor and saved a little of his small income to
relieve their needs ; he was to be found at their
beds, when they were ill or dying. Through his
amiability and sincerity he overcame the suspicion
of the Council, and the same Council which had
put him under supervision of the police, offered
him the freedom of the town. The case of the
Marquis of Vico was not singular in its kind. It
was repeated over and over again in this terrible
time, when the children of the Reformation had
to sacrifice their earthly happiness with a bleeding
heart in order to gain heavenly bliss. A stream of
fugitives left Italy ; at their head the eloquent
Ochino, who had ventured to ask : " He who created
you without your aid—cannot He re-create you without your aid ? " and therefore he was among the
first dangerous heretics against whom a summons
was issued. A great number of fugitives followed
him : men belonging to the old nobility, former
priests of high rank, rich merchants, and highly
cultivated women. They had to leave everything
behind in order to retain their freedom ; along
secret paths they tried to reach the snow-bound
passes of the Alps and the Swiss frontiers, ever in
danger of being betrayed into the hands of fierce
persecutors. He who remained behind, inexorably
went to the dungeon, the rack, the scaffold, or the

stake. In Venice the condemned fugitives were rowed to the sea in a boat at midnight. A plash was heard—a low shriek of farewell, woefully resounding over the dreamy sea—and all was over. Geneva had its full share of the fugitives, and Calvin received and consoled them, taking care of them like a shepherd of his flock. He was their protector, and when wisdom made prudence necessary, he was compassionate. When everyone suspected the marquis, the Chancellor of the hostile Emperor, Calvin opened his door to him and welcomed him most heartily. This welcome given by Calvin was the beginning of his rehabilitation, and this was completed when the Reformer dedicated to the marquis his exposition of the first Epistle to the Corinthians.

What an imposing series of detailed elaborate Bible commentaries by Calvin appeared in these turbulent years of Geneva ! In 1546 and 1547 the two Epistles to the Corinthians appeared ; in 1548 six commentaries ; in 1549 two ; in 1550 three. Thus Calvin expounded thirteen books of the Bible in a period of five years, while he was overwhelmed with other work, without mentioning the numerous writings done in the same period of time. Each commentary was an important event, an historical fact in the Protestant world.

" They mark," says Bungener, " a revolution in the study of the Bible, and in this respect they not only take the first place in the history of theology, but also in the history of the human mind. Common sense dethrones book-learning ; it is truth that is sought for in every verse and word, in the broadest and shortest way. Many passages have undoubtedly been improved, but only by following Calvin's very method. In a word, biblical knowledge owes him what every branch of knowledge owes a man, who transfers it to the range of facts and bases it on observation and experience. He may make mistakes, but he will have paved the way for all further progress of knowledge, and in this sense he will have a right to consider as his what will afterwards improve some part or other of his work. Besides, with regard to Calvin one should not suppose too soon that one has understood better or seen better than he. Modern exegesis has often felt surprised at the discovery that what it considered as new was already to be found in Calvin's writings ; frequently his elucidations, formerly rejected, are now considered the best. Even in those things finally, which he could not know, and on which travelling, archæology, and other branches of knowledge did not throw light till after his time, his astute mind was often competent to see the truth in spite of all the errors and ignorance of his age. The different schools in the Middle Ages had only studied the Bible as a subject for exercises or book-learning. The field of the Holy Scriptures was dug for the sake of the digging, not the finding, it was dug again and again without bearing any fruit. The Reformer, however, never used his spade in vain, he would not open even the smallest furrow, if it could not bear fruit, if it could not produce an idea inspired by God. Though without any fervour, Calvin's commentaries are full of life, and owing to their characteristic truthfulness, their lack of fervour is a new element of power and authority. The reader realises that the author is a man, who says only what he can prove unobjectionably. Hence the result, which surprises at first, when the reader remembers that the author is Calvin, the strict Calvin. This may be explained, because he feels at ease with the author, who conducts him through the field of the Bible, relating what he has seen himself, showing the flowers for a moment only, the fruit for a long time, and offering those fruits most willingly, which seem the soundest and most nourishing. Yet he is more than a guide ; he consults you in some measure, making use of your experience and kindly urging you to increase your knowledge. It is as if the reader also holds the pen in his hand, feeling the author's superiority only through the pleasure of hearing him say clearly and ingeniously, what he has thought himself or at least wished to have thought."

Yet the charm of Calvin's writings is greatly surpassed by the charm of his personality, and one does not do justice to Calvin if one judges him only from his writings. On the contrary—one gets a wrong idea of his life, if one does not penetrate into his soul, his heart, the impulses of his inner self. There was a severe trait in his character—a matter of course in a man who was called upon to be a Reformer. He was also quick-tempered and irritable, while his irritability, a serious fault, acknowledged and repented of by Calvin himself, was increased by his violent bodily sufferings and an opposition often fierce and frequently diabolic. As the sun breaks through the clouds, so his inborn amiability broke through his fits of ill-humour. When the showers were over the sun shone in the famous Cannon Street in Geneva, where any child knew the bright house of John Calvin, surrounded by a shady garden. It was like going on a pilgrimage ; from all corners of the earth foreigners came here to enrich their minds, but more so to find consolation for their hearts. He was called the Pope of Geneva. This was going too far. He was the Father of Geneva, nobody can deprive him of that title of honour. Bossuet designated Calvin as a gloomy genius, which shows that the pious Bossuet looked at things from a gloomy point of view when he used this expression. Calvin had a cheerful mind, he liked to laugh and joke with his friends. When old Bonivard was going to be married for the fourth time Calvin roared with laughter. It is true—he did not often laugh. At that time there was not much to laugh about ; it was a time when the children of God were thrown into dark dungeons and persecuted like wild beasts, when the martyrs gave up their souls to Christ at the stake. Calvin had powerful influence through his works, but this influence was increased by his irresistible charm. There is a Calvin, come down to us through tradition, with a parchment face, with ink instead of blood in his veins, and with a heart of granite. This Calvin, this gloomy genius, stands in the ruddy glow of Servet's stake, with a harsh grin on his cruel, heartless face, and those who have hated this Calvin and his doctrine have exclaimed for more than three centuries : " This is Calvin ! " But is this true ? Is not this a falsehood ? Is not this vile calumny ? The real Calvin was a man of flesh and blood, a sincere friend, who gratefully acknowledged the slightest kindness. He spread warmth around him, his friends liked to be in his company, the Cops, the Cordiers, and so many others found no rest before they breathed the air of the town which has been called the town of Calvin. He has been called stingy, he has been called a hypocrite ; a Roman Catholic author has called him a child of Sodom. And all this he had to bear ; his memory has been mocked and derided, because he burned with zeal for his faith, and the following words were wrung from his soul : " Even a dog barks when his master is attacked, should not I raise my voice when the majesty of God is attacked ? "

Stingy—was he stingy ? A notarial document records what he left behind ; we have his last will, the famous testament, which the Reformer made shortly before his death, and which contains the following :

CALVIN *(after Holbein)* [*Face page* 262

As for the few earthly goods which God gave me
to dispose of, I appoint as my sole heir, Anthony
Calvin, my beloved brother, but only for honour's
sake.   I bequeath to him the silver beaker presented
to me by Mr. Varennes, requesting him to be satisfied with this, as he will be, I am sure, as he knows
that I do it for no other reason than to leave the little
I have to his children.   Further, I bequeath ten
crowns to the University and as much to the poor
foreigners' fund.   Further, the sum of ten crowns to
Johanna, daughter of Charles Costan, and his half-
sister on his father's side.   Further, forty crowns each
to Samuel and John, sons of the above-mentioned
brother, my nephews.   Further, thirty crowns each
to my nieces, Anne, Susan, and Dorothy.   As to
their brother David I give him only twenty-five
crowns, as a punishment, because he is frivolous and
unsteady.   As far as I know, this is all that God
has bestowed upon me in the form of means, books,
furniture, household matters, and everything else."
Adding these sums together we get two hundred
and twenty-five crowns !   And to realise this
amount, everything, the library, the manuscripts,
and the furniture had to be first turned into money.
But all his goods did not even bring in that amount,
but only two hundred crowns—that was all ; it is
Beza who records it.   When we consider Calvin's
character, we cannot help wondering.   When he
himself or his family are concerned, money seems
to have lost its value ; but if others are concerned,

Calvin turns a practical merchant, thinking of every penny. Is not it remarkable ? Calvin refused to marry an immensely rich lady of noble birth. " What is money to me ? " he said. " A dowry of purity and virtue is sufficient for me ! " Yet when one of his friends wished to marry, he thought money very important. He knew the young girls of the town, the surroundings even of Neuchâtel. In this wonderful brain of his, that noticed and retained everything, was recorded how they were educated, what their character was like, what virtues and what faults they had, besides the extent of their dowries. The very unselfishness which made him despise money for himself urged him to value it for others. If a young man of his community came to Calvin to be advised about his intended marriage, Calvin would leave his most profound studies to tell him that a household means money, and that a man must calculate the cost before he begins to build the tower. How Calvin worried to get a wife for Viret ! And how many did he help by word and deed in this respect ! But his care went much farther. With what fatherly tenderness did he watch over the interests of his friends' children; he took interest in all of them ; his shoulders, which, like an Atlas, bore the cares of a Protestant world, also bore the cares of all his friends. Calvin was interested in the smallest details of everyday life, especially when others were concerned. He possessed in an unwonted degree the gift of all great

demagogues, of paying attention to details, to trifles.
For him there were no trifles, everything was important, and this explains the intensity of his actions.
Now we begin to understand why the house in
Cannon Street attracted such numbers of people.
There not only the brain of European Protestantism
was at work, but also the heart. Here flowed in
a stream of letters from England, France, Poland,
Russia—Calvin's house was the international post
office of Protestantism. Each foreign letter was a
matter of great importance, at a time when letters
took the place of newspapers. The news that a letter
had arrived was spread like wild-fire, and its importance was increased by the bearer, who was almost
considered as an ambassador. In Calvin's house
gathered people bearing the most respected names
that were known in Geneva. Other points of view
were shown by these letters; old plans were put
aside and new plans of campaign were formed.
Under Calvin's roof gathered the general staff of
Protestantism; there the chances were calculated;
from here the missionaries of the Gospel were sent
into the wide world without purse or scrip. They
did not hesitate. They united the stoical courage
of the Russian anarchist with a burning love of
Christ and humanity; wherever in any part of
Europe a hard furrow had to be sprinkled with
blood, that the seed of the Gospel might grow in it,
there these heroes were ready to shed theirs;
wherever the fire of the stakes required fresh fuel,

they offered their bodies. They were the sons of Calvin ; on the firm rock of predestination their house was built, and while they were singing their immortal psalms their souls triumphantly rose to heaven. In Geneva Calvin had a hard fight and a bitter struggle. The Libertines had to be converted into Calvinists ; the stubborn pride of the free burgher had to be bridled by discipline ; men full of the pleasures and enjoyments of life had to be put to the yoke of strict morals. Merry, dancing, wanton Geneva, which had surpassed all other towns in unbridled pleasures for centuries, was then called upon to surpass the others in strict morals, purity, and earnestness of life. Geneva was to become the Jerusalem of Evangelical Christianity. A Christian state, a Christian town, a Christian household. A Christian !—that was Calvin's ideal ! And does not a Christian's life form a chapter of the *Institution ?* Geneva found itself in a singular time and in extraordinary circumstances.

Like a horse surrounded by hornets the town was surrounded by grim enemies, longing for the moment when they could divide it among them. It was like a lost post, projecting and solitary ; like a weak camp amidst hostile lines of battle, like a ship with burning sails trying to reach the harbour.

Michelet, the famous French historian, in a moment of inspiration gave his impression of this wonderful spectacle in the following famous words : " At the moment of the death of King Francis I,

one hundred and fifty families fled to Geneva ;
soon there were fourteen hundred families, consisting of at least five thousand souls. This French
élite founded with an Italian élite the real Geneva,
that wonderful place of refuge, situated among
three peoples and existing only through its moral
power. Over against the immense and terrible trap,
into which Europe fell by the desertion of France,
nothing less than this heroic training-school was
necessary. Now the struggle begins. Loyola is un-
dermining the ground ; above the ground, Spanish gold
allures and the sword of the Guises murders. And
in this narrow, closely surrounded corner, this garden
of God, the bloody roses in honour of the freedom
of the soul are budding under the hand of Calvin—
Reformer ! " Geneva was the spiritual centre of
Protestantism. And the spiritual centre of Geneva
was Calvin. He had become so through the astute-
ness of his learning, the resoluteness of his character
and his zeal for God, the flames of which were only
extinguished by the dark waters of the Jordan of
death. Most striking was the simplicity of his life ;
profound and sincere was his contempt of the world
and all its shining glitter ; a wonderful influence
had his strict puritan way of living had on the
life and character of people and nations. It entered into their brain, their soul, and their blood—
it strengthened humanity's nerve. From where did
the prostrate Huguenots get their valour which
still excites our profoundest admiration ? What

inspired the Dutch to attack the Spanish tyrant in his own waters ? Who taught the Scottish Covenanters to struggle and to die ? Calvinism has retained its force, as purifying leaven, for centuries ; it has influenced the lives of the noblest spirits in England, and are not the fathers of the powerful American Republic children of Calvinism ?

" Thou art condemned by God, Calvin ! " exclaimed his antagonists, " for thou sinkest into the grave without descendants ! "

" I have thousands of them," was Calvin's reply. Calvin was mistaken—there were millions of them. And now—after four centuries—his memory is being blessed in five parts of the world.

However, this excellent instrument in the hand of the Lord, was not a faultless instrument. We have already mentioned his temper ; he could be most vehement ; in his debate with the despicable Caroli, who accused him of heterodox opinions respecting the doctrine of the Holy Trinity, he flew into a passion, which alarmed his enemies and startled his friends. Calvin had two mortal enemies : they were Rome and his temper. But let us be fair and not forget that body and soul are closely connected. During the last twenty years of his life Calvin suffered a great deal from most painful diseases. He was seldom without pain, and during the intervals between the attacks of the gravel and stomach-ache he had to endure the fierce and often vicious attacks of his embittered enemies. This made him frequently lose his temper, it made his words harsh and his pen biting. However, in the Bible which he has expounded, was a description of Moses, who had to struggle against the same sinful irritability, and by the grace of God became a leader of the people, surpassing all in gentleness. Calvin stared at this picture, and in spite of many stumblings he obtained much self-control which took root in his Christian humility.

A Spanish nobleman was once greatly astonished at the house of Admiral de Ruyter, and the same sensation was once experienced by Cardinal Sadolet, when he knocked at the door of John Calvin. With unfeigned astonishment he looked at its windows and its front, at the small, humble dwelling, and his astonishment knew no bounds when a simple man, dressed in black, opened the door. This man was the great Reformer himself. We know what this house contained : furniture lent to Calvin by the town. The inventory had been written in duplicate, one signed by Calvin, the other by the secretary of the town, mentioning the following pieces of furniture : two walnut bedsteads, another bedstead of carved maple, a walnut square table, a maple bench for same, a walnut sideboard, two walnut trunks, a walnut carved cathedra, a desk, four long tables of pine-wood, two walnut tables, a dozen wooden chairs. Besides, Calvin possessed some pieces of furniture bought by himself. In his study there was a table and a bench for same, another bench for visitors, and a big bookcase and steps—that was all ! Not a chair, not even a sofa. And in this simple bare workroom were forged the swords of real Damascene steel, which inflicted such deep, bloody wounds. The front of the house was to the north, from where the cold winds blow, the back to the south, towards the warm rays of the sun. There was the garden, Calvin used to walk in it with his friends : Farel, Viret, his brother Anthony, and his Geneva friends ; from this garden Idelette, no doubt, got her vegetables. The windows still command the same view as they did four centuries ago. On the left rise the Jura Mountains, with their lofty summit ; on the right the majestic Alps ; in the middle lies the blue lake glistening in the sunlight. Calvin must often have enjoyed this magnificent prospect, for, although the Alpine Club was unknown then, Calvin had an eye for the beauties of nature. He admired nature, he enjoyed it ; and he who described the stars in his sermons in such enthusiastic, eloquent words, must have observed them glittering in the sky over Geneva at night. He delivered his sermons, his lectures, even some of his essays without MS. In those days there were but two sources which he could consult : the Bible and the Fathers. The Bible Calvin studied incessantly and persistently ; the Fathers he studied in the night, when time did not permit him to do so by day. Among the sixteen hundred million people living on earth, there are probably not a hundred who by practice have obtained such an excellent memory as Calvin possessed. It has been called incomparable ; it struck people at a meeting in Lausanne, where he quoted long passages from the Fathers— by heart—as accurately as a phonograph. In that wonderful brain, ideas were piled up as in a big, well-provided warehouse ; they formed a well-rounded, complete system ; while Calvin had all the treasures of his knowledge at his disposal to enlighten the congregation and to resist the enemy. He looked after the religion and morals of his fellow-citizens without neglecting their hygienic and social interests. In this town dissoluteness had been associated with dirt and neglect, but with the strictness of the Calvinistic ideas the hospitals and the schools were improved. Calvin liked fresh air ; he had the windows opened, as vitiated air would cause infection, and while he prayed in the pulpit for the aversion of the plague, of the black death, he said at the same time that man is not an inanimate object, but that he has got a mind in order to use the means conducive to his health. Geneva owed its good hygienic rules in the sixteenth century to nobody else but Calvin. His many-sided genius seemed to have a knowledge of everything. He gave Robert Etienne valuable hints about the art of printing, and Etienne owed the greater part of his reputation as a printer to this advice. If an inventor applied to the Council, Calvin was called and had to inspect the new invention, the new branch of industry, the complicated instrument—if he lived in Germany now, the Emperor William would probably have asked his opinion on Zeppelin's airship. Neither surgeon nor dentist could get a licence for carrying on their useful occupations, till he had been subjected to the penetrating looks of Calvin. If he nodded assent and said, " It is right ! " it was right, nobody doubted it.

Sully, the powerful minister of King Henry IV, was highly praised for what he did in the interest of French industry. This praise he deserved, yet Sully had a predecessor long before in Calvin, who made the industry of Geneva, which had become dull, flourish again, and provided the town with new sources of welfare by his advice to erect cloth- and velvet-weaving mills. In this way he benefited the town, where he had come as a stranger. However, he never forgot the country to which Noyon belonged. He loved France, he wrote a great many of his works in the French language, and while he dedicated his principal work to the King of France, his heart was turned to his beloved French people. The national aspirations had not a greater influence, because his look ranged over all Europe. And from the lofty Nebo, which he had climbed, the national boundaries had to fade and the national colours to pale, for the grand task of winning the world for the Reformation.

John Huss ! Martin Luther ! John Calvin ! Huss appeals to the Slavonian race, Luther to the Germanic race, Calvin raises all barriers to appeal to the world. Huss has been called the awakening genius of the Reformation, Luther sings its triumph in songs, which make the German mountains re-echo ; Calvin is the unwearying worker, completing the task of both by embodying the Reformation in a system, which commands the admiration of Christianity to this very day by clearness of ideas, acuteness of expression, and inexorable, never-shrinking consistency. He agrees with Huss in the doctrine of predestination, with Luther in the doctrine of vindication, but he does not stop here, he resolutely continues his remarkable expedition along abysses, in the company of angels and devils, and when he has reached the utmost extremity of human thought, he clasps his hands to exclaim in adoration : " Oh, the depth of the riches both of the wisdom and knowledge of God ! How unsearchable are His judgments, and His ways past finding out ! "

CHAPTER XXVIII

DAYS OF JOY AND SORROW

CALVIN'S name had obtained European fame, and his works, bearing a universal international stamp, had found their way to the confines of European Christianity. He dedicated several writings to princes and kings with the purpose of making them strong supporters of the Reformation. He had cast his eye on Gustavus Vasa, the cautious and valorous King of Sweden, on King Christian of Denmark, and on King Radziwill of Poland.

In a moment of inspired self-consciousness Calvin wrote to the Polish King :—

"I who am the messenger of the King of Kings and His herald, have to proclaim His Gospel—I summon you in the name of this King to promote the extension of the Kingdom of God before all things. All, the great and the small, the high and the low, must be roused from their dangerous slumber. It is especially the duty of kings and princes to support this good work with all their power.

"God has granted them their high rank only that they may enlighten and improve others by their faith and example !"

Four such letters he wrote in one day, which proves what an extensive correspondence he had with princes ! However, while his looks were cast on Poland, he heard the cheers in the streets of Paris welcoming Henry II and his consort, the sly Catherine of Medici, and these cries were blended with the shrill cry of anguish of the suffering Evangelicals. This period was momentous on account of the heat of persecution, but no less momentous on account of the victories of the faith. A blood-witness from Geneva, who ended his life in the flames, showed such constancy, that the hands which had to do the executioner's work began to tremble. The executioner himself confessed the faith, for which he had tied the martyr to the strangling-pole, and he went to Geneva to be strengthened in his belief by Calvin. Anthony Laborie, thrown into the damp dungeon, complained of not being allowed to suffer more for his Lord. He left a wife and children behind, consoling them with most touching letters. He gloried in being oppressed, and deploring his weakness and worldliness, he conquered the world. When he had set foot on the scaffold, he thanked the executioner that he had come to deliver him from the close cell of his body. Many of the spectators shed tears, and in religious enthusiasm, while the flames were rising, he exclaimed : " I see Heaven open ! " He said these words with such force and such conviction, that the crowd involuntarily looked up and stared at the clouds.

And Heaven received the soul of this Stephen of the Reformation. The harder the wolves pressed, the closer the sheep of Christ kept together, and in spite of the unheard-of persecutions, small congregations were formed. One dark night, the servants of the Inquisition discovered a small light in a remote part of one of the streets in Paris. They heard besides the soft tones of a solemn psalm—it was the Hymn of Simeon. Then there was silence— there was praying. The priests had little difficulty in instigating the people, for the people were already restless, turbulent, and excited by the defeat of St. Quentin, the Northern Pavia, where Coligny's valour had not been a match for the better discipline of the Spanish-Dutch Army, under Lamoraal van Egmond. In a moment the people were ready to take vengeance on the Protestants for the national calamity. It was a little past midnight. And twenty-one Reformers were condemned to the stake. Among them was a young woman. She dressed all in white and went to the scaffold, as if she were going to a wedding-party. None of them hesitated ; youths went to the stake with the submission of greybeards, for whom the world has no charm, and the greybeards with the fire of youths, who see the glory of the future.

Calvin, Farel, Beza did everything that was in their power to come to the aid of their distressed brothers in the faith. " Thirty of our brethren," thus Calvin complained to a German prince, " are still pining in a horrible dungeon at this moment. The Waldenses are persecuted anew. One of their preachers is undergoing a terrible imprisonment. In Dauphiné especially, people are raging at everybody who is a Protestant. Cardinals themselves undertake to lead the investigations of the Inquisition which has been established. The King of France tries to deceive the German princes by making them believe that he only wishes to disturb the Sacramentarians in his realm, but I swear before God and the angels that not to believe in the Mass is a sufficient reason to be persecuted to death in France." However, the palm tree was growing in spite of oppression. Though in the reign of King Francis I and King Henry II more than fifty thousand Huguenots are said to have lost their lives, and the Inquisition, working in the Spanish way, made most strict investigations, Protestantism was spreading steadily.

Amidst the hostile fire the organisation of the Churches was being effected, and under the influence of Calvin, who always had the unity of the Church in view, the first national Synod was held in Paris. The Synod made a very poor impression ; it lacked all outward splendour. And how badly attended it was !—the meeting consisted only of the representatives of eleven Churches, including the community of Paris, by which they had been summoned. Yet it was an impressive gathering. They were heroes who had gathered here. They risked their lives, for they might be caught by the hirelings of Rome every moment and be led to the scaffold. Yet they did not hesitate for a second, and angels must have guarded the doors of this Synod, which laid the foundation of an organisation, for which the materials had been collected during a whole generation. The Reformed Church of France increased rapidly, now that the communities had been united into one body. Every day the army increased, which had woven the crucified Christ on its banner, and ere long there were two thousand communities, the members of which consisted of water-carriers and wood-cutters, as well as the highest aristocracy of France. The Prince of Condé, Admiral Coligny, and the King of Navarre belonged to them. And with what spirit these nobles were animated may be heard from Jeanne d'Albret, who exclaimed with never-shrinking resoluteness : " I would rather cast my dearly-beloved son together with my crown into the sea where it is deepest, than go once to the Mass ! " Jeanne d'Albret was Queen of Navarre. And her son afterwards became Henry IV, called the Great. Coligny was Admiral of France and Lord of Chatillon. Calvin's first letter reached him during his imprisonment in the Netherlands ; it was an admonition to bless the solitude into which the hand of the Lord had led him and to listen attentively to His voice. The next year Coligny was liberated from the Spanish prison. Well might he gratefully look back to the gloomy dungeon, brightened by the light of the Gospel ; as one new-born he returned to France to prepare, in quiet retirement at his country-seat, for the high distinction of falling as the noblest victim to the terrible Bartholomew's night. Calvin strengthened his faith, roused his zeal. Calvin had become the spiritual adviser of all Protestant France.

However, the day broke when the Reformer had to put down his pen and, like the common burghers, take up arms, for the storm which was then raging in Protestant France, next turned to Geneva. Without doubt, Geneva was the hotbed of heresy ; if it could be extirpated this would be the end of vindication through faith. Then the connection between faith and liberty became evident. While France was gathering its forces to plant the papal flag on Protestant Rome, the town was put into feverish haste to build and fortify its bulwarks. While printing-machines groaned and laboured to print the writings, which Calvin had published as a defence and attack, this remarkable man was already busy surrounding the Gospel with bulwarks. He worked himself in the entrenchments—the author of the *Institution* had become a warrior. The words burgher and Protestant began to be synonymous at Lake Leman ; the Geneva citizen was under military and spiritual regulations ; in the camps strict notice was taken, whether the arms were sharp and the doctrines pure. The storm

passed ; only in the distance the flags of France
had been waving, and more closely than ever
Calvin kept his eye on the Church under the Cross
in France, as he called the Protestant communities
there.

During the times of anxiety which he went
through, there were some bright moments in which
he beheld the blue sunny sky, and in those moments
he glowed with enthusiasm, so rare in his life.   Indeed, it is remarkable what he wrote then—it is the
triumphal shout of the general, feeling the approach
of victory.

" It can hardly be believed," he wrote, " with
how much zeal our friends devote themselves to
the propagation of the Gospel ! As desirous as they
are to ask benefits of the Pope, as eager are they
to request that they may be allowed to serve the
Churches under the Cross. They besiege my door
in order to get a part of the field to cultivate—never
had King more zealous servants than mine are. They
contend with each other for the posts, as if the
Kingdom of Jesus Christ were already firmly
established in France. I try to keep them back
sometimes. I show them the detestable edict, com-
manding the destruction of every house where our
divine services are held. I remind them of the fact,
that in more than twenty towns the relievers have
been killed by the people, but nothing can arrest
them in their course."   Calvin felt happy, when
he realised that he was considered as spiritual leader

by these heroic martyrs ; he was proud of it—not for himself, but for the sacred cause which he defended.

However, a cup of bitterness was put to his lips, and Farel wrote : " So it pleases the Lord to try this His servant, our beloved brother Calvin, that he may not pride himself on the greatness of His revelations."

How was it possible ? While the Reformer had cleansed the Augean stable in Geneva with an iron broom, had improved the morals and prevented licentiousness, his own dwelling had become a house of adultery. Shame covered his face, when the matter became known, and secret enemies whispered : " There is the brother-in-law of an adulteress ! " A violent rage and a more violent grief tore his heart asunder. All Geneva was astounded ; the community mourned, as if the ark had fallen into the hands of the Philistines, and people wondered sorrowfully how in the world it was possible that Calvin had been deceived with his eyes open. How things happen ! Calvin had no suspicion ; he trusted his servant, who had robbed his master for at least two years without the latter's noticing it in the least, and at last the scoundrel committed adultery with his master's sister-in-law. What a sombre spectacle it was when Calvin, with his brother Anthony, had to repair to the Church Council. Anthony stated at this gathering, in a faltering voice, that his wife, Anne le Fert, who had been let off seven years before through lack of evidence, had been caught in the act of committing adultery with his brother's servant. The case progressed slowly. The adulteress persistently denied her guilt, and Calvin seemed broken down by the shame which had been brought on his family. "This domestic sorrow almost overwhelms me," he sighed ; "the judges find no reason to set my brother free, and I see in this blindness a righteous punishment for our blindness, for during two whole years I was plundered by the thief and did not see anything !" At last the judges pronounced the divorce, and Anne le Fert was banished from the town for ever, covered with shame. Five years later a new shame tore Calvin's heart asunder. First his sister-in-law—then his stepdaughter, the child whose mother had been Idelette van Bure. This cut him to the quick, for the memory of his dearly-beloved wife was sacred to him. Judith was her name. It was again the same disgusting story—adultery ! And this woman had been praised so highly by Farel at her marriage ! "A model of a chaste virgin ; an example of piety rich in Christian virtues "—thus Farel had denominated her, and behold ! her marriage ended in adultery. . . .

This time Calvin did not remain in the town ; the scorn and shame were too great ; he fled to the country, that he might not be seen by anyone.

Hark ! the knells are tolling ! Man is going to

his last home. " Seventy years," says the Psalmist,
" or, if we are very strong, eighty years." Then all
is over. Then the dream is dreamt, beginning with
a cry and ending with a sob. The famous Melanchthon experienced this. Alive and well and dead
within a week ! The accurate chronicler made the
following note : " Magister Philippus Melanchthon
reached 63 years and 63 days, and died."

On the Thursday before Easter Melanchthon had
already heard the gentle knock of the messenger of
death. Though unwell he had gone to church, in
order to attend the Lord's Supper with the community. The day after—on Good Friday—he had
even delivered a sermon on Isaiah LIII. He slept
calmly that night, and on awaking he felt as if he
had become young again, the sunny days of his
youth seemed to have come back, and it was as if
he were a boy in church listening to the words, " I
have greatly desired to eat this Passover with you
before I die." He was seen in the street on that
Saturday, going to the printer's—it was the last
time that the beloved Magister was seen in the
streets of Wittenberg. When he came home, Melanchthon felt exhausted, and on Easter Sunday the
churchgoers told each other with dejected faces,
that Magister Philippus Melanchthon was seriously
ill. This meant death ; Melanchthon was sure it
did. And while a secret yearning for home moved
the silver cords, he said to a friend on Easter Monday : " I long for my deliverance and to be with

Christ." In his study a bed had been placed ; there he lay down, and this was to be his death-bed. All the professors were present. They surrounded the couch with sad and gloomy thoughts. And among these professors Melanchthon's dying eye discerned a girl weeping. " I have loved you very much, dear niece ! " he said. " Be always obedient to your parents and the joy of their lives as much as you can ! Trust God—He will not forsake you. I will pray Him to protect and bless you ! " All knelt down near the bed ; a crowd of people had assembled outside, waiting in fearful suspense ; all Wittenberg was moved. A passage of the Holy Scriptures was read to the dying man, who repeated these words in a whisper : " That they all may be one, as Thou Father art in me and I in Thee ! " " Do you desire anything else ? " he was asked. And he answered with the yearning eagerness of a stranger, who sees his native mountains gleaming on the horizon : " I only desire to go to Heaven." The sun set, the day declined ; it was over, and there was great distress in Wittenberg. Calvin felt grievously deserted when the sad tidings reached him.

" Oh, Philip Melanchthon," he exclaimed, " thou who now livest with God and our Lord Jesus Christ —thou shalt await me there until death shall have united us in the blessed enjoyment of eternal peace ! "

Melanchthon dead ! his sister-in-law an adulteress ! he himself ravaged by increasing bodily suffering, verily Calvin experienced that this world is a vale of tears for God's children !

Surprise is felt on hearing that Calvin suffered from malarial fever in mountainous Geneva ; but we must add that Geneva of the sixteenth century, from a hygienic point of view, could hardly be put on a level with Geneva of the twentieth century.

It was surrounded by marshy moats which polluted the air, and in this respect it was no exception to the other towns and districts, which, until the seventeenth century, were hotbeds of infection just as low tropical countries are now.

Calvin had, besides, a tendency to rheumatism ; he was gouty and his lungs were not sound. He was consumptive ; but his consumption confined itself to violent vomitings of blood or oppressive bronchitis, while he probably died of gravel.

This rheumatic tendency was the source of many complaints which made his life one long succession of sufferings ; but to give truth its due, we must add, that this man, who inspected hospitals to ensure good medical treatment and who gave Geneva those excellent hygienic prescriptions, on the other hand did everything to foster his own tendency to disease. Forcibly and impressively he held forth on the sixth Commandment, but in complaining of his inborn slothfulness and sluggishness he was in danger of being his own murderer through excessive work. And this exhausting labour, combined with a sedentary life and endless cares for his reformatory task, sapped his vitality.

A physician of our time would have closed his books before his very eyes, would have taken him by the arm and said : " Come, Professor ! To the mountains ! To the Alps ! Everything else will come right ! "

But at that time they also knew that rest and mountain air were good for one ; Calvin knew this too, and yet he took no rest.

His cares were too many ; his zeal too great ; and in the fire of this zeal the fragile thread of his life was consumed.

Had this zeal been less—he would have suffered less and lived longer. But, on the other hand, he would not have produced the excellent work for which his followers venerate and love him, and the son of the cooper of Noyon would never have become the most prolific of Reformers.

CHAPTER XXIX

A TORCH OF SCIENCE

CALVIN, the man of Predestination, saw in every-thing, unity, firmness, regularity, and order ; in the fixed and unshakable decree of the Supreme Being he perceived the foundation of the laws of Nature as well as of the spiritual and moral laws ; and it was this conviction which was such a powerful motive and incitement to tread the broad field of science with a firm step.

He was not the man to avoid but to rejoice in that which God has given to the world, and instead of neglecting the temporal he wanted to make it subservient to the glory of God and the salvation of mankind.

The Roman Catholic Cardinal Borromeo had once during a destructive plague epidemic ministered to the sick and consoled the dying with the heroic courage of a Christian ; but Calvin, who also was prepared to risk his life, did more by adopting excellent hygienic measures.

So the man of Predestination was at the same time the man of science, and from 1541 he always rose and went to bed with this thought uppermost in his mind : " How can we give Geneva a University ? "

The unrest of the times prevented the realisation of this great plan, but in 1558 a favourable wind swelled the sails. Calvin had opened a national subscription, which realised the, at that time considerable, amount of ten thousand guilders, while some excellent teachers, in every way fit for the work at a university, had repaired to Geneva, driven to this by a dispute with the hard-handed Government of Bern. So the general conviction gained ground that God was smoothing the way for the founding of a University, and the Council no longer hesitated to put their hand to the plough.

For this purpose Calvin had already selected a large garden planted with vines and which was the property of the town. On March 25th, 1558, a committee of experts, conducted by Calvin, surveyed the site ; three days afterwards they already brought out an extensive report.

It was a favourable report. The healthy site was commended ; the building would offer an unrestricted view of the lake, while at the north side sufficient space would be left for a promenade.

The Council approved and they immediately set to work.

Calvin was full of enthusiasm ; he forgot the fever which heated his blood, and seemed ten years younger. He was frequently seen on the building-ground inciting the masons and carpenters to speed ;

it was extremely irksome to a man of his activity when the builders had no bricks to build a wall, or were short of roof-tiles ; but in spite of adversity it was possible to open the college, which was to form the nucleus of this famous University, on July 5th, 1559.

Geneva was that day in festive guise ; all work was suspended ; the church-bells rang out merrily in the warm summer air, and a select company streamed to the large and spacious Church of St. Peter.

The Government came strongly to the fore on this day on purpose, for there was a political side to this ceremony. Formerly a University had been offered Geneva on condition that they accepted the Duke of Savoy as their protector. That they had thought too high a price—so they refused. And now—two centuries after—Geneva, as a sovereign power, founded this University, independent of Savoy, as a lasting monument of her independence.

Roman Catholic Europe was dumbfounded at this audacious act. No one could understand this. In the sixteenth century a Pope, an Emperor, or a King was required to found a University, and this small insignificant town said : " I will do this alone, with God's aid."

And behold, it was done ! Everyone whose heart was in the right place helped, and the poor five-pence offered by a simple Genevese baker's wife sounded through the centuries with a brighter

jingle than the gold-pieces which that sombre
heretic-hater, Philip II, spent on the founding of
the University of Douai—with the intention of
frustrating the Genevese attempt.

The University was small as yet, but it would
grow. Calvin had not asked for more than was
reasonable : five professors, of whom he was one.
The subjects of Greek, Hebrew, and philosophy had
one professor each assigned to them, while the
vacancies of medicine and law would later on be
filled.

The Government had issued a proclamation :

" It is by the great mercy and grace of God," so
it ran, " that it has been given to this town to
become at once the foster-mother of piety and
science. And we shall find cause to appreciate this
glorious blessing yet more highly when we remember
the time in which this plan ripened. We all remember the storms which for many years ravaged our
republic ; the conspiracies of criminal citizens, the
instigations from without, the efforts of Satan to
destroy this stronghold of piety, which day by day
threatens and diminishes his rule. Owing to this,
the execution of our plan was long thwarted, but
at length perseverance and trust in God won the
day. There will doubtless yet be many who censure
this undertaking as too rash, but whosoever pays
attention to the guidance of God and is accustomed
to direct his affairs, not according to human wisdom,
but according to his trust in His immeasurable

power, will judge otherwise, and impressed by the grandeur and the blessing of this work will hope for the best."

Every citizen who read this proclamation understood whose perseverance and trust in God were especially meant, and more than ever, every eye, dim with tears, was turned on this man of God, who, with a pale emaciated face, but with a quiet enthusiasm in his soul, sat there among the councillors.

Amid profound silence the Reformer rose. In a short speech he communicated to them the resolution of the Council to found a University within the walls of Geneva, and then in a fervent prayer invoked the blessing of the Supreme Being on this new institution. He stood on Mount Nebo ; in his mind's eye he saw the lustre which this torch of science would spread throughout Europe.

Then the Town Secretary came forward to read the confession of faith and the statutes, which were to be binding on teachers and students alike, while Beza, who had been appointed rector, conjured them in a touching speech to remain faithful to their vocation.

The University was the fruit of prayer, and like dew and sunshine that prayer rested on it.

The success of the new institution was almost unequalled from the very beginning. No less than nine hundred young men from all parts of Europe were enrolled as students during the first year ; an almost equal number, mostly French and English refugees, were formed into evangelists and teachers by attending Calvin's theological lectures.

And the Reformation in the Netherlands would scarcely have prospered so well, had not this stream been fed at the limpid source which bubbled up to the surface on the shore of Lake Leman. But Calvin was not easily satisfied. He was for ever on the look-out for defects and shortcomings, and he was ceaselessly engaged in trying to obtain the best teachers for his University.

He tried to make them understand that the small salary paid at Geneva was more than compensated for by the honour of the post ; he assured them that the flower of Italy were eager to obtain a chair, and that the students of Geneva marched victoriously throughout the length and breadth of France, spreading the Gospel as they went—like a merchant praising his wares, so did Calvin praise the University to obtain the most excellent teachers.

What an enormous flight did this institution of Calvin's take ! From its foundation until the latter half of the eighteenth century it was the great University for the literary and theological education of Protestant Europe.

" Send the wood to us," so they said at Geneva, " and we will send you the arrows cut from it in exchange ! " And this was done. Such an arrow was Louis of Nassau, brother to the great William the Silent ; Marnix van St. Aldegonde, the poet of the immortal " Wilhelmus hymn," was another arrow; Francis Junius, preacher under the cross, afterwards the famous professor at the newly-founded University of Leyden, was a third arrow.

The town itself plucked the richest fruit from its institution. Next to the Church, nothing contributed so much to bring about that wonderful change from an unknown and insignificant town into a world-famous school of new creative thought. The Genevese people themselves were seized by a passion for knowledge. Everyone was anxious to be taught; it became a general competition; and thus was born a cultured and literary Geneva.

There was now an extensive choice of candidates for the Council; henceforth they were drawn from every class; and in the midst of those anxious times which the republic had to pass through, a strong and self-conscious nation was formed. Owing to the extension of education, the town was spared the poverty of the proletariat, and the only aristocracy known was the aristocracy of piety and culture, of morality, talent, and patriotism.

The citizens mutually trusted each other, they formed a living wall to protect the fortress against the attacks of the enemy, and in the hour of danger they showed what a small republic, by trusting in God and keeping its gunpowder dry, is capable of.

It was the Gospel that had leavened the mass, and which in Calvin's hands had wrought a wonder such as is scarcely to be equalled in Christendom.

Geneva had been morally regenerated. It was

necessary, for how else could it have become the light-giving torch, the training-school and refuge of the nations ?

The town had denied itself, destroyed itself, all places of amusement were demolished, its dancing-rooms were closed, and it became the school of heroes and martyrs, of the chosen among the elect, who passed through the flaming gates of the stake to reach the life eternal.

And at this sight, which became a spectacle for angels and devils, a cry of joy escaped from the breast of the stern law-giver of Geneva : " The old has passed away, behold everything has become like new ! "

The famous college where Calvin lectured has changed but little in the course of centuries. A humble porch formed of massive columns gives admission to the building. The granite of the pillars is weather-beaten ; no wonder ! they have stood there so long.

And in the arched roof of this porch there are three inscriptions which indicate the character of the instruction given there. The first inscription, in Hebrew, runs as follows : " The fear of the Lord is the beginning of wisdom " ; the second is in Greek : " Christ has become to us the wisdom of God " ; while the third is in Latin and repeats the saying of the apostle James : " The wisdom which comes from above is pure, peaceful, and full of mercy."

When a stranger asks to be conducted to the house of Calvin, a certain writer says : " Then do not take him to the house in Cannon Street, but to the tiny college which Calvin founded and the threshold of which he crossed so often. Show the stranger the arms of Geneva ; show him those three inscriptions which testify to the Latin, Hebrew, and Greek, which is taught there and say to him : ' Those arms, those texts, this old building, this monument of our history which years have not changed : this is the house of Calvin.' "

CHAPTER XXX

IN GREAT OPPRESSION

WHILE Geneva was nearing the harbour, the ship of French Protestantism drifted on the high seas with torn sails. The antithesis of the Reformation held France breathless, and the dates 1559 and 1560 are written with blood in the annals of the Huguenots.

They were traced to their most secret conferences; they were treacherously surprised; like sheep they were led to the slaughter.

A word of disapproval about the celebration of Mass might cost a life; the reading of the Scriptures, the singing of a psalm was punished by death.

To a former Augustine monk a free pardon was offered if he would agree to call the woman to whom he was married a concubine. He willingly went to the stake to maintain his wife's honour; he died for the sake of her reputation, and thus he fulfilled the law of Christ.

It is pathetic and touching in the extreme to hear how delighted those martyrs were, when on the last day of their life they were permitted to indite a letter to Calvin. They did not wish to leave this world without expressing their earnest thanks to this man for his Gospel words, the embracing of which sent them to their death, and it is impossible to read those epistles without shedding tears.

What must have been Calvin's feelings on receiving those last avowals of friendship ? Through him they had become martyrs ; he was so truly one with them that the flames of their stakes scorched his throat and their wounds rent his heart.

But he was not allowed to reveal his feelings, for he was the general who had to forget himself, in order to win this great and furious battle. Again and again the agonies of his fellow-believers fell on his heart like blows, but he fought against his anguish like a hero and repressed his sorrow, to secure new victories to the realm of Christ.

The stakes and strangling-poles were at the height of their glory ; the suffering was terrible, while the streets resounded with the anguished cries of parents, who were dragged out of their houses by a mad mob and sacrificed to the fury of the populace. Their children, left orphans, wandered weeping through the streets, poor, neglected, and hungry. They were accursed because their parents were accursed, and human pity turned away from them because capital punishment was the price paid for assisting heretics or their relatives.

The Parisian dungeons in which the Protestants were confined were dark, damp holes ; in one of those holes the air was so foul that a candle could

not be kept burning there. The poet Marot had
become acquainted with those prisons and he compared them to hell. The worst of those dungeons
was a deep cellar, which received neither light nor
air from outside ; it was impossible to stand erect
there or to sleep, while the back part was full of
water. This cellar had no stairs and was reached
by means of a trap-door ; the prisoner was lowered
into those black depths attached to a rope which
passed over a pulley. At the end of a fortnight the
wretched prisoner was either dead or mad. . . .

King Henry II, that bloody persecutor, who,
acting on the advice of a cardinal and a concubine,
had resolved to extirpate Protestantism from his
dominions, root and branch, one day expressed
a desire to meet one of those heretics, just for the
fun of the thing. The cardinal gratified this whim
and sent for a tailor who was known to be rather
foolish. But through this simple son of the people
was fulfilled the saying : " Thou shalt be dragged
before kings and governors for the sake of My name ;
and this shall happen to you as a testimony. Re-
solve then in thy heart not to think beforehand of
what thou shalt reply, for I will give thee speech and
wisdom."

The King's shameless mistress was present. She
wished to find out all about this, but she found this
tailor to be more than a match for her.

" Be satisfied that you have polluted France,
madam ! " he said, with inexorable sternness ;

" but do not attempt to mix your poison and filth with such a holy and hallowed thing as the true religion and the truth of our Lord Jesus Christ."

The King rose from his seat, furious ; he ordered the trial of the tailor to be hastened, assuring him at the same time that he himself would be present at his execution. And the King kept his promise. The King was seen standing before the window of a large mansion, his face turned to the stake on which the martyr was to be burnt.

The crowd saw the King ; even the martyr saw him. And the look of that man amid the flames was so awe-inspiring, that the King turned his face away and swore never again to be present at a scene like this, as the pleasure of seeing heretics being burnt was too dearly bought in that way.

Calvin heard of this. Then this Elijah's prayer escaped in holy wrath from his lips : " May the Lord in His omnipotence punish such horrible cruelty. Amen ! "

And this prayer was heard.

The persecutions continued. There was no justice left in France ; the last flood-gates that might have turned this tide of human blood were opened when the high tribunal met.

All the judges were present, and the deliberations had been going on for about two hours when the King entered, his face sombre, with a silent gesture.

Anne du Bourg, the brilliant lawyer, was speaking, in a tone of burning indignation ; he denied the right to persecute. He was risking his head—that he knew full well, but without an instant's hesitation he went on.

Then the King rose. His eyes flashed ominously.

He whispered to Montgomery, the officer on guard, to at once place du Bourg behind the horrible gratings of the Bastille. And while seated at dinner he ordered six others to be taken into custody.

It was thus this terrible King understood the free administration of justice.

Du Bourg's imprisonment took place amid those brilliant festivities which Paris at that time witnessed, and the groaning of the victims was lost in the shouts of rejoicing with which the streets rang.

It was certainly worth while. Two royal marriages were impending ; the Duke of Saxony was to espouse the King's sister, and Philip II of Spain the King's daughter. In honour of these royal couples a princely tournament was held in the neighbourhood of the gloomy Bastille, where Du Bourg chanted his mournful psalm.

At this tournament the French Court shone in all its lustre ; the King, in a brilliant many-coloured coat of mail, was the hero of it all.

The flower of the French nobility was present : Duke Alva, with his merciless face, was seen, and Alphonse, the eldest son of the Duchess Renata, had come to Ferrara for this occasion.

Du Bourg heard the shouts of joy ; the air was filled with the gay sound of trumpets, and the cries of "Long live the King" were heard above it all.

But all at once the shouts of joy were silenced ; cries of horror reached the ears of the prisoner ; then all was silent, silent as death.

What had happened ?

The King had held sham-fights with three of his knights, when he hit on the idea of inviting Montgomery to a fourth. And with his own hands he handed him the weapon which was to cost him his life. A thrust of the lance pierced his right eye ; the wound grew worse, and this same King who, forgetting a former oath, had sworn that his eyes would delight in the sight of Du Bourg's flaming stakes, was to appear before the judgment-seat of the Supreme Being before his victim had drawn his last breath, while the officer who had laid hands on Du Bourg had been destined to become the instrument of this horrible end.

And in the fatal issue of this brilliant tournament many Protestants saw the finger of God.

And it was whispered from mouth to mouth that the royal corpse had been placed in front of hangings, into which these significant words were woven : " Saul, Saul, why dost thou persecute me ? "

The King was dead. And the light-hearted Parisians shouted : " Long live the King ! "

Thus did Francis II, the son of Henry II, ascend the throne. He was a mere boy ; fifteen years of age ; weak in body and mind, entirely unfit to take

in hand the reins of government, on which the
Guise faction and Catherine de Medici cast covetous
eyes. The mother of the young prince was forty
years of age. She was distinguished by learning and
ingenuity ; faithful to the traditions of her race, she
encouraged the attempts of artists and scholars,
which however did not prevent her from satisfying
her ambition by means of shameless intrigues. She
was extremely cunning ; a human life counted for
little in her eyes, as St. Bartholomew's night proved.
But she knew how to control her hatred when necessary for the furtherance of her political interests,
and assumed the mark of friendship to mislead her
enemies.

She coveted the crown, but being a foreigner there
were many obstacles in her path ; and while sharing
the government with Duke Francis of Guise and the
Cardinal of Lorraine, she hoped for a time when the
monarchy would be hers.

But there were still others, who, by reason of their
descent, might claim the crown ; the three brothers
Bourbon, the eldest of whom became King of
Navarre through his marriage with Johanna d'Albret. He had embraced the Reformed faith, but
not with all his heart. Irresolute and wavering,
he was ruled by his favourites. More than one sharp
arrow was directed at his heart by Calvin, without
curing him of his half-heartedness, and this King,
of whom the Protestants expected so much, turned
his back on them at the critical moment.

The second brother bore the title of General, and had not brains sufficient for a corporal, while the youngest brother, Prince Louis of Condé, was a man of undeniable courage and bravery, a capable general, earnestly devoted to the Huguenot cause ; he was, however, inconstant, without perseverance, and no match for the cunning diplomacy of his enemies.

In the summer of 1560 King Henry II died ; December 23rd of the same year witnessed Du Bourg's death.

In the chapel at eleven o'clock in the morning of that day the sentence was read to him, in which he was condemned, as an obstinate and implacable sacramentarian heretic, to be hanged and hoisted on a gallows, to be placed in Grève Square in front of the town hall : a fit spot—beneath which a fire was to be lit, and the afore-mentioned Du Bourg to be thrown into it and burnt to ashes.

At three o'clock on this short day of December the hangman appeared, the prisoner was placed in a red cart, with a priest beside him. Then the gloomy vehicle moved forward, surrounded by four hundred foot-soldiers and two hundred horse-soldiers, all of them with swords drawn, to prevent the danger of a riot. For Anne du Bourg was a celebrated and beloved man, the nephew of a French Chancellor and a generally respected lawyer.

The streets were crowded, one could have walked on the heads ; and the cart which was conveying the martyr to the scaffold could scarcely proceed through the dense mass of people.

Du Bourg seemed absorbed in reflection ; his thoughts had already passed the threshold of eternity ; his lips were moving, he was singing psalms in a low voice. And Calvin relates that his face was illuminated with joy when the scaffold was reached.

Arrived at the place of execution, he took off his mantle and coat—with the tranquillity of a tired child that undresses before going to sleep—safe in its mother's care.

The hangman put the rope round his neck, on which Du Bourg, looking at him in surprise, exclaimed : " Is not that unnecessary, since I am to be slowly burnt ? " The hangman replied, that in consideration of his high station in life the sentence contained a secret clause, according to which he was to be strangled first and then burnt, to diminish his suffering.

Then Du Bourg cast a last look at that Babel which shed the blood of God's beloved children like water, knelt down on the scaffold, and exclaimed : " Oh Lord, my God, do not desert me, that I may not desert Thee ! "

A few moments after his body swung high in the air, on the gallows, while the crowd, awestruck, exclaimed : " Jesus ! Maria ! " Then the executioners lit the fire and the body was cast into the flames to be burnt to ashes.

Calvin was full of anxiety ; the persecutions went on, and it was to be feared that the bow which was too tightly drawn would some day snap.

He walked to and fro full of care, surveying the French battle-field from his high watch-tower.

He foresaw the possibility of the Protestants forming a political party, and that not the cross, but a waving banner would become their symbol. That was the cause of his anxiety. The most effective victories which could elevate the Church of Christ in his eyes, were the victories gained on the scaffold and at the stake, while the triumphs gained in a bloody war only got a shrug of his shoulders. Have his predictions concerning France turned out false ?

And had the Reformation, like a spiritual Nile-stream, been allowed to fertilise the fields with its blood for another ten years, might not France have become an impregnable fortress of Protestantism ?

There was the " Amboise Conspiracy." That was the beginning ; there the fatal knot was tied which bound French Protestantism to politics.

The conspiracy was set on foot by a nobleman, La Renaudie, who organised a meeting at Nantes, to which he invited the most violent opponents of the Guises, both Protestants and Catholics, in order to put a stop to the growing power of the Guises, which threatened to become a danger to the State. In glowing language he described the critical state of their country ; he appealed to those present to assist him in breaking down the tyranny of these ambitious men ; by imprisoning them and having them sentenced at a sitting of the States General.

The meeting, at which the most embittered enemies of the Guises were present, agreed to this resolution on condition that nothing was to be undertaken against the King or the Government, while Renaudie told them that at the right moment Condé would place himself at the head of the movement.

The conspiracy was betrayed, the Court was removed to safe Amboise, and the Guises took a bloody revenge, while Condé, who swore to his innocence, was taken into custody.

Calvin alluded to this fatal conspiracy in a letter to Coligny. It was necessary, as it was rumoured that Calvin had given his full approbation to this conspiracy.

Where did people get such talk from ? Calvin was altogether opposed to it ; with the utmost decision he rejected the aid of carnal weapons, in a fight where God's Word is the sword of Gideon, with which great deeds are done. His feelings were diametrically opposed to the aspirations of those men, who, with gloomy eyes and compressed lips, awaited the signal to avenge the blood of the martyrs on the cruel Church of Rome. Calvin thought such a deed a crime, which the Church, under the Cross, would one day repent of.

But the reins slipped from Calvin's hands.

And at this unusual sight of rebellion and mutiny

in his own ranks, the Reformer uttered this mournful complaint : " Alas ! Alas ! I never thought to see the day when we should have lost all trust in those that call themselves the faithful; must then the Church of Geneva be thus scorned by her children ? "

The Church of Geneva—that was Calvin. He was the heart of that Church. And identifying himself with that Church, he was its interpreter in calling the use of carnal weapons an abuse.

For a moment we are surprised and confused by this new principle put forward by Calvin. But it is no new principle ; Calvin remains consistent ; and he draws a sharp line between possession and conquest. Let Christianity march forth to conquest ; all knees must bend to the name of Jesus Christ, the Lord of all. But in this march of conquest the weapons to be taken must not be guns or swords ; the only weapons must be faith, an inward resolution, good works, and the patience of the saints. It is a spiritual strife. And when souls have been won for the cause of the great King, then the Government should form a magistracy corresponding to this condition.

The Church under the Cross, that was Calvin's ideal of the suffering and struggling community of Christ in France. And amid the clash of arms he stood on his spiritual watch-tower, and undaunted he flung his powerful protestation against war into the face of the fighters.

He had no rest ; his two letters written to his

brothers in France in June and November, 1559, were full of touching earnestness. He did not address himself to one small community, but to all the Churches ; to the two thousand Protestant communities, to the Huguenots, who, sword in hand and singing their powerful martial hymns, were preparing to fill the world with their immortal fame.

Suffering—nothing but suffering—that was the task which Calvin commended. He assured them that the dark clouds would disperse and that God would send His light to make their hearts rejoice. He would console them better than a mother. He would take pity on his poor persecuted sheep and would pull out the fangs of the bloodthirsty wolves or change them into lambs. Thus spoke Calvin. But the persecutions were continued with undiminished violence, and the latent hope, that the death of Henry II would bring a change, had vanished into smoke.

" During the reign of Francis II," so Beza says, " the fury of Satan was unrestrained, so that we may say of his rule, which only lasted seventeen months, what Jesus says in the Gospel of St. Matthew that, had those days not been shortened, no one would have been spared ; but they were shortened for the sake of the elect."

New edicts for the destruction of the heretics were issued ; in every Parliament a special committee was charged with condemning everyone suspected of being an adherent of the Evangelical truth, to be

burnt to death. Paris and Toulouse, Dijon and
Bordeaux, Lyons, Poitiers, and many other towns
were zealously employed in extirpating all Protestant
heresies ; it was a general competition as to who
could set aflame the largest number of stakes. But
amid this rage, Coligny came forward from the solitude of his country-seat, and unconcerned for the
consequences, publicly placed a petition for freedom
of conscience and public worship at the foot of the
throne, on the opening of the meeting of notables.

Calvin's stern face lit up when he heard of this
courageous act, and, full of admiration and restrained enthusiasm, he wrote to the Admiral :
" We have every cause to praise God for the rare
courage which has been given you, to proclaim His
Glory and to further the extension of the realm of
Christ. Even if everyone were blind or ungrateful,
even if all your labour should seem lost—be satisfied, in the conviction that God and the angels
approve your deed ! "

Again a King died who had not been a King, the
child Francis II. Gloomy clouds of death seemed to
drift over the French throne. Two kings within two
years ! Henry II died in 1559 ; Francis II in 1560.

And the people again cried : " The King is dead—
long live the King ! "

It was Charles IX, then a boy of ten, who, twelve
years after, amused himself with firing on his defenceless Protestant subjects from the window of the royal
palace.

The royal mother soon dried her tears, and sharp-witted as she was, she gave Condé a post of honour instead of sending him to the scaffold.

She wished to win over the Bourbons by favours without estranging the Guises, and she gave the Chancellor l'Hôpital the command to convene the States General within the walls of Orléans. The relief thus afforded the Huguenots was great ; psalms of speedy delivery were sung ; it was whispered from mouth to mouth that l'Hôpital, this Roman Catholic statesman, had a heart and not a stone in his bosom.

Much more could be said of this excellent states-man.

He was a noble and upright man ; he had an open eye for the miseries of a country rent by fierce internal dissension ; at the opening of the States General he spoke words of peace and reconciliation.

He had discovered that Christianity preaches love, not bitter disputes, that it was high time to be led by gentleness, and abolishing the mutual nicknames, to retain only the honourable name of Christian.

So the programme faintly outlined by l'Hôpital aimed at the true salvation of his country ; but alas ! his oars were too short to row against the stream. The States General adjourned without having done anything, and the Bill, consisting of 150 clauses, drawn up by the Chancellor, to improve at any rate the most crying abuses in Church and State could not be carried, owing to the scornful opposition of the clergy, the officials, and part of the aristocracy. Yet there were unmistakable signs of the wind veering. The Queen-Regent and the whole Court were present at the sermon preached by the Bishop of Valence, who was known to be in favour of the new doctrine ; many noble families held Protestant services in their castles ; the Reformation even penetrated into the apartments of the Royal Palace.

Here and there a Roman Catholic Church was used for Protestant worship, and a flood of refugees, who returned from Geneva, repeated with French enthusiasm the strong fervent expressions of faith they had caught from Calvin's lips. The Chancellor kept up his courage. Now that the Reformation was taking such an enormous flight, he foresaw that a bloody civil war would be inevitable if the reconciliation were not on a sound basis. It was just these terrible dangers which would promote a reconciliation, and with the consent of the Queen-Regent he convened the famous meeting of Poissy, in order to bring about an arrangement between Catholicism and Protestantism.

On August 23rd, Beza arrived at Poissy. He had already been staying in France for several months ; the previous winter he had held one of his famous hedge-sermons outside the walls of Paris in a heavy shower of rain, attracting six thousand hearers, and two months afterwards, this number, during an

afternoon sermon, had risen to twenty-five thousand.

The Court looked forward to meeting this man
whose name was so famous in the Protestant world,
in a state of intense expectation, and Beza afterwards communicated his impressions to Calvin.

" When I had exchanged a few words with
Admiral Coligny," he relates, " I was greeted by
the King of Navarre and Condé with the utmost cor-
diality."

Beza was one of Calvin's most excellent pupils.
He had a gentle character ; kindliness was written
on his face ; Geneva, which would not give Calvin
leave, could not have sent a better substitute.

The 9th September was the auspicious day of the
opening of the conference. A throne had been
erected in the large hall of the convent, and on this
throne Charles IX, the child of twelve, seated himself.

On his left sat Catherine de Medici, on his right
his brother, the Duke of Orléans and the King of
Navarre, and behind him the highest nobility had
taken their seats. It was a most impressive gathering ; six-and-thirty bishops and archbishops, besides
a great number of graduates and clergymen of
various ranks, were present.

Silence was commanded, the noise ceased, and the
child sitting on the throne spoke a few words, learnt
by heart, which opened the meeting.

Then l'Hôpital rose to explain again the state

of affairs in an earnest speech ; he predicted the
fall of the State if party-disputes did not cease, and
proposed as a fair demand that the Protestants
should be heard in their own defence.

Duke Francis of Guise, the grim enemy of the
Reformation, then approached to usher in the
Protestant preachers.

There were eleven of them, as the twelfth, Peter
Martyr, had not arrived. And every preacher
brought two representatives elected by the communities, so that altogether the embassy consisted
of thirty-three members.

There was a general movement to see those
notorious heretics ; all eyes were turned to those
simple men, soberly attired in their black gowns,
who, with heads bared, walked towards the balus-
trade which separated them from the throne.

Beza was the foremost. It was whispered that
this man was Calvin's shield-bearer, and it had to be
acknowledged that he was worthy to bear the shield
of the David of Protestantism. In this historical
arena where the children of the Reformation had
to confess their faith, Beza moved as freely as if at
home in his study. Free and unrestrained in his
manners, well formed, with noble, regular features,
born from head to foot an aristocrat, in the full
vigour of his manly strength, this man could not
but create a deep impression.

It had become very quiet ; the fall of a pin might
have been heard ; and amid this solemn silence,

Beza said in a firm, respectful tone : " If we wish this meeting to be crowned with success, O King, we must, first of all, implore the blessing of God on it."

Then he knelt down without waiting for a reply ; all the Protestants knelt down with him.

It was an affecting moment ; the sheep of Christ, sheltering under the wings of their invisible Protector, in the midst of the wolves. . . .

Then the Protestants rose : " May the Lord," said Beza, " guide this meeting, to the glory of His Name, the confirmation of France's happiness, and the salvation of the whole of Christianity ! "

The glory of God's name, the happiness of France, and the salvation of Christianity—such was his programme.

He then held his famous speech. But when in the fire of his speech he used the expression : " Christ's body is as far removed from the sacred bread as heaven is from earth," the gathering burst into fierce cries of indignation.

" He blasphemes God," they cried. " Why should we stay here any longer ? "

It would have been more prudent of Beza not to have used this strong expression, for which he offered his excuses to the Queen-Regent the following day. It had been his intention to bring out the spiritual meaning of the bread and wine at the Holy Communion, and in his anxiety to be faithful to his convictions he had used an expression which might just as well have been omitted.

But Calvin thought differently. He was a man who liked exactness in all things, and he declared that God had guided Beza's mind and tongue when he uttered those offence-giving words. So the different opinions about the Holy Communion were to be the wedge which would irrevocably split Christendom asunder.

Or was it yet possible to bridge the gulf which yawned between Protestantism and Catholicism ? And could a formula be found to satisfy both sides ?

Among the Catholics there were many hearts which bled because of the schism, and they prayed to God for deliverance. And deliverance actually seemed at hand ; in a conference between two Roman Catholic priests and two Protestant ministers, of whom Beza was one, the happy formula was found which could be signed by all.

It ran as follows : " We believe that when partaking of the Communion, Christ truly imparts to us His body and His blood through the power of the Holy Ghost, and that in a spiritual sense we eat the body of Christ and drink His blood through our belief in that sacrament, in order that we may be flesh of His flesh and bone of His bone. In this sense we accept the presence of the blood and the body of Christ at the Holy Communion."

There was great rejoicing over this beginning of a reconciliation ; the Cardinal of Lorraine declared that such had always been his opinion concerning this point ; and Calvin, driven to his bed by a violent attack of rheumatism, felt his heart rejuvenated, while he wrote to Beza : " The Lord be praised ! He will exalt us, even to the clouds, that we may embrace the feet of Christ and look down on His and our enemies with triumphant eyes."

But Calvin had been carried away by his enthusiasm ; the conference adjourned without having come up to the expectations, and the famous formula signed by Protestants and Catholics, was rejected as heretical at the great meeting of Poissy.

Nevertheless the edict of January, 1562, may be termed a consequence of the conference of Poissy.

The freedom of worship, for which the Protestants had long asked in vain, was now granted them, on the understanding that they should hold their services by day and outside the towns.

Calvin was satisfied. " If only we are allowed to keep this freedom," he argued, " then popery must inevitably totter to its fall."

The Huguenots had no less cause to rejoice, while Beza, full of fervent gratitude, wrote : " He who never permits His sheep to be tried above their strength has had mercy on His new-born lambs and the shepherds who had begun to graze them."

Beza remained in Paris for the time being. Catherine de Medici desired this ; and Calvin also desired it. But their motives were different. Calvin thought of the future of French Protestantism, the Queen-Regent of the future of her rule. Her soul was filled with distrust of the great power of the

Guises in which she saw a menace to her authority, and she asked Coligny how many Huguenot communities there were and how many soldiers they could raise.

The reply must have gratified her. The Protestants were five million in number ; there were 2150 communities, and this number was always on the increase.

But Beza did not like to hear this talk of soldiers ; he wished to keep the Reformation apart from politics, and tried to prevent the fatal alliance at the same moment that the French Reformation was already afloat on the political waters with all sails set.

The suction had been too strong. In a cleverly drawn-up manifesto Catherine de Medici appealed to the Huguenots to aid her in maintaining her authority against a faction that, with a false Catholic device on their lips, aimed at overthrowing her government. Instead of being mutineers and firebrands, the Huguenots were all at once changed into faithful subjects ; to be a Protestant was to be a true Royalist ; and the common enemy was the Duke of Guise, who plotted to obtain the throne, and who was at the same time the most furious heretic-hunter.

Beza was in Paris. He preached daily. And the psalms of the Huguenots sounded bolder than ever. For they knew the Queen-Regent had become their friend. They had been oppressed long enough—now there was an end of it. They had been led to slaughter like sheep, but everything had its appointed time, and they would now use their fists, should the enemy dare to come. They no longer tolerated the interruption of their religious services ; the police had been warned by the authorities to help them if they had well-founded complaints, and one evening the streets of Paris witnessed the strange spectacle of a Protestant mob conducting thirty-six Roman Catholic priests to prison.

It was at this time that Calvin dedicated his splendid exposition of the Prophet Daniel to all true believers in France.

Even then his enthusiasm had already left him ; like a prophetic perspective, gloomy visions passed before his mind's eye, and full of sad reflections he wrote in his dedication : " You will have to fight long and fiercely—I foresee a bloodier and more stubborn struggle than you may possibly believe."

Twelve months after, he finished his lectures on the Prophet Jeremiah and was about to commence the Lamentations.

The Lamentations—it frightened him. And he anxiously asked himself whether this might not prove to be a bad omen. It had dawned in the East ; but the red streak on the horizon had not been the splendour of the sun, but the reflection of blood, the warm gushing blood which would stain the lovely hills and valleys of France.

CHAPTER XXXI

THE MASSACRE OF VASSY AND ITS CONSEQUENCES

AMID the intoxication of their rapidly increasing power, the Huguenots were thunderstruck at the news that King Antony of Navarre had gone over to the Roman Catholic camp and the standard of the Guises.

They called it an incredible piece of news, and its truth was questioned when the first shock was over. But it was all in vain ; the truth could no longer be denied, and the man who had been proud of being called the head of the Huguenots, went over to the enemy bag and baggage.

" Sire," the Spanish Ambassador had said to him, " if you return to the old faith, my high commander, Philip II, will restore to you your kingdom of Navarre or else Sardinia as a compensation." " Sire," the Spanish Ambassador had added, " Charles IX is mortal and his brother also. Well, then, what is to prevent you from ascending the French throne when you have cast off your Huguenot guise ? "

The King of Navarre had heard enough. Beza tried his utmost to keep him for the Huguenot cause, Calvin wrote long urgent letters ; Johanna d'Albret shed bitter tears—it was all in vain. " The pity I feel for your fears," Calvin wrote to her, " show me their depth and bitterness. But however that may be—it is much better to be sorrowful for such a cause than to be indifferent to your spiritual interests."

Maltreated by her husband, overcome with grief and sorrow, she proceeded to her states of Bearn. She left her son behind, begging him with a troubled heart to remain faithful to his mother's creed. He did not. Nevertheless he always had an affection for the Church his mother clung to with such heroic faith ; and although not a member of that Church— he always remained its protector.

So King Antony of Navarre had become the ally of the Guises ; France never saw more unnatural alliances than in those days.

On one side stood the Guises, King Antony, the former head of the Huguenots, and Montmorency, a relation of Coligny's. On the other side stood Condé, King Antony's brother, Coligny and his numerous Huguenot adherents, and Catherine de Medici, who, in her heart of hearts, abhorred the Huguenots.

But the unnaturalness of these alliances was only surpassed by the hatred of the factions ; by the religious bitterness raging in their hearts. One spark was sufficient to set France aflame, and the massacre of Vassy was not a spark, but a flame which reached the gunpowder stores.

Was the Duke of Guise guilty of the massacre of Vassy ?

Between the Guises and Vassy there existed an old feud ever since the first-named had obtained the usufruct of the town.

Nevertheless the inhabitants of Vassy were of a vigorous, independent spirit ; the majority of them earned their living in various trades and industries, and they held a lively spiritual intercourse with the democratic citizens of the large town of Troyes.

After the conference of Poissy a Protestant Church was founded at Vassy ; the authorities warned them that this took place within the jurisdiction of the Guises, the bitterest enemies of the Reformation. The preacher took no notice of this warning ; the services commenced with a meeting of a hundred and twenty persons at the house of a linen-weaver, the next day there were six hundred.

Six hundred hearers out of a population of only three thousand ; that was a record ! Vassy was converted ; it had been won for the Reformation, and under the blue vault of heaven the famous hedge-sermons were held. Guise was warned ; he sent some soldiers to assist the officer of justice in suppressing the small church, but with no result. Then the Bishop of Châlons appeared, together with a famous monk, armed to the teeth with scholastic wisdom, who was to explain the true state of affairs to the inhabitants of Vassy. The Bishop invited the most important inhabitants of the town to come and hear this man, but they replied that not for all the treasures of the world would they consent to listen to a false prophet, and they went to their own preacher.

The Catholics were indignant ; with the Bishop, the officer of justice and other authorities at their head, they marched to the meeting-place of the Protestants.

The preacher was in the pulpit ; the Bishop wished to speak, but the preacher cried out that he was no bishop, no true shepherd. " You do not preach," the preacher said, " you do not feed your flock with the Word of the Lord, and your appointment is not ratified by the people."

The Bishop departed amid loud cries from the people ; obscene words were shouted after him, and this scene, which put one more in mind of a revolution than of the Reformation, made things worse.

The Bishop departed full of bitter rage ; Guise stamped his foot with fury, but he controlled himself and bided his time. He wished to teach Paris a lesson—Paris, which for five months had thought the Guises dead, by suddenly dealing a heavy blow to break the enemy's power, which would show them that he was still living. But his courage was more than matched by his cunning. He raised a troop of soldiers which made one think of war, but at the same time he took with him his brother, the Cardinal, his son, who was yet a child, and his wife, who was expecting a second child, when he set out on his expedition. Thus he was afterwards able to declare, with his hand on his heart : " It took place accidentally, else I should not have dreamed of taking my wife ! "

In reality the Duchess did not witness the horrible spectacle ; she was in the neighbourhood, outside the walls of the town.

The Duke might have supposed that the inhabitants of Vassy, in the face of a menacing Roman Catholic force, would give in and surrender a few heretical ringleaders to be strangled. But this did not happen. And when the Duke heard the church-bells ringing in the distance and it was reported to him that the Huguenots were going to their meeting-place, he cried out : " Let us be present at it ! " This command was greeted with joyful exclamations. Vassy was a small but flourishing town ; it would be worth plundering. . . .

Near the gates of the town they met a citizen dressed in black. This black dress was enough to excite the suspicions of the soldiers ; they stopped him and shouted : " Are you a Huguenot preacher ? Speak up—where did you study ? "

The man could prove that he was a bootmaker ; his hands showed it. Besides, he had never studied at Geneva. So he escaped with the fright.

Arrived at the monastery, the Duke dismounted. He dined there, and afterwards walked up and down the long corridor with the prior and the officer of justice, and seemed very excited.

The Catholics who had gone to mass, were told not to leave the church on any account; then the Duke gave his soldiers a sign to advance to the shed where the Protestants were gathered together. And the Duke followed them.

At a distance of twenty-five paces two musket-shots were fired at the window of the shed. And, overturning some people who were trying to lock the doors, the soldiers rushed into the wooden building, raising the terrible cry: "Slay them! Slay them!"

The gathering consisted of about 1260 persons, most of them of the trading-class. There were among them five linen-weavers, a butcher, a wine-merchant, a bailiff, and a schoolmaster. The most important citizen among them was an alderman of Vassy. The Catholics assert that the Protestants commenced hostilities by throwing stones, an assertion which sounds extremely improbable, when we bear in mind that the Protestants were confronted by enemies who were armed to the teeth.

When the Duke arrived, three Huguenots had already been killed, and his presence was a further incitement to proceed with the massacre. It was easy work; the Protestants were unarmed, defenceless they served as targets for the soldiers; they were dispatched like sheep—one of the Duke's lackeys afterwards boasted of having murdered six Huguenots. Surrounded inside and outside by the

hostile hordes, some of the Huguenots tried to
escape through the thatched roof, and mad with
fear they jumped into the town moat to save their
lives. Some of them feared to take the dangerous
leap, while the Duke shouted from above: "Down
with you, rascals!"

The cries of the dying resounded far and wide,
and reached the ears of the Duchess, who, impelled
by human compassion, begged her spouse at least to
spare the pregnant women. And thenceforth pregnant women were spared.

The Huguenot preacher, who had only recently
come from Geneva and who had remained in the
pulpit, managed to escape amid the general confusion, and had almost reached the door when he
stumbled over a corpse and was seized, and, heavily
wounded, taken before the Duke.

The Duke rudely asked him what had moved him
to lead the people to rebellion? Whereupon he still
had strength to reply: "My Lord, I am not a rebel
—I have only preached the Gospel."

Guise contemptuously turned his back on him,
and left him to his lackeys who treated him cruelly.

His end was touching. With his dying lips he
stammered the psalm of praise: "Into Thy hands
I commend my soul. Thou hast delivered me, oh
Lord, thou God of Truth!"

The young Cardinal leaned exhausted against the
wall of the churchyard, his eyes fixed on the horrible
spectacle. The Duke showed him the volume which

had been found in the pulpit ; the Cardinal opened it and said : " It is the Holy Bible ! "

Sixty of those peaceful church-goers, whose only crime had been that they had served God according to their conscience, were dispatched on that fatal Sunday of the 1st of March ; the number of the wounded was simply innumerable.

A cry of anger and horror rose from the Protestant camp when the massacre of Vassy became known, and with the rapidity of a prairie fire the fatal news spread throughout the length and breadth of France. Drawings were made of the scene of the murder, the art of illustration was born, and the pamphlets inscribed by the drawing-pencil made a deeper impression on the people than those inscribed by the pen had ever made.

Guise felt lonely and deserted. Even his wife and his brother, the Cardinal, could not justify his conduct. But his fox-like cunning did not desert him. He went to Nauteuil, where he defied the outburst of public indignation with his dreaded and illustrious name, and invited the old Marshal of France, Montmorency, to pay him a visit.

Montmorency did so ; he had no objection to crossing the threshold of this French Achan.

Then the Duke was saved. And so sure was he of his triumph that when the Queen-Mother invited him to Saint-Germain, he replied that he had prepared a feast for some friends at Nauteuil.

The Marshal conducted the Duke of Guise to

Paris with an impressive retinue of armed noblemen. Condé was still in Paris, but his forces were
small in number, and he had not much support from
his brother, the Cardinal of Bourbon, for this man,
who bore the title of lieutenant-general to the King,
was not quite responsible for his actions. He ordered
both Condé and Guise to depart. Condé went, but
Guise did not. And Montmorency, who had become
his advocate, told the Parliament that the venerated
voice of the people had induced the Duke to remain
in the capital.

Was this true ?

Guise had, on his entry into the town, been very
coolly received by a large part of the populace. At
the corners of the streets in the squares, there had
been people who, notwithstanding the brilliant
military array which escorted the Duke, had clenched
their fists and shouted imprecations after him.

The Duke acted his part masterly. He declared
with affected grief, that at Vassy he had done
nothing but protect his honour, his wife, and his
child, that he knew very well they aimed at his
life, and thirty assassins had been sent to Paris after
him. He begged them to look into this matter, and
the truth would be confirmed. He had never abused
his power, and now he no longer had any power,
because he had handed it over to the King, into the
hands of his Marshal. He asked for nothing but
justice ; he would voluntarily go to prison if the
Government wished it, and where he had com-

mitted an error he was willing to submit to the consequences.

Thus spoke the murderer stained with the innocent blood of Vassy, who, in reality, by means of his forces, held the town and Parliament under his control, and who ordered the child, called Charles IX and King of France, to follow him, the king of murderers and of the civil war, to Paris.

From this fateful day the French Protestants assumed the white sash, while Guise and his adherents followed the red banner. For red was the colour of Spain, of King Philip II, and of the massacre of Vassy. . . .

So the Duke was the victor, before the civil war had begun ; he called himself the true defender of the Catholic Church, and accepted with complacency the homage of a people excited to frenzy, and seized the reins of government.

The King of Navarre was an easy tool in his hands ; and this tool went to Fontainebleau to fetch Charles IX and the Queen-Mother, a woman who had only just given the Protestants permission to take up arms.

On April 6th the King was already in Paris, and six days afterwards a fresh murder was committed at Sens. Sixty killed at Vassy, a hundred at Sens— the thirst for blood was on the increase. The signal for wholesale murder had been given ; the Seine and Loire were red with blood ; in long rows the unburied corpses floated down the stream towards the

sea. In vain did Beza hasten to the Queen-Mother
to demand satisfaction for this violation of an edict
issued by the Government itself. He received no
satisfaction, and the King of Navarre, forgetting
duty and honour, had the insolence to remind him
with a mocking smile, that it was the vocation of
God's Church to be beaten without making resistance. But Beza could find the right word at the
right time.

Looking into the eyes of the traitor King with
proud dignity, he said with cutting severity :
" Sire, it is certainly true that the Church must
receive blows without giving blows in exchange,
but remember it is an anvil which has worn out
many hammers ! "

The Protestants were not unaware of the seriousness of the moment. They examined their conscience
and turned over the leaves of their Bible, looking for
texts which would justify armed resistance. Their
hand yet wavered ; for they lacked a French Knox
who dared to preach from the pulpit the Holy War
of the Lord and the Crusade of fire and steel against
false prophets.

They applied to Geneva for advice. Calvin admonished and warned them ; he spoke of the left
cheek which has to be turned to the enemy when the
right cheek is smitten. His letters were like hammers
to impress them with the truth, that only a spiritual
strife is permitted, and that the death of the body
is of small consequence if only the soul is saved.

The Huguenots had done so—up to the important year 1562. With untiring patience they had endured the most cruel persecutions ; with sublime disregard of death and with a song of triumph on their lips, they had gone forth to die, and in the last agonies of death still strengthened and comforted by the tender words of consolation which Calvin sent them in his letters.

They were yet willing to deny and forsake themselves, but their wives, their children ? Were their families to be defencelessly butchered ? They had to obey the authorities, but who were they ? Was it not high time to overthrow the power of the Guises, who guarded the young King and his mother like prisoners ? The Huguenots took to arms, although they had received no summons. They formed into bands and without order or discipline, without a leader or guide, they marched in the direction of Paris.

Condé, a prince of the blood royal, was their natural commander, now that the King of Navarre, his brother, had deserted them.

But Condé, who was as thoughtless as he was devoted, waited for Coligny. For this great patriot possessed the cool judgment, the clear head and the firm will which Condé so sadly lacked.

Coligny kept them waiting. Courier after courier stormed his castle to beg him to buckle on his armour in the face of this threatening danger, but his eye saw farther into the future than the eye of the near-

sighted prince. He shrank back at the thought of
a civil war. He knew that the Huguenots were in the
minority, and that this minority would be still
further diminished by the chances of an unlucky
war. He knew that only a month previously, Condé
had asked the Protestants of Paris for ten thousand
dollars, and that he had obtained no more than sixteen hundred, and at Paris Condé's condition had
been so precarious that, according to a certain
sharp-witted man, the servants of the Parisian
priests could have hunted him out of the town.

The worst thing was that this weak Protestant
party was not united, but was divided into two
factions ; the Protestants, pure and simple, who
were prepared to risk everything for the faith, and
a fickle crowd who, through different circumstances,
chance, a grudge against prevailing abuses, had
drifted into the Protestant camp.

That was the party which Coligny had to lead, to
command, to save in spite of itself ; opposed by
three-fourths of France and a Spanish King.

In every civil war women appear on the scene—
Kenau Hasselaars, who, wishing to believe the impossible, make it attainable by the turbulent passion
of their souls. There was Madeleine de Roye,
sister to the Admiral, who had preceded her brothers
on the path of the Reformation ; her daughter
Eleanore, recently married to the Prince of Condé;
Claude de Rieu, the wife of Dandelot, who with
touching conjugal fidelity had shared his gloomy

prison at Milan; Queen Johanna d'Albret, who made good her husband's desertion by redoubling her devotion to the cause; Charlotte of Laval, the woman who was worthy of being the wife of France's greatest hero. Tortured by gloomy forebodings, Coligny sat in his castle while his ear caught the cries of distress of his persecuted fellow-believers. His wife, Charlotte of Laval, shed hot tears. She complained that her husband, otherwise one of the most faithful, had now betrayed the Church and surrendered his brothers in the faith unprotected to the Guises. But she was mistaken. It was a woman's passion which spoke in her, while he, a great states-man and general, calculated the consequences.

" Charlotte," said he, " put your hand on your heart! Examine your conscience! Speak. Are you capable of bearing the scorn, the reproaches of a people which judges according to success? Are you capable of bearing flight, poverty, hunger—the hunger of your children, Charlotte? Death at the hands of the hangman? Your husband dragged to a dungeon? Think it over—I give you three weeks!"

" Three weeks!" she cried passionately; " do not heap on your head the victims of three weeks!" That word decided him. From his sense the wife had appealed to his heart, and he thought he heard the voice of the Lord in it. Now thought and deliberation were at an end, he no longer inquired about the number of his friends or of his foes, and jumped into the saddle : he and his heroic brother Dandelot, to fight in the holy wars of the Lord.

The first error of the French Protestants had been to choose the weak King of Navarre for their head ; the second was that they accepted Condé as a substitute for the unfaithful King.

For not Condé, but Coligny was the man who could have brought the fight to a successful issue ; and the difference of opinion, the gulf between their ways of thinking, their aspirations, their inclinations, darkened the Admiral's eye when seated at the same supper-table with the Prince.

Already on the day after that Sunday it came to a violent altercation, as Condé and the nobility wished to apply for foreign assistance, while Coligny opposed it with might and main. He was one of the true national party, and called it tempting God to beg for assistance from abroad, as the Guises had done. The die had been cast meanwhile—the passionate French blood knew no other way out. Condé galloped to the south with a brilliant troop of noblemen, amid shouts of joy and applause. And the gay and joyous Protestants entered the gates of Orléans with him.

Coligny followed at the head of the burly, stern Calvinists. He planted the Protestant standard in Orléans ; he put the trumpet of war to his lips, to call spiritual Israel to arms, and he wrote on his banner : " The Glory of God and freedom to King and Country ! "

Beza was also present. The vigorous advocate of the Reformation at Poissy became the military chaplain of the armed Huguenots, and appointed a solemn day of prayer and repentance to invoke God's blessing on their arms.

The whole kingdom seemed all at once changed into one huge armourer's workshop. The Huguenots needed no incitement to arm themselves. The death-agonies at Vassy had startled them, and the cries of distress at Sens had decided them. They seized their swords to defend their lives and the lives of those most precious to them ; and they got into a state of over-exertion and over-excitement in which they would have been capable of committing a murder merely to prevent another murder.

At the same time the plague was raging in the towns. In Orléans ten thousand people, in Paris eighty thousand were carried to their graves, while those that survived were preparing to tear each other to pieces. Within six weeks the French Calvinists were under arms.

The Duke did not feel at ease ; he was disagreeably surprised ; the Spaniards that Philip II had promised would not arrive till August, and now it was April. In his anxiety Guise wrote to the Catholic cantons of Switzerland to hurry on with their auxiliary troops, and by promising a large amount of money he tried to raise mercenary troops in Germany.

The clergy of his church provided him with the money. Forced to it by his need, he put the knife to their throats, and their terror was the key with which he opened the Roman Catholic money-box.

He had still another weapon : that weapon was intrigue, the secret game of diplomacy, for which his fingers seemed to have a special aptitude.

He used the name of the young King, and the crafty stage-tricks of the Queen-Mother, together with the splendour of the royal court, to obtain the victory. She had seduced the King of Navarre ; she was capable of seducing Condé. To keep up the show, he left the Chancellor l'Hôpital with her ; the noble-minded Catholic, who had to cover the base practices of Francis of Guise with the cloak of his virtue.

The Protestant reaction on the massacre of Vassy was deplorable. Roman Catholic shops were plundered, monks were maltreated ; priests were murdered. But to acknowledge the truth, these were isolated cases, and Protestant revenge confined itself on the whole almost exclusively to the images of convents and Roman Catholic places of worship. The saints were torn from their pedestals and destroyed ; the famous relics, of which so many miracles were related, were summoned to perform another miracle to prolong their existence. It was a wholesale destruction of images ! a rude dissipation ! a horrible deed.

Calvin never approved of such deeds ; his soul abhorred violence ; he was a man of order and discipline.

But was the destruction, the damage, irreparable, as it was said ? Was not rather the massacre which destroyed the lives of so many Protestants irreparable ? Much has been said concerning the anger of the Catholics when the misdeeds committed by the Protestants in their revenge became known. What had the Protestants done in Picardy, in Champagne ? Nearly everywhere they were persecuted to death for the wrong which had not been done by them, but to them. The old mother of the Guises completed her revenge on the unhappy town of Vassy by dismantling its fortifications and demolishing the walls, while savage soldiers were quartered on the inhabitants. It was the prelude to the future dragonades, and the grave-diggers at Vassy were busily employed. Then the Spaniards that Guise had asked for to assist him, arrived from across the Pyrenees. Their barbaric cruelty exceeded the highest expectations. The hard-hearted Gascon Montluc, a man of blood, who boasted of having adorned every tree on his road with corpses, relates that those black devils, whom he had supplied with two hundred women to do with as they liked, had preferred cutting open their bellies, even of the pregnant women, in order to destroy the little Protestants. Is it then surprising that the Protestants who had been called to arms, longed to be at home to defend their families ? Or that Coligny was compelled to call in foreign aid, which the enemy had been doing for the last two years ? Dandelot travelled to Germany, another ambassador went to England.

It was a civil war which would decide the fate of the Guises and the Bourbons, but this war was at the same time a war of religion which would settle the dispute between the Roman Catholic and the Protestant faith. Thus the leaders understood the case. That was why Guise had applied to Spain ; why Condé applied to Queen Elizabeth, while Calvin ordered the churches to raise the pay for the mercenaries.

With the liveliest interest and a heart full of cares Calvin watched the foaming tide of the civil war. He had a keen eye for the great difficulties which the Reformation had to pass through, because in its course it crossed the tortuous paths of politics, but he was of opinion that the war had been pressed on them, and he followed the campaign with bated breath.

The brave Dandelot had a difficult task at the German courts. The difficulty was to open the eyes of the Germans to the real state of France, and to clear away the mountain of lies and slanders which blocked up their view. He was surrounded by swarms of spies of the Guises who penetrated into the cabinets of the German princes and stole the Protestant letters from their tables. It was only by means of infinite patience and inexhaustible perseverance that Dandelot succeeded in obtaining a partial success, and returned to France at the head of six thousand German soldiers to assist the Protestants in their need. Coligny was in Orléans with a select body of brave men, while the rest of the Protestant army had degenerated into guerilla-bands, which overran the country, stealing and plundering, and who had taken as their war-cry, " an eye for an eye and a tooth for a tooth."

Those bands made terrible havoc. Their passions had been let loose. But their barbarity was far excelled by the storm of Roman Catholic fury which changed beautiful Provence into a desert.

Never has war been waged more horribly. Listen to an account of how religious hatred raged in Provence !

" Sommervire and his followers now had the whole of Provence in their power, and the plan to eradicate the Protestant religion was carried out with inhuman cruelty. Its followers were shot, cut down, hanged, thrown from bridges, from windows, from high walls on to the pikes of the soldiers. Many were buried or burnt alive, others were beaten to death, stoned, killed by opening their veins. Living persons had their entrails, their eyes put out, their limbs cut off one by one. The corpses were thrown to the dogs—hewn-off heads were used at games of ball. . . ."

CHAPTER XXXII

A REFORMED FEMALE JUDGE

WHEN we see a kind human face, after having witnessed so many inhuman horrors, our souls feel refreshed, as if we had met an angel.

Look up, and you will see such a kind human face!

Do not be afraid—to-day we are quite safe here on the high road connecting Orléans and Paris.

To-morrow the troops of Guise will march past, the snorting of their horses, the clatter of their swords against the cuisses, and the rattling of the gun-carriages will fill the air.

But to-day we are safe. Do you see the woman on the pinnacle of yonder castle turret? Your eyes are keen—do you not recognise that woman? Consult your memory! Your face tells me you do not recognise her. No wonder—thirty years change a human being. Especially in the sixteenth century.

Oh, she has changed much, this young charming Duchess Renata of Ferrara! Her hair has grown grey; deep wrinkles have furrowed her face; she has got old.

Amid troubles and difficulties has her ship of life

sailed over the high seas. When Calvin left Ferrara, an exile without hearth or home, to seek a quiet place of refuge in the North, he did not forget this spiritual child of his. He was sore afraid that she would not be able to take the last decisive step, but would halt at the cross-way, where Margaret of Valois had remained, disheartened, with the sad complaint on her pale lips : " The wind is so piercing and my heart so cold ! And I am so hungry, so thirsty and so benumbed ! "

Like Margaret of Valois she could not tear herself from the Unity of the Church ; she was one of the moderate party, which wasted its strength in the hopeless attempt to keep together what could not be united, and which was completely defeated at the Council of Trent.

But Ignatius Loyola and the persecutions which broke out in Italy, helped her when arrived at the cross-way to take the path of the Reformation. Her attitude became more and more decided. The Jesuits were surprised at her neglecting the fast-days, and no longer going to mass or confession. The Jesuitic spies also discovered the strange fact of her secret correspondence with that arch-heretic Calvin, and from that moment they left no stone unturned to persuade the Duke to have her tried before the spiritual tribunal of the Inquisition.

But it had to be done with the necessary circumspection, as Renata was the daughter of a King, and sister-in-law to Francis I. Any insult to the Duchess

he would certainly have taken very ill, and the
Pope's policy at the moment did not make it desirable to take vigorous measures. The longed-for
hour to recall this unfaithful daughter of the Church
to a sense of her duty had struck when Francis I
died, and Henry II was trying to wash away his
sins in the blood of the martyrs.

The grand-inquisitor was sent to Ferrara to bring
her back to the fold of the Church. Those were
anxious days for the Duchess. She stood there alone
and deserted. The Duke did not understand her,
neither did her children; Margaret had already
passed beyond all earthly strife; her old friends were
excommunicated, banished, or languished in dungeons, while Geneva was unattainable. But Calvin,
her spiritual father, did not forget her.

He prayed for her and wrote : " When you are in
great anxiety, be assured that I feel my share of it.
May the Lord keep you in His Holy care, and guide
you, through the Holy Ghost, that you may glorify
Him more and more ! "

He did more . . . he sent the young, courageous minister, Francis de Morel, to console and
strengthen her in her anxious circumstances. De
Morel, a born nobleman, who shrank from nothing,
managed to meet her in spite of almost insurmount-
able difficulties ; she regained her constancy of
mind, and bore herself like a heroine in replying
to the speeches of the grand-inquisitor. But with
this her fate was also decided. In the middle

of the night a closed carriage drove to the door, she was ordered to get in, and at a smart pace the carriage was driven to the state-prison, which had been got ready for her.

Then unbelief overmastered her ; her strength was broken and nothing was left but a poor weak woman, who, after a week's imprisonment, sent for the grand-inquisitor. The face of the Jesuit beamed with satisfaction ; he had triumphed ; the Duchess was prepared to confess her sins, and at his hands she received the Holy Communion. She regained her liberty, her children. Once again she took up her abode in the palace, and the Duke praised her because she had behaved like a sensible woman.

But the Duke's joy was surpassed by the sorrow and dismay in Protestant circles. Nobody felt the blow which had been struck at Protestantism more deeply than Calvin ; her fall was worse than a lost battle ; on that gloomy evening when she received the Holy Communion at the hands of the grand-inquisitor, the last bulwark of the Reformation on Italian ground had been lost.

Nevertheless the heart of the Reformer was filled with tender compassion ; his great knowledge of human nature enabled him to understand how great her anguish must be, and instead of threatening with the fire of God's Holy wrath, he consoled her with promises of the Lord's infinite mercy.

How Calvin managed to send her those letters

puzzles us. The Jesuits were cruel and crafty spies, it was almost impossible to slip through the meshes of their nets. And yet it took place repeatedly; cunning was matched by cunning, and again and again the Jesuits were outwitted.

For six long years, life for the Duchess passed in sad monotony. Then the Duke was stretched on his death-bed. She was his faithful nurse; she attended to the least of his desires, and promised the dying man to fulfil his last wish, and to break off her correspondence with Calvin.

This resolution caused the Reformer bitter pain; he had not expected this, and his reply was full of restrained anger when he wrote: " In promising this you have sinned, and offended God; yet this promise is not binding. You know, madam, that Herod was not only praised for keeping the oath, which he had sworn lightly and unthinkingly, too well, but that he was also doubly damned for it."
" I do not say this," he continued, " to press you to write to me, but in order that you may feel no stings of conscience where God leaves you free. I have done my share, madam, in informing you of this."

That ought to have been sufficient for the Duchess.

Renata's eldest son now became the reigning Duke. One thing this young man knew: he was dependent on the Pope, his liege lord, and this liege lord still suspected his mother of heretical feelings.

It was a case of bending or breaking ; she would either have to devote herself exclusively to the Roman Catholic Church or to leave the country ; that was the alternative ; there was no other way for the young Duke.

Then Renata chose the latter.

Calvin warned her ; he was afraid that her wavering attitude would be pernicious to her in France, and that the stifling atmosphere of the French Court would complete her ruin.

Yet she persevered. And it was a sensible resolution. In the midst of the raging passions and slaughter which succeeded the conspiracy of Amboise, she entered the gates of Orléans. She was frightened at the state of things ; she saw her beloved country on the verge of ruin. And Francis of Guise, the grim and triumphant enemy of the Protestants, was her son-in-law. . . .

He greeted her with courtesy ; it flattered his pride that the Duchess Renata was the mother of his wife Anna of Est, and the daughter of a famous French King. Surely it was with his consent that Anna travelled several days in advance to meet her mother, and his eye rested with approval on the family group when the grandmother nursed his little boy on her knees.

How fortunate that God had hidden the future from her sight ! Had the bloody vision of that future appeared before her mind's eye she would have been crushed by sorrow, and have fled from this child, who now looked up at his grandmother with a sweet smile, in unutterable horror ; for this child, flesh of her flesh, and bone of her bone, would in the St. Bartholomew's night become the assassin of her noble friend Coligny.

From the pinnacles of this castle Renata can see on the far horizon, rising above the trees, the proud towers of Châtillon, the hereditary possession of the Colignys.

And with a certain preference did she select this castle and the town of Montargis belonging to it, as her abode in order to be in the neighbourhood of this excellent man. Her father's warlike spirit seemed to come over her when she entered the castle.

It was a gloomy castle with small windows, dark passages, and narrow stairs—a rude contrast to the graceful and charming country-seats in Ferrara. It had besides long been untenanted ; the courtyard was overgrown with grass and weeds, while the twenty-yards-high walls, which rose perpendicular from the river, were in a ruinous condition.

But nothing could shake her resolution. Here she had a fixed point where she ruled absolutely ; and amid the waves of the civil war which beat tempestuously over France, it was of the greatest importance to fortify that point.

Many alterations were necessary, but in the first place the fortifications had to be repaired. The Duchess recruited a small select band to man the castle ; guns were placed on the walls ; the walls were strengthened ; the gates were made heavier, the trap-doors examined, and the embrasures and loopholes were cleared of the encroaching weeds. Then she resolutely set to work to clear out other more noxious weeds in her estate : the bitter religious hatred which existed between Catholics and Protestants in her dominions.

The Catholics were in the majority and were annoyed when the Duchess declared herself to be in favour of the Protestant religion. They fell upon a Protestant congregation and murdered a great many of them. The Protestants attacked some Roman Catholic churches in revenge, knocked the images to pieces, and committed many other misdeeds which made the papists furious.

The Duchess would not tolerate such things. She ordered the Catholics who had murdered Protestants, and the Protestants who had attacked Catholic churches, to be severely punished. She had her private chapel adapted for Protestant worship, but she would not suffer the preaching to degenerate into reviling, and she gave the ministers strict orders to eschew all improper and offensive expressions. Hot-blooded Protestants did not understand her, and the Genevese Reformer was besieged with complaints about her strange conduct. To eyes clouded with passion, her wise policy seemed half-heartedness, and her reserve, fear of man.

Calvin was reminded that her wavering had always been the cause of her misfortune, and that a man like Morel, who once before at Ferrara had visited her at the right time, might become the strong oak to which the weak ivy could cling.

But those zealots were mistaken. The Duchess was no longer the weak ivy ; her character had been refined in the fire of suffering, and proud and self-conscious, as beseems a daughter of kings, she went the path she had chosen. Young Morel came ; the Duchess herself had urgently requested this. But he was not able to change her point of view. His youthful impetuosity was dashed to pieces on the rock of her ripe experience ; she rebuked his severe and rigorous spirit, which would prevent the celebration of mass within her dominions, and took on herself the defence of a Catholic Church which was threatened by the Protestants.

For this passionate Morel it was something unheard of, something above his comprehension ; and he was surprised at this woman, who was three centuries in advance of her time. He was out of temper, embittered, annoyed ; he doubted whether she were a true-hearted Protestant, and in his letters to Calvin he gave him to understand this unequivocally. But, on the other hand, this woman confused him completely, for she opened wide the gates of Montargis for all persecuted fellow-believers in the neighbourhood ; more than once he was struck dumb at the large sums of money she handed him for the suffering Protestants, while with warm devotion she offered them her private chapel for the celebration of the Lord's Supper, for baptism, and the solemnisation of Protestant marriages.

The earnest striving of the Duchess could not long remain hidden to Morel's honest mind ; his coolness disappeared, and he began to write letters to Calvin which testify to a cordial appreciation. It was not necessary. The eagle's eye of the master had seen farther than his disciple. He had already recommenced corresponding with her, and in January, 1561, he sent her one of those encouraging and consoling letters of which he seemed to possess the secret. He reminded the Duchess that, in order to tread the right path, we must break with all earthly ties. Many difficulties yet awaited her, but if only she continued to fix her hope on Him, Who would complete the good work begun in her, all would be well. She was not to cease supporting the poor followers of Christ, for in doing this, she was a fellow-worker in God—a title, desirable above all others. The traveller hastens on his road, when evening begins to fall. Therefore he admonished her to use her increasing years as an incitement to leave behind her a good testimony in this world.

" If you remain strong and persevering, I hope that God will make your generosity and fidelity so productive of good that all the faithful will bless your return to France and confess that God has truly had mercy on them through you, and that He held out His saving hand when He brought you back to your country in your old age."

All distrust was gone ; they had been mistaken. And many a Huguenot's eye grew moist when he heard that she, the mother-in-law of Francis of Guise, had set out for the meeting at Poissy together with Beza and Morel.

CHAPTER XXXIII

THE SWORD OF THE HUGUENOTS

ONCE again traversing the gloomy road from Poissy to the civil war, we are dismayed. For forty long years, more than the average length of human life, the Protestants had not thought of resistance or opposition ; like sheep they had been led to the slaughter, without uttering a cry. They had suffered themselves to be tortured, strangled, burnt, buried alive. But the constant influx of new members, especially of the warlike nobility, had caused a turn of the tide which now demanded a quick and bloody decision.

The Duchess was at Montargis when the storm burst, and hers was the task to dress the wounds which had been inflicted by her hard-handed son-in-law. It was feared that the Roman Catholics, who formed the greater part of her subjects, might attack the Protestants ; so she resolutely ordered the gates to be closed, the drawbridges to be raised, and the guards to be doubled.

Montargis became the great place of refuge for the Protestants who fled from the sword of the Guises, but the gates which had been unlocked for the Protestants, once again opened to admit the Catholic peasants, who dared not await the arrival of Guise's pillaging troops. The people streamed into the castle ; within a short time its walls harboured many hundreds of fugitives : young men, old men, women and children, who lamented and stretched out their hands to the Duchess.

Renata helped and consoled ; her pity performed wonders of mercy ; she stood godmother to the children that came into the world amid this misery. And amid this sea of distress which streamed in through the lofty castle gates, she did not forget Orléans, but sent large sums of money to those two heroic women who practised the works of Christian charity in the hospitals overcrowded with plague-stricken patients.

Calvin's heart was moved when the tidings from Montargis reached him.

" Speaking according to the world," he wrote to the Duchess, full of gratitude, " a princess must feel insulted at her castle being turned into a hospital, but I think that no more honourable title can be given it, after all the mercy you have shown to God's children, who find a place of refuge with you. I sometimes think that God has left you this opportunity in your old age, to enable you to pay your former debt to Him, caused by your timorousness in days gone by. Naturally I only express myself according to the ordinary way of speaking, for even if you had done a hundred or a thousand times more, you would never be able to discharge the debt you owe Him for the good He daily showers on you. But I mean this, that He honours you greatly by using you for such a task, by making you bear His name in order to glorify Himself through you, by revealing His Word to you, that inexhaustible source of blessings, and by making your house a place of refuge for the followers of His Son. So rejoice, for with many reasons for sorrow, you have also reason to rejoice now that God reveals His approbation by choosing you, in order to be glorified through you ! "

But her care and anxiety increased ; the Guises were ever gaining ground ; the basin of the Loire fell into their hands, and with Bourges the last bulwark of the Huguenots in central France succumbed. Renata might now expect the triumvirate ; Anna of Est, who had travelled in advance of the victorious army, brought her the tidings. It was a sweet consolation to the Duchess that Anna was the messenger, for Anna was very fond of her mother ; from her mother she had inherited a warm heart for those that were unhappy and oppressed, and in her filial love she tried everything to soothe the Duchess. There was no need for the Duchess to be anxious ; it was not a religious war ; no one would have to suffer for his religion ; they only aimed at subjecting the rebels who were a danger to the State, but Renata sadly shook her head ; she warned the preachers on her estates to depart at once, and brought the fugitives inside her strong castle. One thing gladdened her heart : the arrival of Charles IX. And the pleasure seemed mutual when the young King paid his respects to his grand-aunt.

But her fervent prayer to be allowed to speak to him privately in order to explain the true state of affairs to him was not heard. Her son-in-law frustrated her plan ; the King's visit was made so short that it was impossible for her to exchange a confidential word with him. And she had to consider herself lucky when, on her pressing, a royal command was issued which prohibited pillage and arson within the territory of Montargis on pain of death.

The troops of Guise were surprised ; such a mode of warfare was not at all to their liking. But the discontented officers became a little more reconciled to this limitation when they were told that one of them was to be appointed commander of the town, and that the Protestant services in the private chapel were to be held only for the Duchess and her retinue.

In this manner did the Duchess and her son-in-law part. And when she met him again, the grim enemy of the Reformation lay stretched on his death-bed. . . .

Francis of Guise hesitated which way to take, Orléans or Rouen ; then a council of war was held and the army marched up to the walls of the populous town of Rouen. The inhabitants perceived the red banner of the Guises with fear and trembling ; the King of Navarre, who formerly had been the head of the Huguenots, was commander-in-chief of the forces which were to besiege the town.

It was stoutly defended, but the Guise army proved too powerful for the Huguenots. The town was stormed, and through the breach which they had made, the flood of furious soldiers streamed into the town.

During eight days the wretched town was left to the unbridled passions of the undisciplined soldiers ; then the judicial murders followed ; the preacher Marlorat, a gentle, amiable man, highly esteemed by Protestants and Catholics alike, who had been present at the conference of Poissy, here confirmed his faith with his blood.

But even the days of the King of Navarre, the victor of Rouen, were numbered. During the siege a musket-shot was fired from the walls, and the King was carried to his tent with a serious wound in his left shoulder. This ball put an end to his short dream of glory and splendour ; on October 15th he was wounded, and he died a month after, on November 17th. On his death-bed he saw the terrible mistake of his life : with eyes full of tears he confessed his sin, and confessed Christ, in whose name his soldiers had murdered the noblest citizens of Rouen.

Condé had meanwhile received his German mercenaries, and now no longer delayed marching to the capital at the head of an impressive force. A panic seized the Parisians when the rumour spread: "The Huguenots are approaching!"

The fright was general; one of the magistrates almost died of fear; three thousand Spaniards were expected, and instead ten thousand armed Protestants appeared at the gates. . . .

But the gates of Paris were impregnable, for they were defended by the Queen-Mother. Near a windmill she had a meeting with Condé; she approached him with her most charming smile, and three precious days were wasted.

We are surprised, and ask how on earth it was possible for Condé to talk and waste his time while France, in her last extremity, was looking up to him as her saviour.

What was he thinking of?

What had happened to the iron Calvinist?

What fatal net held him ensnared?

For three days the Queen-Mother and the beautiful Delilah of her Court held Condé captive; then they turned their back on him for the Spaniards were approaching. So the Huguenots had their leader back again, but he did not lead them; he was led, for the German mercenaries wanted their pay and marched to the coast to receive the money Queen Elizabeth had promised. The principal force of the Guises marched parallel with them; close to Dreux the Catholics offered to give battle to the Huguenots, and Condé considered it a point of

honour due to his princely blood to accept the
challenge. It was in the middle of winter. The
Protestants numbered twelve thousand, the Catholics
seventeen thousand men. But even had the number
on both sides been increased tenfold, the importance
of the battle would not have been greater, for this
first battle between the Catholics and Huguenots of
France decided the fate of French Protestantism.
When Calvin met his colleagues on the memorable
morning of this battle, he said that during the night
he had heard a loud noise as of trumpets sounding.
The noise had been so distinct that it could not
have been imagination, and he begged his colleagues
to join him in a prayer to God as something important would surely take place on that day. It
was piercing cold that Saturday; a cutting north
wind whistled over the fallow fields when the soldiers
left their watch-fires.

Beza delivered a powerful speech, which excited the
Huguenots to the greatest enthusiasm ; then Coligny
drew his sword, brandished it over his head, and
rushed into the hostile ranks at the head of his
cavalry.

The Huguenots had five thousand, the Catholics
only two thousand horse-soldiers, but the Catholic
infantry numbered fifteen thousand men, while the
Protestants could not muster more than seven
thousand.

Guise, matchless in cunning tricks, did not now
belie his true character. He always acted according

to fixed well-considered rules, which enabled him to justify himself should be become involved in a lawsuit, and this prudence now cautioned him not to fight without the sanction of a King and a Queen-Mother, over whom he ruled.

The Queen-Mother burst out laughing when this question was put to her.

Just then the King's old nurse entered the apartment, and she asked her : " Well, nurse, what do you think of it ? "

" Well, madam," replied the woman, " since those Huguenots are never satisfied, it is time to bring them to reason."

At the commencement of the fight Guise went to the Spanish soldiers, who had made a wall of carts to break the shock of the hostile cavalry, and from this fortified encampment they saw Coligny attack Marshal Montmorency, disperse his soldiers, and take the wounded Marshal prisoner.

Condé attacked the Swiss, and swept over them like a hurricane. But those men remembered that their fathers had beaten the Protestants at Cappeln thirty years ago, and they rose again between the hoofs of the horses, and fought with their usual death-despising courage.

Guise had looked on coolly from behind the barricade of carts, assuring the Spaniards that he was only a captain. But when, after waiting for five hours, his army had no chief officers left, he placed himself at the head of the Spaniards, rallied the scattered musketeers, and put the Huguenots to flight, taking Condé prisoner.

Coligny and Dandelot, however, retained their cool intrepidity. At the head of twelve hundred horsemen they threw themselves in a mad gallop on the victorious enemy, brought him to a standstill, and took prisoner Marshal Saint-André. The Marshal, who had dishonestly enriched himself, ended his life miserably. He quarrelled with one of his former servants ; he begged for his life, but the servant shattered his head with a pistol-shot. So the tables were once again turned, but the balance, heavy with so much blood, stood still, and the battle of Dreux was a defeat for the Protestants, since it had not been a victory.

A victory would have opened the gates of Paris to them, without the Queen-Mother being able to turn back, and the war-hymn, chanted by the victorious Huguenots in the streets of Paris, would have sounded in mighty fanfares, and penetrated to the remotest cottages of France. It would have been a decisive victory for the Reformation ; from the Pyrenees to the Meuse a Protestant nation would have been born, and two centuries afterwards the Marseillaise of the Revolution would not have been raised, had not the Marseillaise of the Reformation been smothered in blood.

With sad surprise the Protestants heard that the Huguenot army had retreated, and that Condé had been taken prisoner. They had expected every-

thing but defeat. They asked themselves why the
Lord led them to this gloomy road ; they were
His friends, His children ; and if there were a traitor
in the army, an Achan, they fervently wished that
He would reveal it to their stricken hearts.

Why had the Lord done this—why ? This
" why " was continually on Calvinist lips ; it
sounded wherever Protestant hearts beat ; and
in those sad days Calvin often preached on the
words : " His ways are not our ways ! "

In the same spirit was Calvin's letter to Soubise,
Governor of Lyons, once his pupil at Ferrara.

" When God takes the sword from our hands, we
must quietly await the time when God will return
it. The submission may be hard to bear, but that
does not matter. God has sorely tried us . . . let
us submit, until He raises us up again. And as it
is God's will to afflict us, we should not rebel."

Thus spoke Calvin ; thus he taught—it was the
Protestant Spartan who here spoke.

Guise shed no tears over the loss of Marshal
Montmorency, who fell alive, and General Saint-
André, who fell dead into the hands of the Hugue-
nots. He was satisfied ; the day of Dreux had been
a prosperous one to him ; Condé, the head of the
Huguenots, in his hands. Fortune smiled on him.

He treated Condé with effusive kindness ; there
was no end to it ; Condé had to share his tent, and
all that was done by Guise to shake the faith of the
Protestants in their leaders.

The Germans soon gave loud voice to it. " Those French weathercocks," they said contemptuously, " one day they want to knock each other's brains out and the next they embrace each other."

So Guise was at the height of his ambition. Not only was he the victor, but the sole victor. The Triumvirate no longer existed. Saint-André was dead, the Marshal a prisoner ; and the Duke, who in the morning had modestly declared that he did not wish to command more than a company, was in the evening lieutenant-general of the kingdom.

He now determined to take short measures with Montargis, as officious individuals had informed him that the Protestant services were once again being held regularly in public, that the Duchess, as absolute mistress, had once again made her dominion a hotbed of rebellion and a place of refuge for Protestant preachers.

While his standard appeared before the gates of Orléans, he carried out his resolution to abduct his mother-in-law, willing or unwilling. And to enforce that resolution, he sent his captain, Malicoine, to Montargis at the head of a strong body of cavalry.

The Duchess's royal blood coursed more quickly through her veins when she heard of the misdeeds of those soldiers ; with her own eyes she saw the blood of her fellow-believers staining the pavement ; and powerless to protect the town, she was yet firmly determined to resist the whole of Catholic

France in her castle. Armed with her woman's cunning, she expressed her surprise at the town and castle being expected to surrender, and that the garrison of a town of which a royal officer had been appointed commander could be suspected. And raising her voice she asked Malicoine whether he remembered that the King was her nephew; she would not yield in obedience to anyone, but she could not but see some fearful misunderstanding at the bottom of it all, and she demanded a new enforcement of the royal mandate before she could consider herself at liberty to give in. So she appealed from her son-in-law to the King, whom she knew to be merely the tool of his subject.

By this appeal she gained time; and time gained meant much. For she knew enough of the political game of chess to be aware that a victorious Guise was as obnoxious to Catherine de Medici as a triumphant Huguenot army; she would hurry on the peace negotiations in order to frustrate Guise's conquest of Orléans, and the fact of Condé being a prisoner, could in Renata's eyes only promote peace.

But Guise had not sent a child to Montargis; Malicoine understood well enough that every moment was precious, and was not going to be imposed upon by an old woman. He informed the Duchess that it would be superfluous and merely loss of time to send for more definite instructions; she could follow him willingly, if she liked; otherwise he would find a way to break her obstinacy by razing her castle to the ground.   Luck seemed to favour him ; a company of artillery was just passing, which was to serve at the siege of Orléans.   And he at once directed the guns against the walls of her castle.

But then the Duchess showed herself in all her greatness.

With the tenderness of a mother-hen spreading her wings over her little ones, she stretched out her arms over the poor wretches who would be left defenceless to the bitter animosity of the enemy if she withdrew her protection.   Their cares had become her cares, their danger her danger.

A short space of scarcely a week had once been sufficient to bring her to a humiliating genuflexion at the feet of a Jesuit priest, but that time lay behind her.   Suffering had refined her, as gold is refined in the furnace, and she wished to remain one with her fellow-believers to the bitter end.

With fearless mien she approached Montargis. " Shoot if you dare ! " she said ; " but I shall place myself in the breach !   And we shall see whether you really have the courage to kill the daughter of King Louis XII ! "

The captain of the Guise army was not easily daunted, yet now he hesitated.   This woman would be capable of carrying out her desperate intention, and the responsibility of her death would fall upon him.   That proved too much for him ; without more definite orders he dared not carry out his plan, and before those orders arrived the fate of his master had been sealed for ever.

In the night following the battle of Dreux, Coligny had rallied his decimated forces ; his lion-like courage was unbroken, and he told his soldiers that nothing had yet been effected, that the work had to be done over again, and that it was their task to crush the enemy on the following morning. But the Germans showed him their wounds, their broken weapons ; and two-thirds of the Huguenot army lay on the battle-field, dead or wounded.

The greatest difficulty for the Admiral was to keep the Germans, who had had blows instead of money, and who turned their faces towards the Rhine, within bounds. He told them that they could claim their money ; they ought not, however, to look for it on the shores of the German Rhine, but at Hâvre, and on their way to conquer Normandy.

The question was now how to transform those warring nomads into a quiet and easily movable column. They carried with them their plunder and the possessions obtained in previous campaigns, in a long train of wagons, which prevented all rapid movement, and they would rather lose a battle than this baggage. Coligny persuaded them to place this baggage in the nave of a large church at Orléans, and left his brother Dandelot, who was threatened by an attack of fever and by De Guise, to defend the town.

In the middle of January Coligny advanced. It
was a severe winter ; the plague depopulated the
towns, while the forests were inhabited by fugitives,
who succumbed to starvation and cold. The
German horse-soldiers called the more loudly for
their pay, and Coligny conducted them to the shore
to show them the storm-swept sea. " The money
would be sure to come," he said consolingly, " but
the sea was too tempestuous," they could see that
for themselves.

The Germans drew their own conclusions ; they
began to pillage in order to compensate themselves,
but they reckoned without their host, as Coligny
would not tolerate lawlessness. He had the first
robber who was caught in the act hanged up by the
legs, as a warning to the others, and by maintaining
an iron discipline he made sure of the victory he
was going to gain.

De Guise besieged Orléans, while Dandelot, with
the fever heating his blood, was its heroic defender.
Every morning at six o'clock a service was held ;
then the psalms sounded out of the depths, beseech-
ing God for deliverance. And De Guise, who never
lacked patience, lost it before these stubborn walls.

" I could bite off my fingers," he wrote in a letter.
And he assured the Queen-Mother that he would
raze Orléans to the ground and kill every living
thing, cats and dogs included.

But the man who wanted to murder everyone
in the town was not to set his foot inside, but to

fall himself by the hands of an assassin. That assassin was a young nobleman called Poltrot, who had fought at Saint-Quentin like a brave soldier, and had passed into Spanish captivity, and there in Spain had seen how Philip II illuminated his reign by flaming *autos-de-fé*.

His heart full of vengeance and murderous thoughts, he returned to France. The terrible plan of assassinating De Guise ripened in this Protestant heart ; soon he spoke of nothing else ; he stretched out his right arm, and said to his comrades : " This arm shall kill the Duke."

He told this to Soubise, by whom he had been educated, to Coligny and many others, but no importance was attached to it.

He entered the service of the Admiral as a spy. He obtained money to buy a strong Spanish horse, rode into Guise's camp and offered the Duke his services.

He called himself a Spaniard. And De Guise, usually very suspicious, believed it, as his accent, his face, his whole appearance confirmed his statement. The Duke expected great things from Poltrot's arrival ; he grew enthusiastic and said : " Fifty thousand francs for you if you steal into the town and blow up the gunpowder-stores ! "

Thus the 18th of February arrived. Poltrot threw himself on his knees when alone, in order to ask the Lord to enlighten him, and he fancied he felt a divine incitement to this deed.

So all scruples had been overcome ; a Protestant Belshazzar, Gerards rose from his knees. Instead of listening to the voice of the Lord in the Scriptures, he followed the prompting of a misleading inward voice, and with a lie on his conscience, this fanatical man prepared to save Protestantism by means of assassination. He awaited the Duke on the outskirts of a forest, at dusk. He had calculated his chances ; his hand did not shake ; he had to let the Duke approach to a distance of six paces and then hit him in the vulnerable point above the arm-pits where there is an opening in the armour.

And so it happened. The shot was fired ; the Duke fell backward, and six days after he died of the effects of this mortal wound.

Like a clap of thunder the tidings resounded throughout the Protestant and the Catholic world ; many Huguenots rejoiced, and more than one Protestant, mastered by his passion, exclaimed : " How fortunate that this murderer has been murdered ! He has had his deserts, and this cruel persecutor of our brethren shall not escape eternal damnation ! "

Did the Duke de Guise really go to that terrible place where Judas Iscariot has his dwelling ? Is it certain that he is eternally lost ? How do we know ? The Duchess Renata was his mother-in-law, and this purified Christian did not shrink from writing to Calvin : " If I knew that the King, my father, and the Queen, my mother, and my late husband,

and all my children were rejected by God, I should hate them with a deadly hatred, and wish them to be in hell, and I should completely reconcile myself to God's will, if He would grant me grace for this." But the same pen from which these awful words flowed, then wrote : " I do not believe the Duke, my son-in-law, to be lost. I know he has been a cruel persecutor ; but to speak candidly, I do not think and do not believe that God has cast him off, as he gave signs of the contrary before he died."

Calvin replied in a remarkable letter, which exposed the stirrings of his heart like a flash of lightning.

" Concerning the Duke of Guise," he wrote, " it has been my constant prayer that God would show mercy to him, although I have also often wished that God would lay hands upon him and deliver the Church from the Duke, if He would not convert him. It was entirely due to me, that before the war, men refrained from ridding the world of him, for only my warning voice restrained them."

With these warnings he defied public opinion, which among both Roman Catholics and Protestants held that the slaying of a tyrant was a deed pleasing to God.

Calvin went even farther—he refused to doom De Guise to eternal punishment. " If we damn the Duke," he wrote to Renata, " we go too far, if we have not a sure and unfailing sign of his reprobation. In such things we must refrain from suppositions and presumption. For there is only one Judge before whose judgment throne we must all appear."

When the Duke of Guise felt the end approaching he continually repeated words from the Scriptures ; he begged his wife to forgive his shortcomings, as he forgave her, and thus he passed the threshold of Eternity. The murderer was taken prisoner and was put to the rack. He confessed all they wished, and mad with torture declared that Coligny had incited him to the murder, while Beza had encouraged him in his plans. Once off the rack he recalled his words to once again confirm them when his limbs broke under the hellish torture. Poltrot's body was torn asunder by four horses, after the flesh had been wrenched off by hot pincers —according to the sentence. And the judges regretted that they could not pass the same sentence on Coligny and Beza, although the latter declared himself most solemnly before God and the French nation to be altogether innocent of the murder.

That the Admiral was suspected of complicity was grist to the mill of Catherine de Medici, the Queen-Mother. It cast a stain on his character, which she eagerly applied to her own ends, and it weakened his influence, which was what she most earnestly desired.

He requested her to have Poltrot's case deferred till after the peace, that it might be thoroughly looked into. But she would not hear of it. This new investigation might have brought to light the innocence of both these distinguished Protestants, and that was just what she wished to prevent at any price.

She attained her purpose. In everything she attained her purpose. The proud dream of grandeur and glory dreamed by Francis de Guise on the evening of the battle of Dreux, she now lived through. The reins of government were in her hands ; she ruled ; the seat on which she sat had actually become a throne.

She had Condé in her power. She kneaded this weak mind like clay. He did not hesitate to submit to the wishes of the Queen-Mother and to conclude a peace, which granted the Huguenots no greater privileges than the January edict, although the Queen promised to grant the Protestants more favourable conditions afterwards and to raise him to the rank of lieutenant-general. These were vain promises ; she never intended to keep them. It did not matter—Condé signed. And again we ask in sorrowful surprise : " Where was the iron Calvinist ? "

An unnecessary question—Condé never was an iron Calvinist ! The iron Calvinist in the Huguenot army bore another name. And this Calvinist, this hero, Coligny, who in the middle of winter had conquered Normandy after a brilliant campaign, his was the right to wage war or make peace, for he had been chosen head of the Huguenots after the battle of Dreux. So the Protestants thought ; so Coligny thought ; and he quickly pushed on to Amboise to say an earnest word at the peace conference.

But he was five days too late—the Peace of Amboise had been signed on March 12th.

For form's sake Condé had consulted the preachers, but notwithstanding their opposition he signed. And the indignation of the great Huguenot leader was so great, that at the meeting he flung the words in Condé's face, that he, Prince Condé, had, with one stroke of his pen, destroyed more churches than had been demolished in ten years.

But arguing was useless—the peace had been signed.

It had been stipulated that no Protestant services were to be held in Paris, and in a few other specially mentioned towns, including the place of residence of the Royal Court. But the Huguenots were permitted freedom of worship on the estates of all high vassals, in the houses of the nobles and in the towns where services had been held when the war broke out, while a general pardon was proclaimed.

So there was peace. And the Duchess Renata put her hand to the plough to heal the wounds the war had inflicted. She opened wide the gates of her castle for the needy and suffering, while her generous character watched over the memory of her son-in-law. It cut her to the quick that his death meant life for the Huguenots ; she braved the appearance of ambiguity by diminishing his crimes, and his tragic end washed out the stains of his character in her memory. She covered his glowing ambition with the mantle of charity, and at the flood of abuse which followed the dead Guise into his grave she burst into tears, while she unburdened her mind by writing to Calvin : " God is not the Father of lies, but a God of truth, and His word is sufficient to protect His children without their seizing the weapons of Satan ! "

Coligny was her faithful counsellor ; the regular services were resumed, while Montargis became a second Geneva. Strict supervision on behaviour was held ; the Church Council was quite independent of the Duchess ; the Princess also tried to help De Morel in his work of evangelisation wherever possible.

Calvin corresponded with Renata to the last ; he admonished, he warned and consoled—it was the voice of a father speaking to his daughter. She had to complain more than once of the masterful and hard tone assumed by De Morel in his sermons, while the latter was surprised that she did not take stronger measures to suppress Catholic heresies. Calvin had to be mediator again and again, a difficult task, which required the greatest circumspection, as both parties were convinced of their being right. But De Morel's fanaticism he could not approve of, he was sorry that the zealous preacher was not always free from vanity and pride, and the gentle love shown by the Duchess brightened the evening of his life.

Generosity, wisdom, and tact Renata needed. When she opened the gates for the poor, the Huguenots poured into the town ; and grown wild in the civil war, embittered by the ill-treatment they had undergone, they now thought they were at liberty to wreak their vengeance on the Catholics.

But Renata thought otherwise. She would not tolerate that the oppressed of to-day should become the oppressors of to-morrow. She said without mincing matters that God had made her the protector not only of her Protestant subjects, but also of her Catholic subjects, and that she would take short measures with regard to criminals who in the name of the purified faith lifted the tills of their Roman Catholic fellow-citizens. She did good to all alike ; hungry monks, wandering along the roads, asked where Montargis lay, for there they should find bread and refreshment. In the midst of a sea of boiling passions which disturbed the land, the manor of Montargis lay like a peaceful and quiet island. The ticklish question of freedom of worship had been settled ; Protestants and Catholics passed each other on their way to church without gripping each other's throats or strangling each other. And this mutual respect for each other's convictions was so strange in those days that eminent men who were concerned for their country's welfare travelled to this singular spot.

The fatal knot tied at Amboise had been cut by the Duchess, as far as her estates were concerned ;

she acknowledged neither Guises nor Bourbons, and exacted obedience to royal authority. The world was full of suspicion, distrust, and bitterness, but the good faith of the Duchess remained untouched. Catholics and Protestants trusted her; steeped in Calvin's doctrine, she walked on with a firm step, without swaying to the right or left.

By the gulfs of hatred which separated the children of the same country, her figure appears in a light all the more charming. She was a true daughter of Calvin, and loved all her subjects; bowed down by grief and cares, her eye lit up when she was able to lessen the cares of others or to assuage their grief. Duchess was her title, but she gained a more beautiful title, and the lady of Montargis has been called " a mother in Israel."

So there was peace in the land.

Was it really peace, or merely a truce to recover breath, to restore exhausted strength and prepare for the mortal fray ? The Catholics infringed on the edict of Amboise wherever they could, and the Protestants did so wherever they felt strong enough to remove the barrier which obstructed their freedom of worship. It was a truce—nothing more. The Huguenots had pitched their camp on a volcano, but before a new eruption of this volcano took place, a long wail of sorrow ascended to heaven from Geneva.

CHAPTER XXXIV

" BLESSED ARE THE DEAD THAT DIE IN THE LORD "

" WE have this treasure in earthen vessels," says the apostle. And fragile and ruinous was the tent in which the Reformer lived. Matters did not improve as the years went by ; it was said that he was ailing, and one Sunday he stopped in the middle of the sermon. A hot burning sensation came into his throat ; he suddenly looked to the ground, and a stream of blood flowed·from his mouth.

It made an anxious, uneasy impression on the congregation ; it was now that they saw how strong the tie was which bound them to the remarkable preacher.

Calvin was carried home ; Geneva was in mourning ; " that will be the end," the people sighed.

It was rumoured abroad ; there was a general rejoicing in the camp of the adversaries, and they flattered themselves that Calvin would take the Reformation with him to his grave.

Rumours of his death had been circulated before, and once it had been reported for a change that he had gone over to popery, bag and baggage.

Calvin recovered, however, and resumed his

work. He knew it would not be for long, and he redoubled his zeal to finish the great work his hand had begun. It was at that time that a special ambassador of France appeared at Geneva, and handed the Government a letter from his young master, Charles IX, with a stern, set face.

The contents of this letter were enough to frighten the Genevese authorities. It was full of the most bitter and threatening expressions. " The Privy Council and States of France," thus ran the letter, " were unanimously of opinion, that the fatal confusion which France was a prey to, was solely owing to the preachers sent out by Geneva. But the French Government no longer intended to look on patiently. They categorically demanded the recall of the ringleaders, who instigated the people, or otherwise France would take her measures."

The menacing letter caused great consternation in the Council, and serious voices were raised to oppose going to extremes with regard to France. But Calvin, whose advice had been applied for, appeared at the town hall, and declared with the calmness of an ancient Roman that the safety of the town did not rest with France but with God. He told the councillors that it would be less dangerous to have the King of France for their enemy than the King of Kings, and warned them not to exchange the strong house built on a rock for the ruinous hut which was built on the quicksands of human favour. He explained to the councillors, as if expounding a mathematical problem, how they would do best to keep on the side of God, enforcing his explanation with the conviction of his unshakable faith. He proposed to modestly make the French King understand that the preachers educated at Geneva went forth on their own responsibility and could not be hindered in their movements by the Genevese Government. The preachers had besides always refrained from touching political questions, and if unrest and discord had notwithstanding been caused by their spreading the Gospel, then this was merely a confirmation of what the Great Sender had predicted.

It is highly improbable that such considerations would have made a deep impression in many council meetings, but these men had been formed in the school of Calvin; they were members of his Church, and through his words they had been initiated in the most holy faith.

They were no zealots, no fanatics. They knew very well that their small republic lay like a deserted post between three powerful Catholic States, and that their town was only half an hour's distance from the French frontier. But the weak can do nothing against the strong, and the might of France could in no case be compared with the might of God, whom they would bitterly insult if they deserted him now.

Calvin was entrusted with the reply to this letter; the French Government was struck with surprise, but could not carry out its intentions, as the Lord prevented it.

At the same time a more threatening storm rose from the side of Savoy. Duke Philip Emanuel, who together with van Egmond had beaten the French at Saint-Quentin, and had reconquered his hereditary duchy of Savoy, was now determined to increase his possessions by the desired annexation of the so eagerly desired town of Geneva. He was not only a soldier, but also a most dangerous diplomatist, and secretly called upon the exiled Libertines, who had connections in the town, to aid him. He understood that gold would be more powerful than steel, and in alliance with Bishop Allardet, he tried to attain his end by bribery.

The Bishop especially was full of courage ; this man thought he knew for certain that they would find confederates among the councillors. But those confederates went straight to Cannon Street with the letters the Bishop had sent them, and when the secret was betrayed, the Bishop had enough of it.

Duke Emanuel laughed at the Bishop's pusillanimity, and Cardinal Borromeo, whose heroic philanthropy was only equalled by his fierce hatred of heresies, brought about an alliance between Philip II of Spain, Savoy, and the Pope, of whom the last-mentioned was willing to pay an amount of twenty thousand ducats to conquer the stronghold of heresy.

The Libertines, who had once boasted so of their

patriotism, approved of it; they approved of everything, if only Calvinism was brought to ruin. But
no blessing rested on this undertaking; two days
before the scaling-ladders were to be placed against
the walls, the secret of the conspiracy was divulged,
and the Government took such vigorous measures
that the enemy dared not attempt an assault.
Geneva was saved; Calvin proposed holding a
solemn day of thanksgiving, and the people streamed
into the churches to thank the faithful Shepherd of
Israel who neither sleeps nor slumbers.

Bishop Allardet, who would have liked to hold
spiritual sway over Geneva, shrugged his shoulders
contemptuously.

"It is useless," he said, "as long as the Protector of Geneva is living; he employs demons, who
frustrate all good plans."

Six months afterwards they received news of
Calvin's decease, and began to breathe more freely.
This time it was positively true, there was no doubt
of it; the arch-heretic, who was served by devils,
because he had sold his soul to Beelzebub, the
chief of devils, was dead, dead as a doornail.
And Granville, that cunning statesman, wrote from
the Royal Palace at Madrid to all friendly courts:
"Now is the time to profit by this man's death.
The Roman Catholic states must unite and set
about it earnestly in order that an end may be
put to the misery of the Church, and heresy be
eradicated. His Majesty is fully prepared to employ

all the resources of the realm for this purpose." All the resources of the realm—who ever doubted it ? Did not Philip II make good his word in the Eighty Years' War ?

But Calvin was still living ; he was again seen in the streets ; and to famous strangers, come to Geneva to see the Reformer, the citizens said : " Look, there goes our Master Calvin ! "

Calvin's appearance in the decline of life must have made a deep and indelible impression on all who met him. He was emaciated and seemed to be nothing but skin and bone, yet his eye was not dim, but full of energy. It was quick and penetrating—a piercing falcon-like glance. His forehead was not high but arched, and denoted an iron will and invincible perseverance, while the strongly developed nose, together with the pale sunken cheeks, yet further enhanced the impression of firmness and keenness. He wore a long pointed beard, which flowed over his chest ; he had black hair, and could not bear a speck of dust on his clothes—the Reformer was very particular with regard to his dress. And as he passed by in his long black gown, with his immovable serious face, more like a spirit than a man, he made an indelible impression of discipline, method, determination and restrained force.

He was the man of logic, of conclusion, of iron consequence, who abhorred half-heartedness. The Reformer was unique ; his words went forth like a river with a smooth bed, flowing along under a clouded sky. When the Lord guided him and made him understand His will and the essence of His word, Calvin bowed before the Divine will, the Bible became the lamp before his feet, and he grasped the salvation offered him, as the mighty who take the Kingdom of God by force.

To do God's will and to help to fulfil it everywhere in life, had become his life's task. That was the incitement to his iron strength, his never-resting activity, and the secret of the success which crowned his efforts.

As he himself testified, his character was naturally shy, sensitive, timorous, and he appealed to these qualities to make Farel understand that he was not fit to be a preacher in turbulent Geneva. But when he saw his mistake, he sought no cowardly excuses, but without a moment's hesitation, like a brave soldier, mounted guard on the spot Farel had pointed out to him.

He was firmly convinced of being one of the elect, and praising God's almighty goodwill, he drew from this conviction the living water, which, above all, strengthened and refreshed him in his journey through desolate wildernesses. The mighty spiritual fights and temptations of Luther, the son of Noyon never knew, and whenever a believer fell into Satan's snares and sinned heavily, he declared that with such warnings before our eyes, we should walk our paths with the greater fear and trembling.

But this trembling is a thrill of awe for the impenetrable majesty of God and His judgments, and not fear for the uncertainty of his own election.

As the shades of evening fell, the Sun of righteousness brightened Calvin's inner being more and more. His life was rooted in God, this same God was the shield of his life ; in this consciousness he approached the end of his existence, as if seeing the Invisible. " Before the face of God and His holy angels, who look down upon us," that is a standing expression in his letters and writings. God and His angels who are ever present, he calls upon as witnesses when his words are liable to meet with suspicion and mistrust. The angels he does not forget, and this is the more remarkable, as so many of those who regard themselves as true sons of Calvin, seldom mention the names of the angels. God and His angels—Calvin points them out to his friends, to warn, to console, to admonish them to be steadfast in their faith and to fulfil their promises. He shouts out to the martyrs mounting the stake that the eyes of the Lord and of His hosts of angels follow their steps and rejoice over them. He compares his own life, which is drawing to a close, to a campaign for God and His holy angels. The eye of the Judge of battles who dwells high in the heavens rests upon him ; he feels it ; and this consciousness heightens his courage. But not only that awe-inspiring eye, the hosts of angels are there too, to show their cordial sympathy, and to encourage him.   And then that cloud of witnesses descending from heaven, whispering in his ear words of consolation and love !

Those are the judges whose opinion is all important to him.   But the world's opinion—what is that opinion worth ?   What does it matter that the world spits in his face ?   What is human praise but night and darkness ?

God, the Supreme Being, and His angels, serve him in the sixfold splendour of their wings—those are the friends in whose vicinity he lives.   Before the Majesty of the eternal Being the tinsel of this world grows pale ;   the eternal lights burn, and in that light how insignificant does the toil and moil of human beings appear, whose only philosophy consists in the despairing cry :   " Eat, drink, and be merry, for to-morrow we die ! "

Calvin asks what task God has set him, and in his innermost soul is convinced that neither fire nor water, mountain nor precipice, human enmity nor satanic malignity shall prevent him from carrying out that task.   Boundaries are extended ;   roads are smoothed ;   impossibilities exist no longer, because God is omnipotent.

To carry out God's will—that was and became more and more Calvin's passion in life.   That was the one thing necessary ;   the bells of eternity proclaimed it loudly with thunder peals through the air. . . .   God and His angels—it sounded through Calvin's words like a hymn.   And on his death-bed

CALVIN ON HIS DEATH-BED (*after L. Hurning*)

[*Face page* 382

he stammered in a broken voice : " Before God and
His angels I confess and repent of my sins ! "

God stood between him and man, and while his
outward form was decaying, his inward being was
being strengthened and glorified day by day according to the image of that holy God. It was stamped
on his face, his whole appearance ; and when the
councillors of Geneva stood in sorrowful silence
round his death-bed, they were struck by the
majesty on that marble face.

Calvin's death-bed, it would be death this time.
. . . He had preached on the preceding Wednesday
—it was feared for the last time. But wrestling
with death, which was sapping his strength, he once
again appeared in the pulpit on the following Sunday
to speak about the conformity of the Gospels.

That was his funeral-song, then everything was
at an end ; death was already busy demolishing the
frail tabernacle. His pains increased, and when they
overwhelmed him, the sufferer turned his eyes to
heaven and sighed : " How long, oh Lord ! how
long ! "

But stretched on his sick-bed by the grim hand of
Death, this invincible hero still went on working
by dictating his thoughts. And when begged to stop
this work, he replied, looking up with his penetrating
eyes : " What ? Would you have the Lord find
me idle when He comes ? "

On March 10th the Council ordered a general
hour of prayer to be held for the Reformer, and

behold ! there was a change for the better ! Some
friends, who had heard of this disquieting illness,
came to visit him, and found him at his writing-
desk fully dressed.

When they entered, Calvin rested his head in his
hands for a time, as he was accustomed to do when
deep in thought. Then he said in a weak, halting
voice, but with a glad gleam in his eyes : " Beloved
brethren ! I thank you cordially for your tender
care, and hope it will soon be unnecessary. In a
fortnight's time I hope to see you gathered round
me for the last time. Then the Lord will reveal
to me, as I hope and believe, what He has decided
concerning me, and He will take me into His eternal
kingdom ! "

The usual meeting of the court of censure was
indeed held at the Reformer's house on March 24th.
He said that the Lord had diminished his physical
suffering, then took a French New Testament, and
read over the remarks he had written in the margin.
He then asked the opinion of his colleagues and
said he wished to correct these notes. The brethren
were surprised at his energy and clearness of mind—
had the people's prayer really been heard ?

Would the angel of death really pass over that
beloved head once again ?

The attending the meeting had greatly affected
Calvin's health, he was very tired, and the following
morning he did not feel so well. But he would
not part from this world without having paid his

grateful homage to the members of the Council. He was carried to the town hall, and, supported by two friends, mounted the steps slowly and with great difficulty.

Thus he reached the well-known council chamber with its four windows, and appeared before the gentlemen of the Council, who respectfully rose from their wooden chairs.

First of all Calvin introduced a new rector for the University ; then with his cap in his shaking hand, greatly moved, he thanked them for the many favours received. The councillors had but a short time before shown their good-will by offering him his salary, although, owing to his weakness, he had not been able to fulfil the duties of his post. And they had the sooner decided to do so, as Calvin was burdened with the support of his brother Antony, who, owing to ill-luck in business, had come down in the world. Calvin had refused the money, and when they had pressed him to accept his salary he had confessed the reason, which was that his conscience would not permit him to accept the money, now that he no longer performed his duties. And there the matter rested. But the Reformer no less appreciated the generosity of the Council, adding that he would now have the honour of addressing them for the last time in that place. So he bade a cordial farewell to all, but old recollections overpowered him ; as in a vision he saw how these courageous men had braved the heat of the day and the cold of the night. The words stuck in his throat, and mournful tears glistened in those stern eyes.

Not one remained unmoved ; the stern men of the Government wept, aye, now they knew how this iron heart had clung with a tender love to Geneva, his second country.

Easter fell on April 2nd. The sufferer had become very weak, but he longed to celebrate Communion with his flock. He was carried to church in a chair. Beza was the celebrant ; from his hands he took the bread and the cup. And at the end of this holy service the audience chanted the song of Simeon : " Lord, now lettest Thou Thy servant depart in peace ; according to Thy word. For mine eyes have seen Thy salvation ! "

It was a touching scene. The angels were present at it. Softly, inaudibly their wings rustled through the lofty building. The audience wept ; deeply moved they sang the hymn, their eyes turned on their departing shepherd. But he wept not ; his soul was full of holy joy ; he saw the golden gates of the eternal Home shining before him. It was his last walk. Once again he wished to address the Council to unburden his conscience, but the councillors would not suffer him to come, but went to him. The Council went in a solemn procession to Cannon Street ; they grouped themselves around his bed to hear his last words.

" Your worships," said Calvin, " I cannot thank you enough for the honour and kindness you have

shown me, and especially for the inexhaustible
patience with which you have borne with my great
shortcomings and faults. I have met with many
discouragements and great opposition in my career,
but that was not your fault, but was according to the
decree of God who tries each of his servants. Wherever I have failed in my duty I earnestly beg you
not to impute this to my will, but to my inability.
For of a truth I may say, that I was devoted to your
Republic heart and soul and, notwithstanding all
omissions and faults, I have always laboured, as
much as was in my power, for the public welfare.
It would also be ungrateful hypocrisy, were I to
deny that God had desired to use me as his instrument in performing certain things. Only this I
repeat ; excuse and forgive if my work in public
and private life has been so insignificant in comparison to what it might have been. Above all,
venerable sirs ! am I indebted to you for so kindly
and gently bearing with my too great vehemence.
This and my other faults I am heartily sorry for,
but I earnestly hope that God has pardoned these
faults.

"Concerning the doctrine I preached to you, I
confess before God and my Saviour that I had no
other desire than to proclaim the Word of God which
had been entrusted to me, in all its purity, while
I feel assured that I have not gone my way in uncertainty. Had it been otherwise, I know well
enough that God's wrath would now be threatening

me, while, on the contrary, I am convinced that my labour and care in preaching His Word have not displeased Him."

He reminded them of the Lord's striking deliverances of the anxious year which lay behind them, assuring them that that faithful God who was then the Protector of the town would continue to be so in the future.

" If you wish God to preserve your Republic in the happy condition it is in at present, guard well the holy place where He Himself lives in your midst, namely, His Holy Church, that it be not stained with sin ! For He has said, that He will honour those who honour Him, and despise those who despise Him. He alone is the great God, the King of Kings, the Lord of all. . . .

" The older ones among you I admonish not to envy the younger ones, should they surpass you. I wish to remind the younger ones that it behoves them, above all things, to be modest, humble, and moderate."

It was a father who before departing takes leave of his beloved children. They asked his blessing, and he prayed with them ; then he gave them his hand and bade them a last farewell. The councillors went home full of sorrow ; never had the town witnessed such a scene.

" When he had finished his speech," says Beza, " he called us to him one by one, and pressed our hands. And we went away, our eyes swimming with tears and our hearts full of unspeakable sorrow."

Those last farewell visits were a sweet consolation to Calvin in his great suffering. Farel, almost eighty, came from Neuchâtel.

The Reformer had written to him not to undertake the difficult journey, but he came notwithstanding, impelled by the mysterious force of love which counts all troubles as nothing.

Calvin was exceedingly rejoiced to see this faithful brother-in-arms once more on earth. They talked of days long past, of strife and victory, and they strengthened each other in the holy faith. Did Farel envy his brother's fate ? Farel was five-and-twenty years older, and had to return to his post. And he would remain behind like a solitary tree in a forest, devastated by the storm. But the parting would not be for long, and so they doubtless consoled each other with the prospect of a speedy, eternal, and blessed reunion. On May 19th, two days before Whitsuntide, another meeting of the preacher's court of censure took place, and it was decided to have dinner at Calvin's house. It was a sorrowful surprise when Calvin was carried into the room, and tears rose in the preacher's eyes when he said : " Brethren, I have come to meet you for the last time and to sit down at table with you."

His strong will forced his body to obey it ; he said grace, partook of some food, and talked as cheerfully as possible to comfort his sorrowing brethren.

But before the meal was at an end, the reaction set in ; he had to be carried to his bed in the adjoining room. All those present were greatly dismayed, but he said with a gentle smile : " The partition-wall will not prevent me from being with you in the spirit."

The end was fast approaching now. And while the Reformer had finished with all earthly things, he was like a traveller, who having bidden farewell to all, waits for the signal to depart.

He was praying almost continually. His breath came and went in gasps ; his voice was scarcely audible—his prayer was no more than a sigh. But those penetrating eyes, turned heavenwards, shone with a wonderful light.

Sometimes when the pains made him writhe, he was heard repeating these words from the Psalms : " Lord, I have not opened my mouth because Thou hast done it."

The sympathy shown him was great and touching, but the Reformer regretted that the sight of his suffering should cause pain to others. In the midst of his greatest pains, this great heart remained full of tender solicitude for others, and while his soul thirsted for personal sympathy he would have refused it in order to cause no pain to others.

May 27th was his dying day. He seemed slightly better in the morning—it was the last flickering of the lamp before it went out for ever. In the afternoon death began to set in, but nobody was aware of it. For the Lord had made His faithful servant's death-bed as soft as possible.

Beza was called ; he rushed to the bedchamber— the sufferer had already crossed the River of Jordan. It was eight o'clock ; the May sun which had shone so brightly the whole day was setting and twilight was falling.

Calvin had retained consciousness, the power of thought, and his voice to the last. And he had fallen asleep ; peacefully, like a child tired out by the long day.

It was Saturday—the end of the week of labour. And on this Saturday ended the life's labour of the great Reformer. When late at night the news of Calvin's death spread, there was much weeping in the town, as a nation weeps when it loses its benefactor.

Cannon Street was crowded with people ; it became a pilgrimage to the Reformer's death-bed, and the Government had to take measures to prevent too great a pressure.

On the following morning the corpse, in its white graveclothes, was put into a wooden coffin, and at two o'clock in the afternoon the funeral took place—according to Calvin's express desire— with touching simplicity. The whole of the Council, all the professors, teachers, preachers, the Church Council, and nearly the whole town followed the body to the grave. A low cry of anguish arose from the crowd.

"My father! my father!" exclaimed Beza, "the chariot of Israel and the horsemen thereof!"

The coffin descended into the gloomy pit; the May sun shone in all its glory, and its beams followed the Reformer into the bosom of the earth. The bells tolled solemnly; the echoes replied softly from afar; and the birds sang their songs.

The blue lake sparkled like a sapphire; unmovable, like a gigantic guard towered Mont Blanc; and the Jura Mountains stretched out their hands to one another, and the doves whispered to one another that it was the Sabbath, the Lord's Day.

The noble grain is laid in the earth—hark! the sods fall on the coffin with a dull thud!

Church of Geneva, why do you lament? The corn is scattered into the furrow with tears, and soon the harvest will be gathered in amid shouts of joy and the song of the sickle.

Blessed are the dead that die in the Lord from this day forth! Yea, saith the Spirit, that they may rest from their labour, and their works do follow them.

No monument marks the spot where Calvin was buried. It is not necessary; angels, whom the Reformer met on his toilsome journey, know the spot and guard it, until the day when the dead shall arise from their graves.